Business, Religion and the Law

"Religious organisations and the business sector are increasingly intertwined as the global economy is moving beyond its modern secular concept. This informative and challenging book provides a groundbreaking account from which scholars, actors, and general leadership have a lot to learn for the sake of their knowledge and strategies".

Professor Marco Ventura, University of Siena, Italy

This book investigates the intersection between business and religion from a legal perspective. Taking a fresh look at some of the most compelling literature in law and religion, it proposes a rethinking of what scholars on both sides of the Atlantic have dubbed "church autonomy" or, more recently, "corporate religious freedom".

The volume explores how, in the wake of a decade of US Supreme Court case law, corporate religious freedom is now increasingly being extended to protect the religious liberty of another corporate entity: the for-profit corporation. By exposing this shift from church to business autonomy in American law, it is argued that a similar narrative has also begun to take place in Europe. Through a comparative and interdisciplinary approach to corporate religious freedom, the work provides the reader with a new, comprehensive, and easily accessible history of the genesis and evolution of this legal category in American and European law.

The book combines material that straddles international law and religion, corporate law, and economic theory. The diversity of views contained within it makes it a valuable resource for scholars and students in law and religion, corporate social responsibility, and law and economics.

Matteo Corsalini is a post-doctoral researcher at the University of Padua—School of Law, Italy.

ICLARS Series on Law and Religion

The *ICLARS Series on Law and Religion* is a new series designed to provide a forum for the rapidly expanding field of research in law and religion. The series is published in association with the International Consortium for Law and Religion Studies, an international network of scholars and experts of law and religion founded in 2007 with the aim of providing a place where information, data and opinions can easily be exchanged among members and made available to the broader scientific community. The series aims to become a primary source for students and scholars while presenting authors with a valuable means to reach a wide and growing readership.

Series Editors:

Silvio Ferrari, University of Milan, Italy, Russell Sandberg, Cardiff University, UK, Pieter Coertzen, University of Stellenbosch, South Africa, W. Cole Durham, Jr., Brigham Young University, USA, and Tahir Mahmood, Amity International University, India

Other titles in this series:

The Internal Law of Religions
Introduction to a Comparative Discipline
Burkhard Josef Berkmann
Translated by David E. Orton

Legal Code of Religious Minority Rights
Sources in International and European Law
Daniele Ferrari

Law, Religion, and Freedom
Conceptualizing a Common Right
Edited by W. Cole Durham, Jr., Javier Martínez-Torrón, and Donlu Thayer

Dignity and International Human Rights Law
An Introduction to the Punta del Este Declaration on Human Dignity for Everyone Everywhere
Ewelina U. Ochab and Brett Scharffs

Law, State and Religion in Bosnia and Herzegovina
Nedim Begović and Emir Kovačević

The Church and Employment Law
A Comparative Analysis of The Legal Status of Clergy and Religious Workers
John Duddington

Business, Religion and the Law
Church and Business Autonomy in the Secular Economy
Matteo Corsalini

For more information about this series, please visit: www.routledge.com/ICLARS-Series-on-Law-and-Religion/book-series/ICLARS

Business, Religion and the Law

Church and Business Autonomy in the Secular Economy

Matteo Corsalini

Routledge
Taylor & Francis Group
LONDON AND NEW YORK

First published 2023
by Routledge
4 Park Square, Milton Park, Abingdon, Oxon OX14 4RN

and by Routledge
605 Third Avenue, New York, NY 10158

Routledge is an imprint of the Taylor & Francis Group, an informa business

British Library Cataloguing-in-Publication Data
A catalogue record for this book is available from the British Library

ISBN: 978-1-032-37562-5 (hbk)
ISBN: 978-1-032-37565-6 (pbk)
ISBN: 978-1-003-34082-9 (ebk)

DOI: 10.4324/9781003340829

Typeset in Galliard
by Deanta Global Publishing Services, Chennai, India

Contents

Table of cases

Court of Justice of the European Union

Case C-188/15, *Asma Bougnaoui, Association de Defense des Droits de l'Homme (ADDH) v Micropole Univers SA*, [2017] EU:C:2017:204.

Case C-188/15, *Asma Bougnaoui, Association de Defense des Droits de l'Homme (ADDH) v Micropole Univers SA*, [2017] EU:C:2017:204, Opinion of AG Sharpston.

Case 29/69 *Erich Stauder v City of Ulm-Sozialamt* [1969] ECR 419.

Case 11/70, *Internationale Handelsgesellschaft* [1970] ECR 1125, 1134.

Case C-68/17, *IR v JQ* [2018] EU:C:2018:696.

Case C-466/00 *Kaba* [2003] ECR-I2219.

Case C-157/15, *Samira Achbita and Centrum voor Gelijkheid van Kansen en voor Racismebestrijding v G4S Secure Solutions NV* [2017] EU:C:2017:203.

Case C-157/15, *Samira Achbita and Centrum voor Gelijkheid van Kansen en voor Racismebestrijding v G4S Secure Solutions NV* [2017] EU:C:2017:203. Opinion of AG Kokott.

Case 196/87 *Udo Steymann v Staatssecretaris van Justitie* [1988] ECR 6159.

Case 300/84 *Van Rosmaalen v Bestuir van de Betrijfsvereinigingen* [1986] ECR 3097.

Case C-414/16, *Vera Egenberger v Evangelisches Werk für Diakonie und Entwicklung e.V.* [2018] EU:C:2018:257.

Case 130/75, *Vivien Prais v Council of the European Communities* (unreported) 27 October 1976.

Case 41/74, *Yvonne Van Duyn v Home Office* [1974] ECR 1337.

Joined Cases C-804/18, *IX v WABE e.V* and *C-341/19 MH Müller Handels GmbH v MJ*, [2021] EU:C:2021:144. Opinion of AG Rantos.

Joined Cases C-804/18, *IX v WABE e.V* and *C-341/19 MH Müller Handels GmbH v MJ*, [2021] ECLI:EU:C:2021:594.

European Commission and Court of Human Rights

Baudler v Germany, App no 38254/04 (ECtHR, 6 December 2011).

Bayatyan v Armenia, App no 23459/03 (ECtHR, 7 July 2011).

Canea Catholic Church v Greece, App no 143/1996/762/963 (ECtHR, 16 December 1997).

Case of Holy Monasteries v Greece, Apps no 13092/87 and 13984/88 (ECtHR, 9 December 1994).

Case of Refah Partisi (The Welfare Party) and Others v Turkey, App nos 41340/98, 41342/98, 41343/98 and 41344/98 (ECtHR, 13 February 2003).

Case of Sindicatul 'Păstorul cel Bun' v Romania *(Application no 2330/09)*. Written Comments of Third-Party Interveners. The Becket Fund for Religious Liberty and the International Center for Law and Religion Studies.

Case of The Moscow Branch of The Salvation Army v Russia, App no 72881/01 (ECtHR, 5 January 2007).

Case *'Relating to Certain Aspects of The Laws on The Use of Languages in Education in Belgium' v Belgium (Merits)*, App nos 1474/62; 1677/62; 1691/62; 1769/63; 1994/63; 2126/64 (ECtHR, 23 July 1968).

Cha'are Shalom Ve Tsedek v France, App no 27417/95 (ECtHR, 27 June 2000).

Christine Goodwin v UK, App no 28957/95 (ECtHR, 11 July 2002).

Church of Scientology Moscow v. Russia, App no 18147/02 (ECtHR, 5 April 2007).

Company X v Switzerland, App no 7865/77 (ECommHR, 27 February 1979).

C. of S. v. United Kingdom, App no 3798/68 (ECommHR, 17 December 1968) 29 CD 70.

Dahlab v Switzerland, App no 42393/98 (ECtHR, 15 February 2001).

Darby v. Sweden, App no 11581/85 (EComHR, 9 May 1989), para. 45.

Ebrahimian v France, App no 64846/11 (ECtHR, 26 November 2015).

Eweida and Others v UK, App nos 48420/10, 59842/10, 51671/10 and 36516/10 (ECtHR, 15 January 2013).

Fernández Martínez v Spain, App no 56030/07 (Third Chamber, 15 May 2012).

Fernández Martínez v Spain, App no 56030/07 (Grand Chamber, 12 June 2014).

Hasan and Chaush v. Bulgaria, App no 30985/96 (ECtHR, 26 October 2000).

Holy Synod of the Bulgarian Orthodox Church (Metropolitan Inokentiy) et al. v. Bulgaria, App nos 412/03 and 35677/04, (ECtHR, 22 January 2009).

ISKCON v United Kingdom (ECommHR, 8 March 1994).

Jehovah's Witnesses of Moscow v. Russia, App no 302/02 (ECtHR, 10 June 2010).

Karlsson v Sweden, App no 12356/86 (ECommHR, 8 September 1988).

Kokkinakis v Greece, App no 14307/88 (25 May 1993).

Kontinnen v Finland, App no 24949/94 (ECtHR, 3 December 1996).

Kress v France, App no 39594/98 (ECtHR, 7 June 2001).

Kustannus Oy Vapaa Ajattelija AB et al. v. Finland, App no 20471/92 (ECommHR, 15 April 1996).

Lee v the United Kingdom, App no 18860/19 (First Section, 23 March 2020).

Lee v the United Kingdom, App no 18860/19 (ECtHR, 6 January 2022).

Loizidou v. Turkey (preliminary objections), App no 40/1993/435/514 (ECtHR, 23 February 1995).
Loizidou v Turkey, App no 15318/89 (ECtHR, 23 February 1995).
Lombardi Vallauri v Italy, App no 39128/05 (ECtHR, 20 October 2009).
Metropolitan Church of Bessarabia and others v Moldova, App no 45701/99 (ECtHR, 13 December 2001).
Müller v Germany, App no 12986/04 (ECtHR, 6 December 2011).
Obst v Germany, App no 425/03 (ECtHR, 23 September 2010).
Perincek v Switzerland, App no 27510/08 (ECtHR, 15 October 2015).
Reuter v Germany, App no 39775/04 (ECtHR, 6 December 2011).
Schüth v Germany, App no 1620/03 (ECtHR, 23 September 2010).
Serbo-Greek Orthodox Church in Vienna v Austria (ECommHR, 2 April 1990).
Siebenhaar v Germany, App no 18136/02 (ECtHR, 3 February 2011).
Sindicatul 'Păstorul cel Bun' v Romania, App no 2330/09 (Third Section, 31 January 2012).
Sindicatul 'Păstorul cel Bun' v Romania (Grand Chamber, 9 July 2013).
Stedman v United Kingdom, App no 29107/95 (ECtHR, 9 April 1997).
Svyato-Mykhaylivska Parafiya v. Ukraine, App no 77703/01 (ECtHR, 14 September 2007).
Travaŝ v Croatia, App no 75581/13 (ECtHR, 30 January 2017).
Tyrer v UK, App no 5856/72 (ECtHR, 25 April 1978).
X and Church of Scientology v. Sweden, App no 7805/77 (ECommHR, 17 December 1979) 16 DR 68.
X v Denmark, App no 7374/76 (ECommHR, 8 March 1976) 5 DR 157.

Human Rights Committee

Sister Immaculate Joseph and 80 Teaching Sisters of the Holy Cross of the Third Order of Saint Francis in Menzingen of Sri Lanka v. Sri Lanka, 3 November 2005, Communication No 1249/2004, CCPR/C/85/D/1249/2004.
William Eduardo Delgado Páez v Colombia, Communication No 195/1985, 23 August 1990, CCPR/C/39/D/195/1985.

International Court of Justice

Ahmadou Sadio Diallo (Republic of Guinea v Democratic Republic of the Congo) (2010), Merits, Judgment ICJ Rep 2007 639.

United States Supreme Court

Altitude Express Inc. v Zarda, 883 F.3d 100 (2d Cir. 2018).
Bostock v. Clayton City., 140 S. Ct. 1731 (2020).
Brief Amicus Curiae of United States Conference of Catholic Bishops; Institutional Religious Freedom Alliance; World Vision, Inc; Catholic Relief Services; Family Research Council; Association of Catholic Colleges and Universities; Thomas More Society; and The Cardinal Newman Society in support of Petitioners

and Supporting Reversal Nos. 14-1418, 14-1453, 14-1505, 15-35, 15-105, 15-119, & 15-191

Brief of Corporate and Criminal Law Professors as Amici Curiae in Support of Petitioners, *Burwell v Hobby Lobby Stores, Inc.* (No 13-354 and 13-356)'

Brief for Lawyers' Committee for Civil Rights Under Law, Asian American Legal Defense and Education Fund, Center for Constitutional Rights, Color of Change, the Leadership Conference on Civil and Human Rights, National Action Network, National Association for the Advancement of Colored People, National Urban League, and Southern Poverty Law Center As Amici Curiae Supporting Respondents (No. 16-111).

Burwell v Hobby Lobby Stores, Inc 134 S Ct 2751 (2014).

Cantwell v Connecticut, 310 U.S. 296 (1940).

Church of the Lukumi Babalu Aye, Inc. v. City of Hialeah 508 U.S. 520 (1993).

Elane Photography v Willock, 309 P.3d 53 (2013).

Employment Division v Smith, 494 US 872 (1990).

Espinoza v. Montana Department of Revenue, 140 S. Ct. 2246 (2020)

Everson v Board of Education, 330 U.S. 1 (1947).

Fulton v. City of Philadelphia, 593 U.S. (2021).

Harris Funeral Homes Inc. v. Equal Employment Opportunity Commission, 884 F.3d 560 (6th Cir. 2018).

Hosanna Tabor v EEOC, 132 S. Ct. 694 (2012).

Little Sisters of the Poor Saints Peter & Paul Home v. Pennsylvania, 140 S. Ct. 2367 (2020).

Masterpiece Cakeshop, Ltd. v. Colo. Civil Rights Comm'n, 138 S. Ct. 1719 (2018).

N*ewman v. Piggie Park Enters., Inc.*, 390 U.S. 400 (1968) 402.

Obergefell v. Hodges, 135 S. Ct. 2584 (2015).

Our Lady Guadalupe School v Morrissey Berru, 140 S. Ct. 2049 (2020).

State v. Arlene's Flowers, Inc, 138 S. Ct. 2448 (2018).

*St. James School v Bie*l, 140 S.Ct. 680 (2020).

Trump, President of the United States, et al. v. Pennsylvania et al. F. Supp. 3d 553, 563.

Wallace v. Jaffree, 472 U.S. 38, 107, 113 (1985).

Zubik v Burwell, 136 S. Ct. 1557 (2016).

United States district and appeals courts

EEOC v. Hosanna Tabor Evangelical Lutheran Church & Sch., 582 F. Supp. 2d 881 (2008).

EEOC v. Hosanna Tabor, 597 F.3d 796, 780.

Fulton v. City of Philadelphia, 2 F.3d 140 (3d Cir. 2019).

Newland v Sebelius, 881 F Supp 2d 1287 (D Colo 2012) (No 1:12-cv-01 123-JLK) 1296.

State v. Arlene's Flowers, Inc., 389 P.3d 543, 550 (Wash. 2017).

State v. Arlene's Flowers, 441 P.3d 1203 (Wash. 2019).

Belgian domestic courts

S A & Centrum voor Gelijkheid van Kansen en voor Racismebestrijding t G4S Secure Solutions nv (2017) *Hof van Cassatie van België* Nr S.12.0062.N.

British domestic courts

Lee v Ashers Baking Company Ltd [2018] UKSC.

French domestic courts

Cass Ass Plén 25 June 2014 (2014) Recueil Dalloz, 1386.

Table of international instruments

United Nations

International Covenant on Civil and Political Rights and Optional Protocol to the International Covenant on Civil and Political Rights, 16 December 1966, 999 UNTS 171 (ICCPR).

International Covenant on Economic, Social and Cultural Rights, 993 UNTS 3.

Universal Declaration of Human Rights, 10 December 1948, UNGA Res 217 A III (UDHR).

UN Economic and Social Council, *Draft International Covenant on Human Rights: Recapitulation of Amendments To Articles 13, 14 and 15*, 24 May 1949, UN Doc. E/CN.4/253.

———-, *Summary record of the 161st meeting*, 19 April 1990, UN Doc E/CN.4/SR.161.

———, *Report submitted by Mr. Angelo Vidal d'Almeida Ribero, Special Rapporteur appointed in accordance with resolution 1986/20 of the Commission on Human Rights*, 24 December 1986, E/CN.4/1987/35.

———, *Report submitted by Mr. Angelo Vidal d'Almeida Ribeiro, Special Rapporteur appointed in accordance with resolution 1986/20 of the Commission on Human Rights*, 6 January 1988, E/CN.4/1988/45.

UN Human Rights Committee (HRC), *CCPR General Comment No. 22: Article 18 (Freedom of Thought, Conscience or Religion)*, 30 July 1993, CCPR/C/21/Rev.1/Add.4.

———, *General Comment No. 33: The Obligations of States Parties under the Optional Protocol to the International Covenant on Civil and Political Rights*, 5 November 2008, UN Doc. CCPR/C/GC/33.

UN General Assembly, *Declaration on the Elimination of All Forms of Intolerance and of Discrimination Based on Religion or Belief*, 25 November 1981, A/RES/36/55.

———, *Draft International Covenants on Human Rights: annotation prepared by the Secretary-General*, 1 July 1995, UN Doc A/2929.

———, *Implementation of the Declaration on the Elimination of All Forms of Intolerance and Discrimination Based on Religion or Belief, Note by the Secretary General*, 7 November 1996, A/51/542/Add.1.

———, *Interim report of the Special Rapporteur on freedom of religion or belief, Ahmed Shaheed, submitted in accordance with General Assembly resolution 71/196*, 12 October 2020, UN Doc. A/75/50302.

———, *Interim report of the Special Rapporteur on freedom of religion or belief, Heiner Bielefeldt, in accordance with Assembly resolution 67/179*, 7 August 2013, UN Doc A/68/290.

———, *Official Records of the Fifteenth Session*, 14 November 1960, UN Doc A/C.3/SR.1021.

———, *Official Records of the Fifteenth Session*, 16 November 1960, UN Doc. A/C.3/SR.1023

———, *Official Records of The Fifteenth Session*, 16 November 1960, UN Doc A/C.3/SR.1024.

———, *Official Records of the Fifteenth Session*, 17 November 1960, UN Doc A/C.3/SR.1025.

———, *Report of the Independent Expert on Minority Issues, Gay McDougall. Addendum*, 18 February 2009, A/HRC/10/11/Add.3.

———, *Transforming our world: the 2030 Agenda for Sustainable Development*, 21 October 2015, UN Doc. A/RES/70/1.

UN National and Economic Social Council, *Summary record of the 116th meeting held at Lake Success, New York, on Tuesday, 7 June 1949: Commission on Human Rights, 5th session*, UN Doc E/CN.4/SR.116.

Conference and Organisation for Security and Cooperation

Conference for Security and Co-operation in Europe (CSCE), *Document of The Copenhagen Meeting of the Conference on the human dimension of the CSCE*, 29 June 1990.

———, *Helsinki Concluding Document. The Challenges of Change*, 10 July 1992.

———, *Concluding Document—of the Madrid Meeting 1980 of representatives of the participating states of the conference on Security and Co-operation in Europe, held on the basis of the provisions of the Final Act relating to the follow-Up to the Conference*, 6 September 1983.

———, *Concluding Document—of the Vienna Meeting 1986 of representatives of the participating states of the conference on Security and Co-operation in Europe, held on the basis of the provisions of the Final Act relating to the follow-Up to the Conference*, 15 January 1989.

———, *Helsinki Final Act*, 1 August 1975.

OSCE/ODIHR, *Guidelines on The Legal Personality of Religious or Belief Communities* (2014).

———, *Guidelines for Review of Legislation Pertaining to Religion or Belief* (2004).

Organisation for Economic Co-operation and Development

Organisation for Economic Development and Cooperation, *OECD Guidelines for Multinational Enterprises* (OECD Publishing, 2011).

Council of Europe

Council of Europe, 'Chart of signatures and ratifications of Treaty' 005 [1950] ETS No.005.

———, *Protocol No. 11 To The Convention For The Protection of Human Rights And Fundamental Freedoms Restructuring The Control Machinery Established Thereby*, 11 May 1994, European Treaty Series—No. 155.

———, *Protocol No. 15 amending the Convention for the Protection of Human Rights and Fundamental Freedoms*, 24 June 2013, Council of Europe Treaty Series—no 213.

Council of Europe/European Court of Human Rights, 'Guide on Article 9 of the European Convention on Human Rights' 1, 9 (31 August 2020).

Council of Europe/European Court of Human Rights, *Practical Guide on Admissibility Criteria* (2020).

Council of Europe/European Court of Human Rights, 'Rules of Court' (2021).

Council of Europe (CoE), *Protocol No. 15 amending the Convention for the Protection of Human Rights and Fundamental Freedoms*, 24 June 2013, Council of Europe Treaty Series—no 213, Article 1.

Directorate of Policy Planning (CoE), *The Council of Europe and The OSCE: Enhancing Co-operation and Complementarity Through Greater Coherence. By Professor dr. juris Geir Ulfstein, University of Oslo*, 23 March 2012, DPP (2012).

European Convention on Human Rights and Fundamental Freedoms, 4 November 1950 (entered into force 3 September 1953) 213 UNTS 221 (ECHR).

European Community and Union

Charter of Fundamental Rights of the European Union, 18 December 2000, C 364/20, OJ C364.

Commission of The European Communities, 'Completing the Internal Market. White Paper from the Commission to the European Council' COM (85).

Commission Staff Working Document Annexes to the Joint Report on the application on the Racial Equality Directive (2000/43/EC) and the Employment Equality Directive (2000/78/EC) SWD(2014) 5 final, Brussels 17 January 2014.

Consolidated Version of The Treaty on the Functioning of The European Union [2012] [2008] OJ C 326/47.

Consolidated Version of The Treaty on European Union [2012] OJ C 326/13.

Council Regulation (EC) 2000/78 establishing a general framework for equal treatment in employment and occupation (EC Employment Equality Directive) [2000] L 303/16.

Council Directive 2004/83/EC on minimum standards for the qualification and status of third country nationals or stateless persons as refugees or as persons who otherwise need international protection and the content of the protection granted [2004] 304/12.

European Commission, 'Study on director's duties and sustainable corporate governance' COMM (2020).

European Single Act [1987] OJ No L 169/1.

Treaty Establishing a Constitution for Europe (unreported) 13 January 2005.

Treaty Establishing a Single Council and a Single Commission of the European Communities, 8 April 1965 (unreported).

Treaty Establishing the European Atomic Energy Community (Euratom) 25 March 1957 (unreported).

Treaty Establishing the European Economic Community, 25 March 1957 (unreported).

Treaty Establishing the European Coal and Steel Community, ECSC Treaty, 18 April 1951 (unreported).

Treaty On European Union (unreported) 7 February 1992.

Other legal orders—Greece

Constitution of Greece, article 3.

Other legal orders—Italy and the Holy See

Agreement Between the Italian Republic and the Holy See (1984), article 2.

Other legal orders—United States

Amendments to the Constitution of the United States of American, Amendment I.

Americans with Disabilities Act (ADA), 1990,42 U.S.C.A. § 12112.

Colorado Anti-Discrimination Act (CADA), CO Rev Stat § 24-34-601 (2016).

Patient Protection and Affordable Care Act 2010 Public Law III-148, 124 Stat 119.

Religious Freedom Restoration Act (RFRA) 42 USC ss 2000bb (1993).

US Department of Labour, Employee Benefit Security Administration, 'FAQs About Affordable Care Act Implementation Part 36' (9 January 2017).

US Department of the Treasury, Department of Labour; Department of Health and Human Services, 'Religious Exemptions and Accommodations for Coverage of Certain Preventive Services Under the Affordable Care Act' (13 October 2017).

Preface

A piece of advice that my PhD supervisor, Professor Marco Ventura, gave me before I started writing this project was that good researchers always focus on the forest, not the trees. Move past the boring details of your thesis, keep track of the "big picture", and call me if you get lost: this is pretty much what he meant.

In hindsight, "big picture thinking" has proved incredibly useful in guiding my choice of which data to analyse and which not to analyse (and *why*) during the process of transposing years of research into a coherent chunk of written material. This, in turn, certainly made the various steps of thesis writing more stimulating and creative. It is, for this reason, that the greatest debt of gratitude is owed to Professor Marco Ventura, who proved to be exceptionally hardworking, enthusiastic, and imaginative in his supervision.

This book brings to a close a research journey that took place in several geographical areas over almost five years. It all started with a period as a pre-doctoral student, first at the University of Modena-Department of Law in late 2017, and then at the University of Leicester—Law School (UK) between January and July 2018. In those years, it was thanks to the help of some people that I took my first steps into academia and started collecting the first data (the trees!) for this volume.

To begin with, I must thank my bachelor's thesis supervisor, Professor Vincenzo Pacillo, who first introduced me to the world of law and religion studies. I also owe a lot to Professor Oxana Golynker and Professor Stefano Bertea for offering me an important pre-doctoral opportunity at the University of Leicester, without which I would not have gotten to this point with this project. Living in Leicester was, in fact, crucial for learning the basics of essay writing in English and how to go through the painful process of crafting academic arguments in a foreign language, such as those contained in this work. In particular, a heartfelt thank you goes to Frances Jones for agreeing to give me free courses in English writing (and for throwing several of my essays in the bin!). I reserve special praise also for some friends from the academic staff and post-grad community at Leicester Law School for making me feel at home in the UK and being a great source of fun and insight. In alphabetical order: Ana Liza, Antonis, Arwen, Cristina, Dan, Paolo, Rossana, Stelios, Theresa, Tom, Valentina, and Vicki.

In October 2018, I finally started my PhD at the University of Siena—Department of Law and also joined Fondazione Bruno Kessler—Center for Religious Studies (FBK-ISR) in Trento, thanks to a collaboration between the FBK International PhD programme and my department. The intellectual atmosphere of these two places allowed me not only to combine the data that I had previously collected into a stronger research proposal but also to learn from countless and great academic minds. This manuscript has benefitted from discussions and exchanges of materials with scholars in Trento, Siena, and elsewhere. A lot is owed to (always in alphabetical order): Silvia Angeletti, Pasquale Annicchino, Osvaldo Costantini, Paolo Costa, Peter Cumper, Michele Dorigatti, Raphaël Durante, Peter Edge, Valeria Fabretti, Gabriele Fattori, Silvio Ferrari, Lucia Galvagni, Frederick Gedicks, Marco Guglielmi, Brian J. Grim, Tania Groppi, Elizabeta Kitanovic, Ronan McCrea, Nausica Palazzo, Enrico Piergiacomi, Andrea Pin, Andrea Pisaneschi, Boris Rähme, Matteo Romagnoli, Isotta Rossoni, Vittorio Santoro, Giancarlo Sciascia, Abraham Singer, Gordon Smith, Winnifred Fallers Sullivan, Elio Tavilla, Jeroen Temperman, Debora Tonelli, Ilaria Valenzi, and Alessandra Vitullo. In particular, I have learned a great deal from Daniele Ferrari, a scholar with a razor-sharp mind and always ready to enjoy a good joke and a drink.

I am deeply indebted to an anonymous peer reviewer of my earlier manuscript 'Religious Freedom Inc: Business, Religion and the Law in the Secular Economy' (2020) 9(1) *Oxford Journal of Law and Religion* 28–55 for offering me crucial insights that have also benefitted this volume.

Thanks also go to all present and past researchers of the *Gruppo di Ricerca e Formazione del Diritto Pubblico Europeo Comparato* (DIPEC) and FBK-ISR who have involved me in their projects and activities. I am glad we crossed paths. I owe a deep depth of gratitude to Elia, Anna, Giuseppe, and Stefano for hosting me in their homes countless times during my stay in Siena. My heartfelt thanks also go to Valentina and Gianmaria who offered me many late-night conversations and early-morning coffees. Floriana and Francesco's wit and phone calls kept me company during the almost endless train travels between Modena, Siena, and Trento. That is why you have also been a big part of this journey. Thank you a hundred times to Isabella Masè for giving me invaluable technical support at FBK in Trento along with an ample supply of funny conversations and evening beers with Filippo. For making all this possible, my thanks also go to Professor Manlio Miele and the "*Dipartimento di Diritto Privato e Critica del Diritto*" of the University of Padova for giving me a wonderful year as a post-doctoral researcher and the time to get the editing of this book under way.

Finally, I was lucky enough to have friends from outside academia that kept me from turning into what is colloquially known as a "nerd" (or at least I hope so). Alex, Alis, Angelo, "Cioppo", Marco, Valeria, Veronica, and Tullio—you have been co-adventurers who came along with me. Thanks for your patience.

Last but not least, thanks to Mom, Dad, Gianluca, Massimo, Stefania, Alice, and Martina. You taught me everything.

Introduction

Matteo Corsalini

This book describes and investigates the intersection between business and religion from a legal perspective. It does so by exploring certain conflicts between the law and the *business* of faith-based organisations against a backdrop of burgeoning jurisprudence on law and religion in European anti-discrimination legislation. Illustrations from the United States (US) are also discussed when they are transferable to the European context or are useful for a better understanding of the phenomenon under consideration.

An important premise underlying this study is as follows: the term "business", as employed here, is conceived in a dual meaning; namely, in a broad sense and a narrow sense. More on these definitions can be found in the "Methodology" section of this introduction. For now, it is enough to note that a broad definition of "business" should invite readers' attention to conventional law and religion issues about the autonomy and self-direction of ecclesiastical entities, including, by extension, their affiliated non-profit offshoots (be they faith-based schools, hospitals, or nursing homes). As counterintuitive as this might sound, the basic idea here is quite simple: there are some areas of ecclesiastical governance that the law recognises to be the sole *business* of churches and not of governments. Such areas flow from the autonomy to carry out worship services and religious teachings as well as from the right to settle property disputes or appoint spiritually qualified ministers without intrusion by state regulation, and the list goes on and on.[1] Stated as simply as possible, "business" in the broad sense can be understood here as referring to the internal spiritual domain of religious institutions, the

1 For a more detailed analysis of the freedoms included in the broader category of "church autonomy", see Chapter I.

DOI: 10.4324/9781003340829-1

protection of which is the indispensable attribute of what scholars have dubbed "church autonomy"[2] or, more recently, "corporate religious freedom".[3]

At this point, a word of caution is needed. In fact, the term "church", in its conventional meaning, risks being excessively underinclusive. It might disadvantage minority or new churches that do not satisfy traditionally accepted characteristics of religion (e.g., the Church of Scientology). Hence, in order to do justice to important nuances, this book uses "church autonomy" where appropriate, but it prefers the term "corporate religious freedom", or "corporate religious autonomy"[4] when discussing the right to religious freedom of religion or belief communities more generally.

Having come this far, it has to be noted that the term "corporate" might also bear a variety of legal meanings. For instance, in US legal doctrine, this term has been used to describe a recent trend in which courts moved initially to protect churches and other affiliated organisations and, from there, to recognising the religious freedom rights of for-profit corporations.[5] Quite intuitively, it is, at this point, that a narrow definition of "business" vis-à-vis religion comes into play.

In principle, "business", in the strict sense, might be defined as the need for commercial enterprises to make revenues by producing and exchanging goods for payment so as to survive in markets. In that sense, this definition undoubtedly also includes churches that, today, have often some level of recourse to commerce.[6] Be that as it may, churches are, in principle, non-

2 See generally Gerhard Robbers (eds), *Church Autonomy: A Comparative Survey* (Peter Lang 2001); Hildegard Warnink, *Legal Position of Churches and Church Autonomy* (Uitgeverij Peeters Leuven 2001); Brett G. Scharffs, 'The The Autonomy of Church and State' (2004) 1(4) Brigham University Law Review 1219–1348; Oslo Conference of Religious Freedom and others (eds), *Facilitating Freedom of Religion or Belief: A Deskbook* (Martinus Nijhoff Publishers 2004); Julian Rivers, *The Law of Organized Religions. Between Establishment and Secularism* (Oxford University Press 2010); Norman Doe, *Law and Religion in Europe: A Comparative Introduction* (Oxford University Press 2011) 114–138; Merilin Kiviorg, 'Freedom Freedom of Religion or Belief – The Quest for Religious Autonomy' (DPhil thesis, Wolfson College 2011); and Jane Calderwood Norton, *Freedom of Religious Organisations* (Oxford University Press 2016).

3 For one of the most recent applications of this formula, see Micah Schwartzman, Chad Flanders, and Zoë Robinson, *The Rise of Corporate Religious Liberty* (Oxford University Press 2016); Jeroen Temperman, *Corporate Religious Freedom and the Rights of Others* (Eleven 2019); and Edward A. David, *A Christian Approach to Corporate Religious Liberty* (Palgrave Macmillan, 2021).

4 On the interchangeability of the term "religious autonomy" with "religious freedom", see W. Cole Durham, Jr., 'The Right to Autonomy in Religious Affairs: A Comparative View' in Gerhard Robbers (eds), *Church Autonomy: A Comparative Survey* (Peter Lang 2001) 687.

5 Micah Schwartzman, Chad Flanders, and Zoë Robinson, 'Introduction' in Micah Schwartzman, Chad Flanders, and Zoë Robinson (n 3) xiv.

6 Granted, today, ecclesiastical entities can no longer rely just on traditional forms of charity and donations to provide for their needs and maintain their ministry. For a legal discussion on so-called "commercial religions", see Peter W Edge, 'Believer Beware: The Challenges of Commercial Religion' (2013) 33(3) Legal Studies 382.

profits, meaning that, say, when they sell religious literature in their stalls, they do not do so to maximise revenues (that is, pure profits generated for the benefit of the individuals controlling them). Net gains, if any, are, instead, retained and redistributed to finance the spiritual activities for which they were originally set up.[7]

All told, the American trend mentioned above is different. It concerns corporate entities that are neither places of worship nor church-controlled organisations and which, above all, have an *entirely* profit-oriented business structure and mindset. What bears note is that, in some cases, these entities also exhibit certain religious behaviours attuned to the moral properties of their founders and owners. For instance, they craft religiously shaped business models, provide goods and services in line with their beliefs, and even close their stores on religious holidays.

Beyond that, and perhaps more strikingly, these "faith-based companies"[8] have recently begun to invoke a right to religious freedom to autonomously oversee their own spiritual (and financial) affairs without intrusion by state regulation, thus de facto behaving as if they were churches. The American retail store Hobby Lobby is an illustrative example in this regard. This faith-based company has, in fact, grabbed headlines and obtained scholarly attention for years, most notably after it won a US Supreme Court (USSC) case in 2014 exempting its Christian owners from providing contraceptives to their female employees on conscience grounds.[9]

While, at this point, European readers might be baffled by the idea of such an explicit mix of profits and religion, this would not come as much of a surprise to their American counterparts. After all, the history of the United States, evocatively named "one nation under God", has been a story about free enterprise, religion, and the confluence of business and religion.[10] Hence the growing interest in academic debates on the other side of the Atlantic on the subject of American religious CEOs (mainly Christian evangelicals) reflecting biblical morality in business.

7 This is coherent with the non-profit funding model described in Henry B. Hansmann, "The Role of Nonprofit Enterprise" (1980) 89(5) Yale Law Journal 836, 838.

8 This term can be traced back to Rex Ahdar, 'Companies as Religious Liberty Claimants' (2016) 5(1) Oxford Journal of Law and Religion 1, 4.

9 This decision and litigation in its wake will be discussed in Chapter IV.

10 For a historical account of the conflation of religion and capitalism in the US, see Kevin M. Kruse, *One Nation Under God. How Corporate America Invented Christian America* (Basic Books, 2015).

Various research fields have made profound inroads in this topic, including sociology;[11] history;[12] management theory;[13] economics;[14] journalism;[15] and more recently, legal studies.[16] To state the obvious, within the latter field, a prime concern has been problematising the legal relationship between profits and religion. One reason that this might be so problematic is that the faith-based commitments of for-profit companies might, in some cases, be feared to not constitute a genuine exercise of religion but, rather, a means to obtain big boosts in the market. At the risk of oversimplification, it is easy to see how faith-based companies invoking and successfully obtaining tax-exempted status (on a par with churches) can obtain a competitive advantage over their secular competitors.[17] In addition, it is also problematic that claims of business religious freedom can result in tensions with human rights laws generally and equality and anti-discrimination laws in particular. In this connection, the USSC has recently developed a pattern of decisions that are now allowing faith-based companies to object on conscience grounds to serving same-sex couples, to covering preventive healthcare services, and to making religiously biased employment decisions.[18]

All things considered, it would not be an irrationality to argue that this new "business turn" in law and religion is virtually reimagining the breadth and scope of the legal category "corporate religious freedom". As part of this fundamental shift, a pattern seems to be emerging. One in which, if corporate religious freedom was, at one time, designed only to provide a zone of *church autonomy* in the management of internal religious affairs (business in a broad sense), it is now stretching beyond traditional houses of worship to cover the *business autonomy* of commercial enterprises in secular commerce (business in a strict sense). On the whole, most of the existing studies on this "business" narrative in law and religion come from the US, whilst European scholarship on the topic is still sparse. Thus, it is a key goal of this book to go some way in filling the gap in European

11 See Bradley C. Smith, *Baptizing Business. Evangelical Executives & The Sacred Pursuit of Profits* (Oxford University Press 2020).

12 See Kevin M. Kruse (n 10); David W. Miller, *God at Work. The History and Promise of the Faith at Work Movement* (Oxford University Press, 2007); Darren E. Grem, *The Blessing of Business. How Corporations Shaped Conservative Christianity* (Oxford University Press, 2016).

13 See Ian I. Mitroff and Elizabeth A. Denton, *A Spiritual Audit of Corporate America: A Hard Look at Spirituality, Religion, and Values in the Workplace* (Jossey-Bass Publishers, 1990).

14 Benjamin M. Friedman, *Religion and the Rise of Capitalism* (Alfred A Knopf, 2021).

15 Marc Gunther, *Faith and Fortune: The Quiet Revolution to Reform American Business* (Crown Business, 2004); Katherine Stewart, *The Powers of Worshippers. Inside The Dangerous Rise of Religious Nationalism* (Bloomsbury Publishing, 2020).

16 Micah Schwartzman, Chad Flanders, and Zoë Robinson, (n 3); Winnifred Fallers Sullivan, *Church State Corporation: Construing Religion in US Law* (The University of Chicago Press 2020).

17 In this sense, see Mark Tushnet, 'Do For-Profit Corporations Have Rights of Religious Conscience' (2013) 99(1) Cornell Law Review Online 70, 80.

18 See Chapter IV.

literature by providing a doctrinal and theoretical reconstruction of this American "business turn" in law and religion.

Having exposed this shift from church to business autonomy in American law, and challenging the terms of the contemporary debate, the claim that a similar narrative has also begun to take place in Europe (and, more specifically, at the European Union (EU) Single Market's level) is then introduced and advanced. This book's objective, then, is to engage in an unprecedented exercise of comparative law that first reconstructs the genesis of corporate religious freedom in the international human rights framework and then trace its evolution (from *church* to *business* autonomy) in American and EU law.

Methodology

In discussing the intersection between business and religion, this research adopts a legal approach that considers scholarship, constitutions, legislation, and case law on corporate religious freedom. For this purpose, four international legal orders are considered: the United Nations (UN), the Organisation for Security and Co-operation in Europe (OSCE), the Council of Europe (CoE), and the EU. As noted, illustrations from the US will be taken when necessary to emphasise a circulation of legal models—that is, the emulation of concepts and legal rules between foreign legal systems.[19] In this sense, this book is also comparative, as it is also intended to draw analogies and look for convergences or divergences between jurisdictions.

In this study, the goal is also to bring a diversity of tools and perspectives to better understand the legal interaction between business and religion. For instance, Part I of this book grounds its conceptual framework in John Locke's (1632–1704) argument that "[t]he only *business* of the Church is the salvation of souls".[20] A brief reconsideration of this claim is a good place to introduce this work's main methodological assumptions.

In short, and as Micah Schwartzman explains, by this phrase, Locke meant to identify a "separation between the spheres of politics and religion", in which the "salvation of souls" is something that lies outside the jurisdiction of states.[21] At any rate, this book does not engage in any level of detail with Locke's political philosophy, an analysis of which is referred to more authoritative scholarship. However, it is precisely Locke's choice of language (*the business of the Church*)

19 For a first discussion on comparative legal research in Italy, see Rodolfo Sacco, *Che Cos'è il Diritto Comparato* (Giuffrè, 1992).

20 John Locke, *A Letter Concerning Toleration* (Bobbs-Merril Company, 1955) 36 (this work by Locke was originally published in 1689) (emphasis added).

21 Micah Schwartzman, 'The Relevance of Locke's Religious Arguments for Toleration' (2005) 33(5) Political Theory 678, 683. In this sense, see also David H. McIlroy, 'Locke and Rawls on Religious Toleration and Public Reason' (2012) 2(1) Oxford Journal of Law and Religion 1, 4.

that has offered much-needed support for developing the idea of what this study has dubbed "business in a broad sense".

In the author's interpretation, this concept suggests that a sole focus on the *commercial behaviour* (business in the strict sense) of faith-based organisations does not do justice to the endeavour of comprehensively exploring the connection between business and religion. Rather, the idea of "business", broadly understood in Lockean terms, also captures patterns of *organisational behaviour* associated with the way that religious institutions administer their internal spiritual affairs. Seen in this way, and drawing on management theory, it can be assumed that religious institutions behave in the manner that they consider to be the most efficient as possible toward the direction of fulfilling their "religious mission"[22] (or, as Locke would put it, "the salvation of souls"). These behavioural patterns, in turn, inevitably have legal ramifications because they might translate into appeals by religious institutions before a court to obtain protection of their organisational autonomy vis-à-vis the state. From the vantage point of management theory, the term "business in a broad sense" can, thus, become a useful semantic device that permits to do two things on a methodological level.

On the one hand, this allows a fresh introduction to conventional legal issues on the autonomy rights of religious institutions by bringing them into this study's macro-theme on "business and religion". On the other, in using the economic metaphor of "business" to describe the internal spiritual domain of religious institutions (a matter purely related to their theologies and doctrines), it is also possible to clarify the author's standpoint vis-à-vis religion.

In fact, if the concept of "business" applied to religion is here used to evoke a certain "managerial rationality"[23] in ecclesiastical governance, then one can imagine how this book does not concern itself with exploring the doctrinal contents of the religious beliefs of faith-based institutions. Rather, this study is more interested in introducing and analysing religion as a "macro social force":[24] an incentive that shapes the way in which religious entities behave, organise their ecclesiastical environments, and even take legal action.[25]

22 See Paul Tracey, Nelson Phillips, and Michael Lounsbury, 'Taking Religion Seriously in the Study of Organizations' in Paul Tracey, Nelson Phillips, and Michael Lounsbury (eds), *Religion and Organization Theory* (Emerald, 2014).

23 This term could be traced back to Yehouda Shenhav, *Manufacturing Rationality. The Engineering Foundations of the Managerial Revolution* (Oxford University Press, 1999) 1 (describing "managerial rationality as a powerful mode of thought and code of conduct in the modern world").

24 In this sense, see Harry J. Van Buren III, Jawad Syed, and Raza Mir, 'Religion as a Macro Social Force Affecting Business: Concepts, Questions, and Future Research' (2019) 59(5) Business & Society 799–822.

25 One author described this idea in terms of a "rationalization" of religion to facilitate the administration of highly hierarchical religious institutions. See Pierre Bordieu, 'Genesis and Structure of the Religious Field' in Craig Calhoun (eds) *Comparative Social Research. A Research Annual. Religious Institutions* (Jai Press, 1991) 6–8.

To support the validity of this approach, it bears note that the use of economic or management language and principles to describe religious discourses as social and behavioural processes is not new. In fact, since the 1970s, some sociologists and economists have been thinking about various aspects of religion by focusing on concepts such as "spiritual capital"[26], "religious marketplaces"[27], "religious products"[28], and "supply and demand of religion"[29]. By and large, this innovative field of study is also known as "economics of religion" and is mainly based on ideas inspired by Adam Smith's *Wealth of Nations* (1776). Perhaps more interestingly, Smith was the first to draw analogies between for-profit corporations producing and selling goods to customers and churches which, in his eyes, had begun to assume many of the organisational traits of the modern and efficiency-oriented industrial firm.[30] In doing so, Smith anticipated, by at least 200 years, insights from the literature in economics of religion and management theory that constitute the intellectual background of this work.

In light of this brief overview, it is the author's opinion that incorporating insights from other social sciences (such as sociology, management theory, or economics) into research in law and religion can be a useful tool for legal scholars to broaden their views and methodologies. In fact, if it is true that the "[l]aw is not, and probably has never been, an independent field of study"[31], this is even more so for those branches of law that deal with religion, a phenomenon of mainly extra-legal nature. This is with the obvious exception of those cases in which religion itself is elevated to a legal source (e.g., Christian canon law, Islamic *sharia* law, or Jewish *halakhah* laws.).

At any rate, it is submitted that the usefulness of applying insights from other social sciences to law and religion is that they can help scholars better understand how religion is changing over time together with the social perception of *what* constitutes a religious belief, ritual, or religious institution. Economic analysis of

26 See Michael McBride, 'Why Churches Need Free-Riders: Religious Capital Formation and Religious Group Survival' (2015) 58(1) Journal of Behavioural and Experimental Economics 77, 78 (describing religious or spiritual capital as "an individual set of skills, experience, knowledge, and familiarity tied to a specific religious group's doctrine, structure, and norms").

27 This term could be traced back to Peter Berger, 'A Market Model for the Analysis of Ecumenicity' (1963) 30(1) Social Research 77–93.

28 The idea of describing religion as a consumer good could be traced back to Laurence R. Iannaccone, 'Sacrifice and Stigma: Reducing Free-riding in Cults, Communes, and Other Collectives' (1992) 100(2) Journal of Political Economy 271–91.

29 Rachel M. McCleary and Robert J. Barro, *The Wealth of Religions. The Political Economy of Believing and Belonging* (Princeton University Press, 2019) 10.

30 See Book V of Adam Smith, *An Inquiry into the Nature and Causes of the Wealth of Nations* (University of Chicago Press 1976). For a more recent work with a specific focus on this argument proposed by Smith, see Robert B. Ekelund, Jr. and others, *Sacred Trust: The Medieval Church as an Economic Firm* (Oxford University Press, 1996).

31 Albert Sanchez-Graells, 'Economic Analysis of Law, or Economically Informed Legal Research' in Dawn Watkins and Mandy Burton (eds), *Research Methods in Law* (Routledge, 2017) 173.

religion, for instance, is based on so-called "rational choice theory", which, in turn, rests on the assumption that individuals are utility-maximisers who weigh the costs and benefits of participation in a religion.[32] By and large, this economic-oriented approach stemmed from observations about how religious tendencies in the West had become increasingly individualistic and hinged more on personal choices than orthodox religious precepts.[33] The popularity of yoga, an Indian meditative practice, among Western Christians who are increasingly motivated by the pursuit of "spirituality" as an alternative to institutional and organised religion is a case in point.[34]

However, and almost without fail, it is not unreasonable to think that the economics of religion as a field of study could be criticised for being reductionist, ethnocentric, if not even downright offensive for orthodox believers. Yet, the mere fact that these studies *do* exist and continue to thrive seems to reveal that, as Marco Ventura explains, the "reality" of religion is objectively changing, albeit in a more or less homogeneous manner throughout the world.[35] In the author's view, it is precisely this changing reality (observed through a scientific lens) that could inspire new generations of legal scholars and professionals to approach issues in law and religion with the scientific rigour of the impartial and detached observer. This, in turn, should help researchers grow more sceptical about accepting conventional understandings of what religion is (or should be) in their legal analyses while, at the same time, maintaining a respectful understanding of the beliefs of others.

If the aim of a social-science approach applying *economic language* to religious discourses is to describe behavioural changes in the way religion is experienced and perceived (i.e., a matter of increasingly individual and personal choice), the same applies to the reverse semantic operation.

To appreciate this point, one can also assume that the growing use of *theological language* among scholars in religious studies to describe secular (and economic) affairs is another indication of how social perceptions of what constitutes religion are changing.[36]

32 Rachel M. McCleary and Robert J. Barro (n 29) 6.

33 See ibid 4. More recent work in the economics of religion has also begun to deal with Eastern countries. See, for example, Sriya Iyer, *The Economics of Religion in India* (Harvard University Press, 2018).

34 In this regard, a classic anthropology paper from the late 1990s coined the now popular phrase "spiritual but not religious". See Brian J. Zinnbauer and others, "Religion and Spirituality: Unfuzzying the Fuzzy" (1997) 36(4) Journal for the Scientific Study of Religion 549–64.

35 See Marco Ventura, *Nelle Mani di Dio. La Super-Religione del Mondo che Verrà* (Il Mulino, 2021) 128.

36 This idea is borrowed from the 2019 position paper by Bruno Kessler Foundation - Center For Religious Studies (FBK-ISR). See Center For Religious Studies - Fondazione Bruno Kessler, 'Religion and Innovation. Calibrating Research Approaches and Suggesting Strategies For a Fruitful Interaction' (2019) <https://isr.fbk.eu/wp-content/uploads/2019/03/Position-Paper.pdf> 7 (posing the following research questions: "[h]as the vocabulary of

Specifically, the idea of "capitalism as religion" was a central theme for sociologist Pierre Bordieu (1930–2002). Trained in the Marxist tradition, Bordieu, in fact, made frequent use of religious metaphors as an overarching framework to describe his critique of the capitalistic socio-economic system.[37] In so doing, some would say that he de facto transformed "this-worldly struggles over material resources and power" into "other-worldly ideals of a 'spiritual' nature."[38] A similar attack on the "religion of capitalism" was made years earlier, in 1921, by philosopher Walter Benjamin in a brief fragment entitled *Kapitalismus Als Religion*[39] and was then revived more recently in 2016 by theologian Harvey Cox in his book *The Market as God*.[40] It is on this intellectual background that Part II of this book has been grounded. However, while the abovementioned authors applied religious language to economics to discuss the "capitalism as a religion" theme from a sociological and philosophical perspective, this investigation takes a different tact.

In this study, Bordieu's, Benjamin's, and Cox's lines of arguments have been, in fact, transposed into an exclusively legal level. To illustrate, in Part II of this book, the adjective "religious" is applied to completely secular for-profit corporations to describe a legal trend that is now reimagining the scope and breadth of the category "freedom of religion or belief" (FoRB). Far from being committed to any political agenda, this methodological approach is based on a purely empirical observation. Namely, if, at one time, corporate FoRB rights were reserved only to protect the organisational autonomy of churches (business in a broad sense), such rights are also now covering for-profit corporations and their secular interests in commerce (business in the strict sense). It is, therefore, the argument of this book that a for-profit corporation becomes "religious" (legally speaking, at least) whenever it enjoys the same levels of immunities as churches under the law.

To push this argument, Part II of this book uses material that straddles three fields of study: (1) law and religion, (2) corporate law, and (3) economic theory. On a final note, it should be stressed that, in developing the second part of this study, much credit is due to some ideas exchanged and discussed at the FBK-ISR to which the author was affiliated from 2018 to 2021. In particular, this work has benefitted greatly from FBK-ISR's "broad understanding" of religion which its researchers explained in terms of: "a non-essentialist, and inclusive understanding of religion, which leaves room for taking new forms of faith, belief,

---

innovation itself become a rhetorical vehicle for quasi-religious discourses? Has innovation itself turned into a belief system and become a sort of religion?").

37 See generally Pierre Bordieu (n 25).

38 In this sense, see Hugh Hurban, 'Sacred Capital: Pierre Bordieu and the Study of Religon' (2003) 15(4) Method & Theory in the Study of Religion 354, 362.

39 For a comment on Walter Benjamin's fragment see Giorgio Agamben, *Creation and Anarchy. The Work of Art and the Religion of Capitalism* (Stanford University Press, 2019) 66–78.

40 Harvey Cox, *The Market as God* (Harvard University Press, 2016).

and spirituality, as well as hybridisations of religious traditions and practices, into account." It is precisely in the spirit of this approach that this research has been carried out.

Structure

This study is divided into two main parts that explore the relationship between religion and business in a broad and narrow sense, respectively.

Part I outlines different approaches to corporate religious freedom in four international legal orders: the UN, the OSCE, the CoE, and the EU.

Chapter I is foundational; it sets the groundwork for a discussion on the more specific sub-topic of corporate religious exemptions from laws of general applicability for further elaboration in Chapter II. On the whole, religious exemptions constitute a system of legal or judicially created accommodations protecting churches in their claims that certain legal principles do not (or should not) apply to them. In other words, they are special concessions that purport nothing less than a positive recognition of the autonomy rights of religious institutions under the law. Seen it this way, the underlying rationale of Chapter I becomes very clear. For if one wants to understand which of the legal orders under consideration are best suited to accommodate religious exemption requests, they should begin by appraising which of them have taken a more favourable stance toward recognising churches as religious freedom claimants more generally. For reasons that will become apparent in Chapter I, only two of the models examined (the CoE and the EU) exhibit sufficient legal and judicial strength to seriously take corporate religious freedom (and, relatedly, religious exemption claims) into account.

Having established that, Chapter II narrows the field of inquiry to these two models and their respective courts: the European Court of Human Rights (ECtHR) and the Court of Justice of the European Union (CJEU). In these contexts, the main tensions between religious demands for special treatment and human rights law concern church-employment disputes and have been broken down into the following queries addressed to the courts: to what extent should religious organisations be permitted to discriminate against ministers and lay personnel in their hiring and firing practices? And more specifically: could a church advance religious reasons for dismissing ministers engaged in non-religious activities (e.g., the teaching of completely secular subjects) that are contractually regulated by civil laws? Ultimately, and in an opposite perspective, can corporate religious exemptions be invoked also to discriminate against lay employees (or potential ones) performing secular tasks (e.g., administrative staff, musicians, gardeners, bus drivers)?

The breakdown of data on *church autonomy* (business in the broad sense) and religious exemptions obtained from Part I will then be used to introduce questions on the *business autonomy* of for-profit enterprises (business in the strict sense) that are explored in Part II.

Having exposed how the CJEU contracted the scope of religious exemptions protecting *church autonomy* in Chapter II, the claim that this court has begun to extend these same exemptions to cover the ***business autonomy*** of secular for-profit corporations is then introduced and advanced in Chapter III.

In support of this argument, this book critically analyses the most recent CJEU case law on the reconciliation of the autonomy rights of what will be called "neutrality-based companies" with their employees' equality rights to be free from discrimination on grounds of religion. The subject of "neutrality-based companies" constitutes the fulcrum of this study and is introduced to describe an economic, normative, and legal phenomenon that is identical, but diametrically opposed, to that of American "faith-based companies". That is, a growing recognition of the right of for-profit corporations to assert before the law the "belief-based" identities underpinning their business models. Phrased differently, in the same way that churches and "faith-based companies" are capable of exercising corporate freedom *of* religion, "neutrality-based companies" can similarly invoke corporate freedom *from* religion as part of their corporate mission and strategy. On a methodological note, it should be pointed out that the adjective "neutral", which is used here to describe companies advancing freedom from religion in contrast to corporations with a religious orientation; however, it is not really even-handed between "religious belief" and "unbelief".[41] As will be seen in Chapter III, neutrality is in itself a value-laden idea that, in fact, inherently presupposes some kind of belief. Be that as it may, and for a lack of a better term, for now, this book will continue to label for-profit corporations exercising freedom from religion as "neutrality-based companies".

That said, and in evaluating the results reached by the analysis of this "business turn" in EU law and religion, the goal of Chapter III is also to show how treating "neutrality-based companies" as corporate freedom *from* religion claimants could help settling employer/employee disputes on more proportionate grounds.

Finally, Chapter IV provides an analysis of how the USSC handles the subject of "faith-based companies" and what legal mechanisms it used to expand corporate religious exemptions to the context of for-profit corporations. In doing so, this chapter begins by discussing major US case law on the ability of business entities to "exercise religion" and then, in the second part, contrasts it with an emerging jurisprudence at the ECtHR level on the intersection between profits and religion.

Legal developments are reflected up until 6 January 2022.

Reference list

Agamben G., *Creation and Anarchy. The Work of Art and the Religion of Capitalism* (Stanford University Press, 2019).

Ahdar R., 'Companies as Religious Liberty Claimants' (2016) 5(1) Oxford Journal of Law and Religion,1–27 (DOI: 10.1093/ojlr/rww001).

41 The author would like to thank an anonymous peer-reviewer for raising this point.

Berger P., 'A Market Model for the Analysis of Ecumenicity' (1963) 30(1) Social Research, 77–93.
Bordieu P., 'Genesis and Structure of the Religious Field' in Craig Calhoun (ed), *Comparative Social Research. A Research Annual. Religious Institutions* (Jai Press, 1991), 1–44.
Calhoun C. (ed), *Comparative Social Research. A Research Annual. Religious Institutions* (Jai Press, 1991).
Cox H., *The Market as God* (Harvard University Press, 2016).
David E. A., *A Christian Approach to Corporate Religious Liberty* (Palgrave Macmillan, 2021).
Doe N., *Law and Religion in Europe: A Comparative Introduction* (Oxford University Press, 2011) (DOI: 10.1093/acprof:oso/9780199604005.001.0001).
Durham Jr. W. C., 'The Right to Autonomy in Religious Affairs: A Comparative View' in Robbers Gerhard (ed), *Church Autonomy: A Comparative Survey* (Peter Lang, 2001), 683–714.
Edge P. W., 'Believer Beware: The Challenges of Commercial Religion' (2013) 33(3) Legal Studies, 382–406 (DOI: 10.1111/j.1748-121X.2012.00252.x).
Ekelund Jr. R. B. and others, *Sacred Trust: The Medieval Church as an Economic Firm* (Oxford University Press, 1996).
Friedman B. M., *Religion and the Rise of Capitalism* (Alfred A Knopf, 2021).
Grem D. E., *The Blessing of Business. How Corporations Shaped Conservative Christianity* (Oxford University Press, 2016).
Gunther M., *Faith and Fortune:The Quiet Revolution to Reform American Business* (Crown Business, 2004).
Hansmann H. B., 'The Role of Nonprofit Enterprise' (1980) 89(5) Yale Law Journal (DOI: 10.2307/796089).
Hurban H., 'Sacred Capital: Pierre Bordieu and the Study of Religon' (2003) 15(4) Method & Theory in The Study of Religion.
Iannaccone L. R., 'Introduction to the Economics of Religions' (1998) 36(3) Journal of Economic Literature, 1465–1495.
Iyer S., *The Economics of Religion in India* (Harvard University Press, 2018).
Kiviorg M., *Freedom of Religion or Belief - The Quest for Religious Autonomy* (DPhil thesis, Wolfson College, 2011).
Kruse K. M., *One Nation Under God. How Corporate America Invented Christian America* (Basic Books, 2015).
Locke J., *A Letter Concerning Toleration* (Bobbs-Merril Company, 1955).
McBride M., 'Why Churches Need Free-Riders: Religious Capital Formation and Religious Group Survival' (2015) 58(1) Journal of Behavioural and Experimental Economics, 77–87 (DOI: 10.1016/j.socec.2015.07.001).
McCleary R. M. and Barro R. J., *The Wealth of Religions. The Political Economy of Believing and Belonging* (Princeton University Press, 2019).
McIlroy D. H, 'Locke and Rawls on Religious Toleration and Public Reason' (2012) 2(1) Oxford Journal of Law and Religion, 1–24 (DOI: 10.1093/ojlr/rws046).
Miller D. W., *God at Work. The History and Promise of the Faith at Work Movement* (Oxford University Press, 2007).
Mitroff I. I. and Denton E. A. D., *A Spiritual Audit of Corporate America: A Hard Look at Spirituality, Religion, and Values in the Workplace* (Jossey-Bass Publishers, 1990).

Norton J. C., *Freedom of Religious Organisations* (Oxford University Press, 2016) (DOI: 10.1093/acprof:oso/9780199689682.001.0001).

Oslo Conference of Religious Freedom and others (eds), *Facilitating Freedom of Religion or Belief: A Deskbook* (Martinus Nijhoff Publishers, 2004).

Rivers J., *The Law of Organized Religions. Between Establishment and Secularism* (Oxford University Press, 2010) (DOI: 10.1093/acprof:oso/9780199226108.001.0001).

Robbers G. (ed), *Church Autonomy: A Comparative Survey* (Peter Lang, 2001).

Sacco R., *Che Cos'è il Diritto Comparato* (Giuffrè, 1992).

Sanchez-Graells A., 'Economic Analysis of Law, or Economically Informed Legal Research' in Dawn Watkins and Mandy Burton (eds), *Research Methods in Law* (Routledge, 2017), 170–193.

Schwartzman M., 'The Relevance of Locke's Religious Arguments for Toleration' (2005) 33(5) Political Theory, 678–705.

———, Flanders C. and Robinson Z. (eds), *The Rise of Corporate Religious Liberty* (Oxford University Press, 2016) (DOI: 10.1093/acprof:oso/9780190262525.001.0001).

———, 'Introduction' in M. Schwartzman, Flanders Chad and Robinson Zoë (eds), *The Rise of Corporate Religious Liberty* (Oxford University Press, 2016), xiii–xxv (DOI: 10.1093/acprof:oso/9780190262525.001.0001).

Shenhav Y., *Manufacturing Rationality. The Engineering Foundations of the Managerial Revolution* (Oxford University Press, 1999).

Smith A., *An Inquiry into the Nature and Causes of the Wealth of Nations* (University of Chicago Press, 1976).

Smith B. C., *Baptizing Business. Evangelical Executives & The Sacred Pursuit of Profits* (Oxford University Press, 2020).

Stewards K., *The Power Worshippers. Inside the Dangerous Rise of American Nationalism* (Bloomsbury Publishing, 2020).

Sullivan W. F., *Church State Corporation: Construing Religion in US Law* (The University of Chicago Press, 2020).

Temperman J., *Corporate Religious Freedom and the Rights of Others* (Eleven, 2019).

Tracey P., Phillips N. and Lounsbury M. (eds), *Religion and Organization Theory* (Emerald, 2014).

———, 'Taking Religion Seriously in the Study of Organizations' in Paul Tracey, Nelson Phillips and Michael Lounsbury (eds), *Religion and Organization Theory* (Emerald, 2014), 3–22.

Tushnet M., 'Do For-Profit Corporations Have Rights of Religious Conscience?' (2013) 99(1) Cornell Law Review Online, 70–86.

Van Buren III H. J., Syed J. and Mir R., 'Religion as a Macro Social Force Affecting Business: Concepts, Questions, and Future Research' (2019) 59(5) Business & Society, 800–822 (DOI: 10.107.171/0770/070067560530139l9884455097).

Ventura M., *Nelle Mani di Dio. La Super-Religione del Mondo che Verrà* (Il Mulino, 2021).

Warnink H., *Legal Position of Churches and Church Autonomy* (Uitgeverij Peeters Leuven, 2001).

Watkins D. and Burton M. (eds), *Research Methods in Law* (Routledge, 2017).

Zinnbauer B. J. and others, 'Religion and Spirituality: Unfuzzying the Fuzzy' (1997) 36(4) Journal for the Scientific Study of Religion, 549–564.

Part I

Church autonomy

1 Framework

Matteo Corsalini

Freedom of religion or belief (FoRB)[1] is said to be one of "the oldest and most controversial"[2] of the liberties that fall under the scope of human rights protection in international law. As a general matter, this legal category is made up of two interrelated dimensions that coalesce into a "two-tier structure"[3] of protection at both universal and regional levels of jurisdiction.[4]

With respect to the first dimension, FoRB confers a "first-tier right" to have (or not to have)[5] a religion or belief as well as to change it according to one's own choice. This "inner dimension" of FoRB ensures the spiritual integrity of the human person in the private sphere of his mind and conscience (*forum internum*). Hence, it is held to be absolute in the sense that it cannot be subjected to governmental authority and interference, as would be the case with, say, state

1 In this book, the formulas "religious freedom" and "FoRB" are used interchangeably. The preference, however, is for the term "FoRB", as its reference to both "religion" and "belief" is more inclusive and consistent with international human rights documents. In this sense, see Marco Ventura, 'The Formula "Freedom of Religion or Belief" in the Laboratory of the European Union' (2020) 23(1) Studia z Prawa Wyznaniowego 7, 9.
2 Malcolm D. Evans, *Religious Liberty and International Law in Europe* (Cambridge University Press 1997) 1.
3 This term could be traced back to Brett G. Scharffs, 'The Autonomy of Church and State' (2004) 1(4) Brigham University Law Review 1219, 1237.
4 See Universal Declaration of Human Rights, 10 December 1948, UNGA Res 217 A III (UDHR), art. 18; International Covenant on Civil and Political Rights, 16 December 1966, 999 UNTS 171 (ICCPR) art. 18; European Convention on Human Rights and Fundamental Freedoms, 4 November 1950 (entered into force on 3 September 1953) 213 UNTS 221 (ECHR) art 9; United Nations (UN) Human Rights Committee (HRC), *CCPR General Comment No. 22: Article 18 (Freedom of Thought, Conscience or Religion)*, 30 July 1993, CCPR/C/21/Rev.1/Add.4, para 1; Charter of Fundamental Rights of the European Union, 18 December 2000, C 364/20, OJ C364; art. 10; UN GA, *Declaration on the Elimination of All Forms of Intolerance and of Discrimination Based on Religion or Belief*, 25 November 1981, A/RES/36/55, art 1(1).
5 In this sense, see Francesco Ruffini, *La Libertà Religiosa. Storia dell'idea* (Feltrinelli,1967) 11.

DOI: 10.4324/9781003340829-3

indoctrination or the use of criminal sanctions compelling individuals "to recant their religion or belief or to convert".[6]

Moving swiftly on, and with respect to the second dimension, FoRB also incorporates a "second-tier right" to manifest religion or belief in the public sphere (*forum externum*). It is important to note here that religious freedom cannot be said to be complete without this outer dimension. Rather, "*forum internum* and *forum externum* should be generally seen as a continuum",[7] as Heiner Bielefeldt put it. *Forum externum*, in fact, legally enhances the *internal* nucleus of a person's convictions by facilitating any individual or group to live out their *external* relations with society and others in a way that is consistent with their all-encompassing ideological views. To do that, the "external dimension" of FoRB generally covers everyone's right "to manifest his religion or belief in worship, observance, practice and teaching".[8] This, however, comes with the caveat that such four manifestations of religion or belief should not be intended to constitute an exhaustive list of the morally inspired actions deserving protection under the "external dimension" of FoRB.[9]

By way of example, the sub-categories of "observance" and "practice" also include the right to submit conscientious objection claims.[10] Speaking of which, these are manifestations of belief that (just like all *external* expressions of religiosity) sometimes might have severe repercussions on the rights of other individuals of groups (whether they are themselves religious). Hence, an obvious difference between the *forum externum* aspect of FoRB and its *forum internum*: while the latter is protected absolutely and unconditionally, the former is not because cer-

6 This hypothetical FoRB interference is discussed in Bahiyyih G. Tahzib, *Freedom of Religion or Belief: Ensuring Effective International Protection* (Martinus Nijhoff Publishers, 1996) 26.

7 UN GA, *Report of the Special Rapporteur on Freedom of Religion or Belief*, 23 December 2015, UN Doc A/HRC/31/18, para 22.

8 See Universal Declaration of Human Rights (n 4) art. 18; International Covenant on Civil and Political Rights (n 4) art. 18; European Convention on Human Rights and Fundamental Freedoms (n 4) art. 9; Charter of Fundamental Rights of the European Union (n 4) art. 10; *General Comment No. 22* (n 4) para 4; *Declaration on the Elimination of All Forms of Intolerance and of Discrimination Based on Religion or Belief* (n 4) art 1(1).

9 In this sense, see Arcot Krishnaswami, 'Study of Discrimination in the Matter of Religious Rights and Practices' UN Doc. E/CN.4/Sub.2/200/Rev.1 (United Nations Publications 1960) 17 (commenting on Article 18 (freedom of religion) of the Universal Declaration of Human Rights, the author argued that: "the intention was to embrace all possible manifestations of religion or belief within the terms 'teaching, practice, worship and observance'"). See also *General Comment No. 22* (n 4) para 4 (reading that: "[t]he freedom to manifest religion or belief in worship, observance, practice and teaching encompasses a broad range of acts.")

10 *Report of the Special Rapporteur on Freedom of Religion or Belief* (n 7) para 23 (discussing more in-depth conscientious objections to compulsory military service). In this sense, see also Heiner Bielefeldt, Nazila Ghanea, and Micheal Wiener, *Freedom of Religion or Belief. An International Law Commentary* (Oxford University Press 2016) (arguing that a right to conscientious objection can be "legally drawn" from the formula "freedom of thought, conscience and religion") 259.

tain practices and rules of religious behaviour might negatively affect the freedoms of others. Seen in this way, and despite textual differences in concrete formulations, human rights law has spelled out specific criteria allowing limitations on the *forum externum* component of FoRB whenever it risks to excessively intrude upon the rights of other human beings. More exactly, under general standards, restrictions must always be "prescribed by law" and "necessary in a democratic society" to protect "public safety, order, health or moral or the fundamental rights and freedoms of the others".[11]

As an aside, another major aspect of the *forum externum* of FoRB is that it enables individuals to "give expression"[12] to their religion or belief "either alone or in community with others and in public or private".[13] All things considered, this is because "religion is seldom if ever solely an individual matter";[14] believers might, in fact, find it meaningful to pursue their religious goals together with other like-minded individuals. Thus, it comes as no surprise that FoRB extends also to accommodate the needs of believers to associate as communities for worship and religious ritual.[15] Religious or belief communities, in turn, might want to set up appropriate institutions of governance needed to carry out a specific mission. These organisations will include a wide spectrum of corporate bodies: from churches and congregations with a primary religious character to entities that combine their stated religious purpose with secular objectives (such as medical care, education, and commercial objectives in faith-based hospitals, schools, and businesses, respectively).

Based on this analysis, it becomes clear that FoRB is a complex and multifaceted right. At its heart, FoRB, in fact, is made up not only of individual and collective elements but also of a "corporate" dimension covering and empowering the rights of religious institutions *qua* corporate actors that are separate

11 See International Covenant on Civil and Political Rights (n 4) art. 18(3); European Convention on Human Rights and Fundamental Freedoms (n 4) art. 9(2); *Declaration on the Elimination of All Forms of Intolerance and of Discrimination Based on Religion or Belief* (n 4) art 1(3).

12 See Malcolm D. Evans (n 2) 312–314 (suggesting that civil courts should appraise not only whether an act is motivated *by* religion or belief but also whether such an act is motivated *by the intention to give expression* to that religion or belief).

13 See Universal Declaration of Human Rights (n 4) art. 18; International Covenant on Civil and Political Rights (n 4) art. 18; European Convention on Human Rights and Fundamental Freedoms (n 4) art 9; *General Comment No. 22* (n 4) para 4; Charter of Fundamental Rights of the European Union (n 4) art. 10; *Declaration on the Elimination of All Forms of Intolerance and of Discrimination Based on Religion or Belief* (n 4) art 1(1).

14 Rex Ahdar and Ian Leigh, *Religious Freedom in The Liberal State* (Oxford University Press 2013) 376.

15 This should not be taken for granted, as some scholars believe that a more general "freedom to assembly and association" is a sufficient protection to collective expressions of religion. See Erik Jurgens, 'Are Freedom of Religion and a Special Legal Position for Churches, Necessary or Even to be Desired in a Liberal Democracy under the Rule of Law?' in Hidegard Warnink (eds), *Legal Position of Churches and Church Autonomy* (Peeters, 2001) 239–243.

and distinct from the individuals holding their offices.[16] Consequently, as to current legal terminology, some scholars tend to distinguish "corporate religious freedom" (or, more conventionally, "church autonomy") from "collective religious freedom".[17] Acknowledging this difference has been crucial to emphasise the institutional and bureaucratic aspects of FoRB that, by extending protection to the corporate rights of religious entities, are also most important for their adherents' capacity to manifest religion collectively.[18] At any rate, the point to be gleaned here is that, once applied to religious or belief organisations, the concept of "autonomy" feeds into FoRB discourses with an important variable: the right of self-determination and self-management of religious organisations *within* a belief community. In this sense, some commentators use the wording "freedom *within* religion" to describe the rights of religious entities to determine for themselves the functioning of their governance structures.[19] More exactly, "freedom *within* religion" denotes an area of autonomy inside which religious institutions can regulate matters of church doctrine and group membership according to their own religious laws and, thus, without the distortion of state regulation.[20]

16 The oldest literature on the rights of religious organisations goes back to the nineteenth-century ecclesiastical law of "separatist" countries that have most successfully kept church and state distant, each within their own sphere of autonomy. Examples include Italy, Germany, Spain, France, and the US. For an analysis of these and other European systems, see Gerhard Robbers (eds), *Church Autonomy: A Comparative Survey* (Peter Lang 2001). In nineteenth-century Catholic ecclesiology, this equal positioning of church and state was emphasised by the so-called "*societies perfecta*" doctrine. In this sense, see Burkhard Josef Berkmann, 'Catholic Church Law: Challenges by Secular Law and Religious Pluralism' (2021) 7(1) Interdisciplinary Journal for Religion and Transformation in Contemporary Society 95, 102; see also Giuseppe dalla Torre, *La Città Sul Monte. Contributo ad Una Teoria Canonistica Delle Relazioni Fra Chiesa e Comunità Politica* (Ave, 2007) 62–64. Instead, in countries with established churches (e.g., the UK and Scandinavia), where there is less awareness of a separation of church and state (and their respective autonomy), scholarship on corporate religious freedom has only recently begun to emerge. For instance, it is generally agreed that the first work on corporate religious freedom in English law dates back to 2010 with Julian Rivers's book *The Law of Organized Religions. Between Establishment and Secularism* (Oxford University Press 2010).

17 See generally Gerhard Robbers (n 16); Hildegard Warnink (n 15). See also Merilin Kiviorg, *Freedom of Religion or Belief—The Quest for Religious Autonomy* (DPhil thesis, Wolfson College 2011) (arguing that "religious autonomy" entails a positive right of self-determination that "adds an important extra dimension to that of religious freedom") 27–28.

18 In this sense, see Merilin Kiviorg, 'Collective Religious Autonomy versus Individual Rights: A Challenge for the ECtHR?' (2014) 39(1) Review of Central and East European Law 315, 317–18.

19 See Brett G. Scharffs, Asher Maoz, and Ashley Isaacson Woolley, 'Introduction. Freedom of/for/from/within Religion: Conceptually Inseparable Rights' in Brett G. Scharffs, Asher Maoz, and Ashley Isaacson Woolley (eds), *Religious Freedom and the Law. Emerging Contexts for Freedom for and from Religion* (2019, Routledge) 6–7.

20 See generally Ronald Minnerath, 'The Right to Autonomy in Religious Affairs' in Oslo Conference of Religious Freedom and others (eds), *Facilitating Freedom of Religion or Belief: A Deskbook* (Martinus Nijhoff Publishers 2004) 291–321.

Phrased differently, there are certain zones of ecclesiastical governance that are the business of the church and not of governments.[21]

In sum, and as already noted in the introduction to this book, it would not be an irrationality to broadly conceive of the term "business" as a shorthand for describing the internal spiritual domain of religious institutions and, relatedly, their autonomy claims vis-à-vis state regulation. From this vantage point, it seems right from the start that an inquiry over the intersection between religion and business (in the broad sense) is likely to be faced with a puzzle.

For if domestic[22] and international legal orders have an obligation to respect the corporate autonomy of religious institutions (read: business in a broad sense), these latter, in turn, can and do violate the personal autonomy of the individuals who operate within them.[23] This dilemma is not merely of theoretical importance. Quite the contrary, such issue has generated real-life litigations that, in Chapter II, will be discussed with examples from the sphere of church employment. It suffices to note here that labour law conflicts have most starkly raised the general points of tension between a church's corporate right to control group membership and some civil laws of the state. To take an obvious example, a religious institution's interest in appointing spiritually qualified ministries and lay personnel is "inseparably connected"[24] to the interest of employees (or potential ones) in non-discriminatory employment.

Ultimately, adding to this complex tension has been the practice of some jurisdictions in Europe and the United States (US) of granting religious bodies exemptions from the applicability of state anti-discrimination laws in employment. Needless to say, all this has come with some costs to the individual autonomy of church employees. Questions over the entitlement of religious exemptions for church employers will, however, be left for further discussion in the next chapter, as it would be going too far to examine them at this early stage of the investigation. For if one wants to engage in a fruitful discussion on corporate religious exemptions within the international FoRB framework, insights into which jurisdictions have taken a more favourable stance toward religious entities as corporate holders of FoRB rights must first be gleaned. Religious exemptions

21 See W. Cole Durham, Jr., 'The Right to Autonomy in Religious Affairs: A Comparative View' in Gerhard Robbers (n 16) 683 (investigating areas of absolute religious autonomy by comparing Europe, the US, and OSCE).

22 For instance, Article 2 of the Italian Lateran Treaty recognises "the sovereignty of the Holy See in international matters as an inherent attribute in conformity with its traditions and the requirements of its mission to the world." Article 8(2) of the Italian Constitution protects "denominations other that Catholicism" by granting them "the right to self-organisation according to their own statutes, provided these do not conflict with Italian law". For a discussion on religious freedom in the Italian Constitution, see Vincenzo Pacillo, *Buon Costume e Libertà Religiosa. Contributo all'Interpretazione dell'Art. 19 della Costituzione Italiana* (Giuffrè Editore, 2012).

23 See Frederick M. Gedicks, 'The Recurring Paradox of Groups in the Liberal State' (2010) 1(1) Utah Law Review 47, 51.

24 In this sense, see Brett G. Scharffs, Asher Maoz, and Ashley Isaacson Woolley (n 19) 11.

in employment are, in fact, special concessions that purport nothing less than a positive recognition of the autonomy rights of religious or belief institutions *qua* institutions as separate and distinct entities from their members.[25]

Seen this way, the present chapter is foundational; it outlines different approaches to corporate religious freedom at the universal and European regional level to set the groundwork for a discussion on religious exemptions in Chapter II. In so doing, this analysis will allow the field of inquiry to be restricted to those jurisdictions that, by granting a certain degree of autonomy to religious institutions, have also edged toward accommodating their claims of exemptions in employment.

The first part of this chapter considers the universal level of the United Nations (UN), the position it took on corporate religious freedom, its legal doctrine on the matter, and some interpretative developments. The second part turns to analyse the posture of the Organisation for Co-Operation and Security in Europe (OSCE), the Council of Europe (CoE), and the European Union (EU) Single Market at the regional level.

United Nations

The starting point for tracking how different jurisdictions handle corporate religious freedom matters is the universal level of the international human rights framework. The following section begins by looking at the United Nations (UN) and its understanding of FoRB as a matter of personal autonomy and conscience of the individual believer. Not surprisingly, therefore, issues over the institutional rights of religious entities have not been considered in depth at this level, whilst the question of religious exemptions, as related to such institutions, has been completely disregarded.

The individualistic approach

It is often said that a serious commitment to the universal protection of "all human beings in all countries"[26] and their fundamental freedoms (FoRB included) began in the twentieth century with the creation of the UN system in 1945 generally, and the adoption of the 1948 UN Declaration of Human Rights (UDHR) in particular.[27]

The modern proclamation of the communal dimension of FoRB is, in fact, fleshed out by this latter document, which in Article 18 states:

25 In this sense, see Jeroen Temperman, *Corporate Religious Freedom and the Rights of Others* (Eleven 2019) 39.

26 See Brice Dickson, 'The United Nations and Freedom of Religion' (1995) 44(2) International and Comparative Law Quarterly 327, 331.

27 ibid 331; in this sense, see also Malcolm D. Evans (n 2) 172.

> Everyone has the right to freedom of thought, conscience and religion; this right includes freedom to change his religion or belief, and freedom, either alone or ***in community with others and in public or private***, to manifest his religion or belief in teaching, practice, worship and observance.[28]

This text, however, is silent about whether the collective dimension of FoRB also covers the autonomy rights of religious institutions.[29]

This is precisely the crux of the matter: should the formula "***in community with others***" be interpreted to mean that it is only individuals, as members of a religious community and its institutions, that benefit from Article 18? Or do religious institutions themselves deserve protection in a similar fashion to their individual members? And if so, does a church derivatively acquire its corporate rights from the freedom of its adherents to collectively manifest religion "in teaching, practice, worship and observance"? Or do churches *qua* corporate legal entities have their *own* rights under international law?

In short, the formula of "***in community with others***" offers the opportunity to imagine churches as all-out rights-and-duty bearers. Of course, this is not to deny the obvious fact that churches necessarily need physical persons to properly work. Be that as it may, there are a number of rights that concern religious institutions *qua* institutions. To take an evident example, a church's right to obtain *juridical* personhood directly concerns its legal status of distinct and separate entity from the *physical* persons holding its offices. In addition, legal entity status is functional for a religious body to unlock further capacities (to hold property, receive financial contributions, employ staff, enter into contracts, sue and be sued, and so forth) which indirectly benefit its adherents.[30]

A first attempt to offer some clarification on these matters can be found in the 1960 study on discrimination in the field of religious rights and practices by Arcot Krishnaswami, Special Rapporteur of the Sub-Commission on Prevention of Discrimination and Protection of Minorities.[31] Krishnaswami's work extensively covered the various issues around the implementation of the rights belonging to religious minorities to practice and profess their own religion. But interestingly, this study has also been largely recognised as a pioneering effort to correct the neglect of corporate religious rights (or so-called "religious association laws")[32]

28 Universal Declaration of Human Rights (n 4) art 18 (emphasis added).

29 See Ioana Cismas, *Religious Actors and International Law* (Oxford University Press 2014) 27.

30 On the importance of the right to legal entity status, see generally OSCE/ODIHR 2014, *Guidelines on the Legal Personality of Religious or Belief Communities* <https://www.osce.org/odihr/139046> accessed 15 October 2020. See also Cole W. Durham, Jr., 'Facilitating Freedom of Religion or Belief through Religious Associations Law' in Oslo Conference of Religious Freedom (n 20) 330.

31 Arcot Krishnaswami (n 9).

32 This term could be traced back to Cole W. Durham, Jr. (n 30)(using this term to describe "the entire range of laws governing entities that religious groups or communities can use in structuring their legal affairs.") 325–26.

by the international community.[33] In particular, Chapter IV of the study briefly addressed questions over the "management of religious affairs". It was in this context that Krishnaswami clarified, for the first time ever, that public authorities cannot interfere at will in the internal business of organised groups.[34] He, thus, recognised that the collective dimension of FoRB includes a corporate right of self-determination. Yet, as Krishnaswami himself admitted, "it is difficult to formulate a rule of general applicability"[35] on corporate religious autonomy. Hence, in spite of everything, his study was not able to resolve questions of religious institutions as right-holders, let alone clarify whether corporate autonomy justifies exemptions from laws of general applicability.[36] Also, Krishnaswami's principles were not codified in international human right law.[37]

In fact, it was the 1966 International Covenant on Civil and Political Rights (ICCPR) (1966) that offered the first legal basis to protect the collective aspects of FoRB. As is well known, the ICCPR gave legal strength to the 1948 UDHR general statements on FoRB, which are not a source of legal obligation, despite their iconic status.[38] Nevertheless, even though the ICCPR vested legally binding powers in the UDHR formula "*either alone or in community*", its preparatory works revealed that, even on that occasion, no consensus was reached on the possibility to bestow explicit autonomy rights on collective religious entities.[39] With this in mind, a brief overview of the ICCPR might, however, help understand the general reluctance to draw an explicit connection between the collective dimension of FoRB and corporate religious rights at the UN level.

The International Covenants on Civil and Political Rights

The ICCPR was adopted by the UN General Assembly (GA) on 16 December 1966 by resolution 2200 A (XXI). It became effective on 23 March 1976 and has been ratified by 173 states.[40] It protects FoRB under Article 18, whose final version reads:

33 In this sense, see Natan Lerner, *Religion, Secular Beliefs and Human Rights: 25 Years after the 1981 Declaration* (Brill 2006) 19.
34 Arcot Krishnaswami (n 9) 49.
35 ibid. 51.
36 In this sense see Nazila Ghanea, 'Religion, Equality and Non-Discrimination' in John Witte and M. Christian Green (eds) *Religion and Human Rights: An Introduction* (Oxford University Press 2011) 215.
37 Julian Rivers (n 16) 38.
38 The UDHR was originally intended only to be "a common standard of achievement for all peoples and all nations." Universal Declaration of Human Rights, preamble. This is also observed in Malcolm D. Evans (n 2) 192.
39 See Jeroen Temperman (n 25) 16.
40 UN GA, *International Covenant on Economic, Social and Cultural Rights, International Covenant on Civil and Political Rights and Optional Protocol to the International Covenant on Civil and Political Rights*, 16 December 1966, UN Doc. A/RES/2200(XXI).

1. Everyone shall have the right to freedom of thought, conscience and religion. This right shall include freedom to have or to adopt a religion or belief of his choice, and freedom, either individually or in community with others and in public or private, to manifest his religion or belief in worship, observance, practice and teaching.
2. No one shall be subject to coercion which would impair his freedom to have or to adopt a religion or belief of his choice.
3. Freedom to manifest one's religion or beliefs may be subject only to such limitations as are prescribed by law and are necessary to protect public safety, order, health, or morals or the fundamental rights and freedoms of others.
4. The States Parties to the present Covenant undertake to have respect for the liberty of parents and, when applicable, legal guardians to ensure the religious and moral education of their children in conformity with their own convictions.

Paragraph I closely resembles the wording of Article 18 of the UDHR. The ICCPR, however, explicitly excludes any mention of the UDHR formula "freedom to change his religion or belief", which was replaced with the milder wording "freedom to have or to adopt a religion or belief of his choice".

Overall, this change reflected an important textual compromise among the drafting parties, as Malcolm Evans explains.[41] Diverging positions on the formulation of the future text of Article 18 of the ICCPR led to extensive debates during its preparatory works. For one thing, the "right to change religion" posed particular difficulties for Muslim states[42] that viewed any possible legitimisation to abandon Islam for other faiths as offensive. Additionally, a number of Western delegates rebutted that if FoRB were shorn of the possibility of discontinuing a belief, it would have not been worthy of legal recognition at all.[43]

41 Malcolm D. Evans (n 2) 201.

42 The suggestion to remove the formula "freedom to change his religion or belief" can be traced back to the proposal of Egypt. See UN Economic and Social Council, *Draft International Covenant on Human Rights: Recapitulation of Amendments to Articles 13, 14 and 15*, 24 May 1949, UN Doc. E/CN.4/253, 3. Saudi Arabia stressed that the words "to change his religion or belief", and "freedom" would raise difficulties for states that had constitutional religions. See UN GA, *Official Records of the Fifteenth Session*, 14 November 1960, UN Doc A/C.3/SR.1021 para 11.

43 See UN National and Economic Social Council, *Summary Record of the 116th Meeting Held at Lake Success, New York, on Tuesday, 7 June 1949: Commission on Human Rights, 5th session*, UN Doc E/CN.4/SR.116, 8 and 11 (Philippines and France). UN GA, *Official Records of the Fifteenth Session*, 16 November 1960, UN Doc. A/C.3/SR.1023, para 8 (Liberia). UN GA, Official Records of the Fifteenth Session, 16 November 1960, UN Doc A/C.3/SR.1024, paras 23–5 (Pakistan). UN GA, Official Records of the Fifteenth Session, 17 November 1960, UN Doc A/C.3/SR.1025, paras 2,6,9,43 and 46 (Philippines, France, Cuba, Netherlands and Israel). UN Economic and Social Council, *Summary Record of the 161st meeting*, 19 April 1990, UN Doc E/CN.4/SR.161, paras 26 and 27 (Yugoslavia and the US).

In light of this, the new formulation in Article 18 of the ICCPR went some way toward recognising a middle-ground position. In effect, whilst the current wording "to have or to adopt a religion or belief" restates the right to hold and maintain a particular worldview, the verb "to adopt" ***implicitly*** hints at the possibility of discontinuing (and, therefore, changing) such belief.[44]

In any case, and as it emerged from the US Secretary-General's annotations to the Draft Covenant, the idea of a right to *explicitly* change religion was contested on several grounds. For instance, it was considered to be redundant, as it was already implied by the concept of FoRB itself.[45] Significantly, it was also argued that an explicit mention of that right would have been excessively supportive of proselytism and missionary activities that, so it was felt, could constitute a threat to public order.[46] As Samuel Moyn explained, the distaste of some delegates for proselytism should be historically traced back to the modern religious warfare that, during the Cold War era, pit the Americans against the Soviets and their programmes of atheistic indoctrination and persecution based on religion.[47] Here, what comes immediately to mind is the Soviet Union's totalitarian aspiration to "remake Soviet man himself by changing the very structure of his beliefs and values through control of the press, education, and propaganda".[48] Within this narrative, it is hardly surprising, therefore, that it was the protection of the personal autonomy of individuals (and not the corporate autonomy of ideologically oriented institutions) that should have been the rationale of Article 18 of the ICCPR in the eyes of the UN drafters.

Perhaps even more so because of this, the UN delegates wanted it understood "that the covenant should not lend its support to any religious body in its proselytising or missionary enterprise, nor should be instrumental in creating any doubts in the mind of any believer of the truth of his belief."[49] This is even

44 Malcolm D. Evans (n 2) 29.

45 UN GA, *Draft International Covenants on Human Rights: Annotation Prepared by the Secretary-General*, 1 July 1995, UN Doc A/2929, para 108.

46 ibid para 116; see also Jeroen Temperman (n 25) 17. See also Andrew Clapham, *Human Rights Obligations of Non-State Actors* (Oxford University Press 2006) (arguing that there are "longstanding concerns at the international level that extending human rights to non-state actors—such as armed groups and corporations (including churches)—might imply excessive legitimisation of their goals and actions.") 33–55.

47 Samuel Moyn, 'From Communist to Muslim: European Human Rights, the Cold War, and Religious Liberty' (2014) 113(1) The South Atlantic Quarterly 63–86 (arguing that FoRB was historically a principle most often intended to marginalise communist secularism). In this sense, see also Pasquale Annicchino, *Law and International Religious Freedom. The Rise and Decline of The American Model* (Routledge, 2017) (explaining that the origins of Article 18 of the UDHR (and, consequently, of Article 18 of the ICCPR) are "related to the battle against communist regimes and their policies of state atheism and persecution based on religion and of religious minorities.") 9.

48 Francis Fukuyama, *The End of History and the Last Man* (The Free Press 1992) 24.

49 UN GA, *Draft International Covenants on Human Rights: Annotation Prepared by the Secretary-General*, 1 July 1995, UN Doc A/2929, para 108.

more evident when looking at Article 18(2), which specifically forbids any kind of coercion impairing a fully autonomous right to have or adopt a religion or belief.

In sum, and in light of the foregoing, any attempt to legitimise corporate religious freedom during the preparatory works of Article 18 of the ICCPR failed and did not produce substantial effects.[50] But on further reflection, and despite the "individualistic"[51] nature of Article 18 of the ICCPR, this provision actually leaves open the possibility for "mild"[52] concessions to the rights of religious groups.

Paragraph I mentions the individual right to "manifest" religion collectively "in worship, observance, practice and teaching", thus, touching on issues that are of great relevance for religious institutions. Be that as it may, this formula constitutes only a formal acknowledgment of the communal dimension of FoRB. Also, it says nothing about which basic freedoms, if any, corporate religious entities can substantially exercise. At any rate, subsequent instruments dealing with corporate religious rights progressively clarified their scope and meaning. This is illustrated below.

The Declaration on The Elimination of All Forms of Religious Intolerance and Discrimination Based on Religion or Belief

A first and substantial effort to elucidate the content of corporate religious rights appeared in the 1981 Declaration on the Elimination of All Forms of Religious Intolerance and Discrimination Based on Religion or Belief (the Declaration).[53] This was an important step because, as noted, it is problematic to deduce the content of these rights simply from the text of the ICCPR itself.[54]

50 Any proposal to recognise this corporate right was rejected. UN GA (n 45) para 116.

51 In this sense, see Pamela Slotte and Helge Årsheim, 'The Ministerial Exception — Comparative Perspectives' (2015) 4(2) Oxford Journal of Law and Religion 171,176–79. see also Malcolm D. Evans (n 2) 3; Natan Lerner, 'The Nature and Minimum Standards of Freedom of Religion or Belief'(2000) 2000(3) Brigham Young University Law Review (arguing that "the international community, suspicious of the validity and genuineness of the assertion of collective and group (including religious group) rights, shifted its emphasis from protecting collective and group rights to affording protection to individual persons on the basis of individual rights and nondiscrimination.") 905, 909.

52 In this sense, see Natan Lerner (n 33) 15.

53 *Declaration on the Elimination of All Forms of Intolerance and of Discrimination Based on Religion or Belief* (n 4).

54 In this sense, see Göran Gunner, Pamela Slotte, and Elizabeta Kitanović, 'Introduction. Human Rights, Freedom of Religion or Belief and the Church' in Göran Gunner, Pamela Slotte, and Elizabeta Kitanović (eds) *Human Rights, Religious Freedom and Faces of Faith* (Globethics.net 2019) 26. See also UN GA, *Interim Report of the Special Rapporteur on Freedom of Religion or Belief, Ahmed Shaheed, Submitted in Accordance with General Assembly Resolution 71/196*, 12 October 2020, UN Doc. A/75/50302 1, 18 (clarifying that "the first steps in developing human rights indicators is to identify the 'normative essence' or the 'attributes' of a given right").

As the title suggests, the primary purpose of the Declaration had to do more with questions of non-discrimination on religious grounds than religious freedom per se.[55] This is perfectly in line with the nature of the UN system which, in a series of UDHR and ICCPR provisions, solemnly proclaims the principles of universal respect for human rights, equality and non-discrimination.[56]

Additionally, underlying this emphasis on non-discrimination were concerns about mounting antisemitic escalations between 1956 and 1960 and Third World pressures against apartheid in South Africa.[57] These events culminated in the UN GA resolutions 1780 and 1781 (XVII) of 8 December 1962. With these, the UN GA instructed the Commission on Human Rights (CHR)[58] to prepare a draft declaration together with a convention on the elimination of religious intolerance. However, it was not until 1981 that the Declaration was finally adopted in GA Resolution 36/55.[59]

On the face of it, the Declaration went beyond questions of discrimination, as it also tried to give specific content to the collective rights of groups *qua* groups. Article 6, which is of the greatest interest for present purposes, offers a concrete catalogue of the collective manifestations of religion that constitute the *forum externum* of FoRB. This catalogue is said to set universal minimum standards of protection for religious collectives[60] and was designed to emphasise the core aspects of religious autonomy.[61] It lists the following freedoms:

a. the freedom to worship or assemble in connection with a religion or belief and to establish and maintain places for these purposes;
b. the freedom to establish and maintain appropriate charitable or humanitarian institutions;
c. the freedom to make, acquire, and use to an adequate extent the necessary articles and materials related to the rites or customs of a religion or belief;
d. the freedom to write, publish, and disseminate relevant publications in these areas;
e. the freedom to teach a religion or belief in places suitable for these purposes;
f. the freedom to solicit and receive voluntary financial and other contributions from individuals and institutions;

55 Malcolm D. Evans (n 2) 230.
56 See Universal Declaration of Human Rights (n 4) Preamble, art 1(3) and 55; see International Covenant on Civil and Political Rights (n 4) Preamble, art 4; 20(2); 24 and 26.
57 See Natan Lerner (n 33) 28; Malcolm D. Evans (n 2) 228.
58 The CHR was a UN monitoring body that was replaced in 2005 by the Human Rights Council. See Rosa Freedman 'The Human Rights Council' in Fréderic Mégret and Philip Alston, *The United Nations and Human Rights. A Critical Appraisal* (Oxford University Press 2020) 182–83.
59 For further reading on the history of the drafting process of the Declaration, see Malcolm D. Evans (n 2) 227–31.
60 Natan Lerner (n 33) 32.
61 Ronald Minnerath (n 20) 310.

g. the freedom to train, appoint, elect, or designate by succession appropriate leaders called for by the requirements and standards of any religion or belief;
h. the freedom to observe days of rest and to celebrate holy days and ceremonies in accordance with the precepts of one's religion or belief;
i. the freedom to establish and maintain communications with individuals and communities in matters of religion and belief at the national and international levels.

Despite this welcome progress, the status of the 1981 Declaration is, however, not entirely clear.[62] In short, although it belongs to what is generally referred as non-binding "soft law",[63] some have argued, however, that its content, including the above catalogue of collective freedoms, has enough normative strength to produce legal effects.[64] Hence, the Declaration could, theoretically, generate state obligations to facilitate the establishment and maintenance of religious or belief corporate entities. Be that as it may, the Declaration's catalogue of rights is non-exhaustive and, more pertinently for the scope of this investigation, does not create any explicit religious exemption from generally applicable laws.[65] In hindsight, it is hard to see how that could be different, as the underlying logic of the 1981 Declaration is to tackle discrimination not only *against* religion but also *by* religious groups themselves on account of their beliefs.[66]

Monitoring mechanisms

To summarise thus far, it has been argued that attempts to recognise the corporate dimension of FoRB at the UN level between 1948 and 1981 were not particularly, or only very partially, successful. Granted, the 1960 Krishnaswami study and the 1981 Declaration's catalogue of religious autonomy rights were the first move toward the recognition of corporate religious freedom. However important they may be, they, nevertheless, constituted only a small step.

With this in mind, this sub-section turns to consider the work of the Human Rights Committee (HRC) and the UN Special Rapporteur on FoRB. On the

62 Julian Rivers (n 16) 43.
63 For a general discussion on soft law in general, see Alan Boyle, 'Soft Law in International Law Making' in Malcolm D. Evans (eds), *International Law* (Oxford University Press, 2006) 141–158.
64 Donna J. Sullivan, 'Advancing the Freedom of Religion or Belief Through the UN Declaration on the Elimination of Religious Intolerance and Discrimination' (1988) 82(3) The American Journal of International Law 487, 488. See also UN Economic and Social Council, *Report Submitted by Mr. Angelo Vidal d'Almeida Ribeiro, Special Rapporteur Appointed in Accordance with Resolution 1986/20 of the Commission on Human Rights*, 6 January 1988, E/CN.4/1988/45, 25.
65 Pamela Slotte and Helge Årsheim (n 51) 176.
66 Malcolm D. Evans (n 2) 84–86.

whole, the former monitors FoRB under the ICCPR, whilst the latter does the same but in the context of the 1981 Declaration.[67]

As will be discussed, despite their lack of legally binding strength, they offered an important contribution in further clarifying the scope of corporate religious freedom.

The Human Rights Committee

The HRC is one of the nine treaty bodies dealing with human rights within the UN architecture.[68] It was created by Article 28 of the ICCPR to ensure state compliance with the ICCPR itself. Under Article 40 of the ICCPR, the HRC scrutinises the reports that state parties submit in relation to the measures that they adopted to give effect to ICCPR rights. By extension, this so-called "reporting procedure" also covers FoRB matters which are dealt under Article 18 of the ICCPR.

In addition to this first function, and on the basis of its experience as a monitoring body, the HCR publishes its own interpretations of specific ICCPR provisions in the form of "general comments".[69] It was in the context of this second function that the HRC clarified the scope of the collective dimension of Article 18 of the ICCPR. In Paragraph 4 of the 1993 General Comment No. 22, the HCR observed that the freedom to manifest religious beliefs covers "acts integral to the conduct by religious groups of their basic affairs", including "the freedom to choose leaders, priests and teachers" and to establish seminars and faith-based schools.[70] At first glance, this does not seem to add much to the content of the 1981 Declaration. Furthermore, general comments are said to be legally non-binding.[71] In any case, because general comments are often quoted by other

67 Pamela Slotte and Helge Årsheim (n 51) 177.

68 The other nine-bodies are the Committee on Economic, Cultural and Social Rights (CESCR); the Committee on the Elimination of Racial Discrimination (CERD); the Committee on the Elimination of Discrimination Against Women (CEDAW); Committee Against Torture (CAT); Committee on the Rights of the Child (CRC); Committee on Migrant Workers (CMW); Committee on the Rights of Persons with Disabilities (CRDP); Committee on Enforced Disappearances (CED). In addition to the nine treaty bodies monitoring the implementation of the nine UN human-rights treaties, the tenth treaty body, the Subcommittee on Prevention of Torture, monitors places of detention in the states parties to the Optional Protocol to the Convention against Torture. See Heiner Bielefeldt, Nazila Ghanea, and Micheal Wiener (n 10) 46.

69 See International Covenants on Civil and Political Rights (n 4) art 40(4). Martin Scheinin, 'The Human Rights Committee and Freedom of Religion or Belief' in Oslo Conference of Religious Freedom (n 20) 191 (describing general comments as a byproduct of the HRC's reporting procedure).

70 UN Human Rights Committee (HRC) (n 4) para 4.

71 Helen Keller and Ieena Grover, 'General Comments of the Human Rights Committee and Their Legitimacy' in Helen Keller and Geir Ulfstein (eds), *UN Human Rights Treaty Bodies: Law and Legitimacy* (Cambridge University Press 2012) 129.

international bodies,[72] some scholars now agree that they form a "persuasive body of jurisprudence"[73] that binds domestic legislation and judicial interpretation.[74]

Conversely, for others, the presumed correctness of this view is rebuttable; even though general comments are sufficiently authoritative to attract state compliance, they remain legally non-binding.[75] Despite the lack of clarity on this issue, the fact that general comments report and communicate the final interpretation that the HRC gives on certain matters after completion of a quasi-judicial procedure might corroborate their legal strength.[76] In practice, although general comments originate from the reporting procedure, they also "draw upon"[77] a third function of the HRC: the compliant procedure under the First Optional Protocol to the ICCPR.[78] This is the part of the HCR's work that is closer to judicial decision-making, as it is in this capacity that it might receive and consider individual complaints alleging violations of the ICCPR.[79]

Linked to this, and as regards FoRB cases settled under the Optional Protocol, some positive developments on the corporate dimension of this right merit attention. For instance, in the 2004 case of *Sister Immaculate Joseph v Sri Lanka*, the HCR, for the first time ever, recognised the right of a group belonging to a Roman Catholic order to obtain legal entity status under Sri Lankan laws.[80] In particular, the struggle for legal recognition testified in *Sister Immaculate* epitomises one of the thorniest issues that many religious or belief minority communities all around the world face on a daily basis in the area of corporate religious

72 See, for instance, *Perincek v Switzerland*, App no 27510/08 (ECtHR, 15 October 2015) para 71 (referring to General Comment 34 on Article 19 of the ICCPR). See also *Ahmadou Sadio Diallo (Republic of Guinea v Democratic Republic of the Congo)* (2010), Merits, Judgment ICJ Rep 2007 639, para 66 (referring to General Comment 15 regarding the position of aliens under the Covenant).

73 The HRC itself has recognised that its views have "some important characteristics of a judicial decision". See UN Human Rights Committee (HRC), *General Comment No. 33: The Obligations of States Parties under the Optional Protocol to the International Covenant on Civil and Political Rights*, 5 November 2008, UN Doc. CCPR/C/GC/33, para 11. See generally Ludovic Hennebel, 'The Human Rights Committee' in Fréderic Mégret and Philip Alston (n 57) 369–370.

74 In this sense, see also Natan Lerner (n 33) 26.

75 For instance, the International Court of Justice (ICJ) clarified that it is now way obliged to model its own interpretation of that of the Committee. Yet, it also acknowledged the great weight of the interpretations adopted by the HRC. See *Ahmadou* (n 72) para 66. For an analysis of the view rejecting the legal strength of the HRC see Helen Keller and Ieena Grover (n 71) 129–130.

76 In this sense see Martin Scheinin (n 69) 192.

77 In this sense ibid 192.

78 See *Optional Protocol to the International Covenant on Civil and Political Rights*, art 1–5. See also Martin Scheinin (n 69) 192 (clarifying the relationship between general comments and the individual compliant procedure).

79 See also International Covenants on Civil and Political Rights (n 4) art 41 and 42.

80 UN Human Rights Committee (HRC), *Sister Immaculate Joseph and 80 Teaching Sisters of the Holy Cross of the Third Order of Saint Francis in Menzingen of Sri Lanka v. Sri Lanka*, 3 November 2005, Communication No 1249/2004, CCPR/C/85/D/1249/2004.

freedom: access to legal entity status. As such, it is no exaggeration to say that quite a number of states with a constitutionally established religion or church[81] are still privileging majority denominations "to which they feel a certain cultural or historical attachment."[82] The end result is that, in countries concerned with the maintenance of traditional state religions, several organisational hurdles for "non-official" minorities are likely to emerge from governments piling excessively burdensome conditions on them for acquiring juridical personhood.[83]

To appreciate this argument, it has to be noted that, in *Sister Immaculate Joseph*, the Sri Lankan government requested the Catholic order to include evidence of the local authority's favourable opinion on the registration.[84] Upon verification that such extra requirement was not satisfied, it then rejected the application. As Jeroen Temperman explains, behind this decision was a clear effort by Sri Lankan authorities to make it difficult for the order to access legal entity status—an effort that was dictated precisely to limit the dissemination of Catholic doctrine that, so it was felt, could have posed a threat to Buddhism, the Sri Lankan state-supported religion.[85]

Also noteworthy is the 1990 decision in *Delgado Paéz v Columbia*.[86] Here, at stake was whether Catholic Church authorities in Colombia could assign other duties to a religious education teacher who advocated a "liberation theology" that the church disapproved. The HRC dismissed the teacher's complaint and found no violation of his FoRB right under Article 18 of the ICCPR. It, thus, concluded that church authorities have discretional powers to decide who should teach religion and the manner in which it should be taught.[87] Although *Delgado* recognised considerable institutional autonomy for religious organisations, Pamela Slotte and Helge Årsheim explain that this decision did not create any special religious exemption for churches *qua* corporate entities.[88] This should come as no surprise, as the HRC complaint procedure is open only to individuals or groups of individuals, while juridical persons *as such* cannot bring claims under this mechanism.[89]

In *Delgado*, the HRC could, in fact, indirectly extend protection to a corporate entity only by virtue of the individual complaint that was brought to its

81 Scholars generally distinguish between three models of religion-state religion in Europe: church-state systems, separation systems and hybrid systems. For a discussion see Norman Doe, *Law and Religion in Europe: A Comparative Introduction* (Oxford University Press 2011) 29–39.

82 Heiner Bielefeldt, Nazila Ghanea and Micheal Weiner (n 10) 224.

83 Recently, this issue has been thoroughly discussed in: OSCE/ODIHR 2014 (n 30) 2020.

84 Jeroen Temperman, *State-religion Relationships and Human Rights Law: Towards a Right to Religiously Neutral Governance* (Brill 2010) 260.

85 ibid.

86 UN Human Rights Committee (HRC), *William Eduardo Delgado Páez v Colombia*, Communication No 195/1985, 23 August 1990, CCPR/C/39/D/195/1985.

87 ibid.

88 Pamela Slotte and Helge Årsheim (n 51)177.

89 See Optional Protocol (n 78) art 1–2.

attention. The same logic also applied to the *Sister Immaculate* case, in which a nun authored a communication to the HRC on behalf of herself and 80 other sisters of a Roman Catholic order. In any case, one cannot help noticing how institutional religious autonomy rights finally seem to have progressively carved judicial meaning out of the HRC's praxis and case law.

UN Special Rapporteurs

So far, it has been shown that the protection of FoRB, at the universal level, "has been firmly anchored in the sanctity of the conscience of individuals".[90] If this approach is undeniably valuable, it is also true, however, that an individual's religious freedom would be impoverished if the corporate dimension of the institution to which he or she belongs was left unprotected.[91] The UN Special Rapporteurs on FoRB seem to have been more sympathetic to this latter view, as will be discussed below.

On the face of it, the Rapporteurs are a category of experts that the Human Rights Council has designated to investigate human rights violations. They are also tasked with developing soft law guiding principles on thematic issues to enrich the corpus of international human rights law.[92] In the context of clergy appointments, for instance, in 1987, Special Rapporteur Angelo d'Almeida Ribeiro expressed concerns about the excessive dependence of corporate autonomy rights upon state authority in so far as "clergymen must obtain a license issued by the State in order to officiate".[93]

In 1993, Ribeiro was replaced by Abdelfattah Amor who confirmed, during his visit in Greece in 1996, the "need to refrain from interfering in the affairs of religion, apart from the restrictions provided for in international law".[94] Also in this sense, Independent Expert Gay McDougall in her 2009 mission report on Greece recommended that "[r]eligious leaders should be chosen by their religious communities, but must be restricted to religious duties that do not infringe fundamental rights".[95] Hence, she urged civil courts to exercise effective judicial review of clergy appointments to guarantee their adherence to constitutional and international human rights law.[96]

90 Pamela Slotte and Helge Årsheim (n 51) 179.

91 Rex Ahdar and Ian Leigh (n 14) 377.

92 See Philip Alston and Frédéric Mégret, 'Introduction. Appraising the United Nations Human Rights Regime' in Fréderic Mégret and Philip Alston (n 58)12–14.

93 UN Economic and Social Council, *Report Submitted by Mr. Angelo Vidal d'Almeida Ribero, Special Rapporteur Appointed in Accordance with Resolution 1986/20 of the Commission on Human Rights*, 24 December 1986, E/CN.4/1987/35, para 56.

94 UN GA, *Implementation of the Declaration on the Elimination of All Forms of Intolerance and Discrimination Based on Religion or Belief, Note by the Secretary General*, 7 November 1996, A/51/542/Add.1, 139.

95 UN GA, *Report of the Independent Expert on Minority Issues, Gay McDougall. Addendum*, 18 February 2009, A/HRC/10/11/Add.3, para 95.

96 ibid.

Interestingly, Special Rapporteur Heiner Bielefeldt took a slightly different approach to the matter.[97] In his 2013 thematic report on FoRB and equality between men and women, he stressed that the decision-making powers of religious leaders must certainly abide by human rights standards. However, this should not be taken to mean that state interferences in clergy appointments are always a priori justified.[98] There is "no general trumping of the equality principle over religious freedom, or vice versa", he clarified.[99] Hence, in refusing to establish a hierarchy of human rights, with the right of religious freedom at its top, Bielefeldt implicitly suggested that a "balancing-approach" is the most suitable for settling disputes in church management. Perhaps this explains why he did not specifically comment on the possibility of crafting statutory religious exemptions that would risk creating an anti-discrimination imbalance between religious institutions and the secular rights of others.

Also, the Rapporteur, Ahmed Shaheed, flagged the need to tackle wrongful restrictions on corporate FoRB rights in his 2020 interim report on FoRB. He recommended promoting the social inclusion of marginalised minority groups via the creation of "specific mechanisms and arrangements at different levels of decision-making ... to overcome the impediments that persons belonging to these groups face in their efforts to play an effective part in the life of the community".[100] This resonates with Target 16.b[101] and 10.3[102] of the UN Sustainable Development Goals (SDG-16). These latter outline the need to promote non-discriminatory laws and equal opportunities also in relation to collective manifestations of FoRB.[103] In this connection, he expressed concerns over (i) onerous bureaucratic procedures limiting the establishment of places of worship,[104] (ii) anti-terrorism measures restricting peaceful religious manifestations also via AI surveillance mechanisms,[105] (iii) the destruction of religious properties and commercial businesses,[106] the underfunding of faith-based

97 In this sense, see also Heiner Bielefeldt, Nazila Ghanea, and Micheal Wiener (n 10) 189.

98 UN GA, *Interim Report of the Special Rapporteur on Freedom of Religion or Belief, Heiner Bielefeldt, in Accordance with Assembly Resolution 67/179*, 7 August 2013, UN Doc A/68/290, para 57, 59, 60 and 61.

99 Heiner Bielefeldt, Nazila Ghanea, and Micheal Wiener (n 10) 190.

100 See UN GA (n 54) para 80(f).

101 Target 16(b) of the SDG-16 outlines the need to "[p]romote and enforce non-discriminatory laws and policies for sustainable development". See UN GA, *Transforming Our World: The 2030 Agenda for Sustainable Development*, 21 October 2015, UN Doc. A/RES/70/1 1, 26.

102 Target 10(3) of the SDG-16 outlines the need to "[e]nsure equal opportunity and reduce inequalities of outcome, including by eliminating discriminatory laws, policies and practices and promoting appropriate legislation, policies and action in this regard". Target 16(b) of the SDG-16 outlines the need to "[p]romote and enforce non-discriminatory laws and policies for sustainable development". See ibid 21.

103 See UN GA (n 54) para 12.

104 ibid paras 22–29.

105 ibid paras 17–21.

106 ibid para 36.

public services,[107] and the expropriation of indigenous sacred sites for commercial purposes.[108] Despite this favourable approach to corporate religious freedom, Shaheed, however, said nothing about the right of religious entities to exercise religion as separate and distinct bodies from the rights and interests of its members. As a matter of fact, his report is explicitly concerned with "persons who on account of their religion or belief, are at risk of 'being left behind'".[109]

In sum, what emerges from this analysis of the work of the UN Rapporteurs on FoRB is a picture in which there is some ambiguity as to who should hold religious freedom (a church or its adherents?) To conclude, while both the HRC and consecutive Special Rapporteurs opened up toward religious autonomy rights, they seemed, however, to adopt a cautious stance to corporate FoRB. If it is true that this approach is coherent with the conventional UN's emphasis on the primacy of the individual believer, then the Rapporteurs definitively confirmed that questions over corporate religious exceptions have never been at issue under this legal order.[110] In other words, it is at least plausible to argue, then, that the Rapporteurs supported the idea of FoRB as a right that belongs more to natural than legal persons.

European institutions

As can be inferred from the previous section, institutional religious entities have not been explicitly recognised as legal entities in their own standing at the UN level. In the quest of examining corporate religious freedom in the international FoRB framework, a number of different and parallel developments at the European regional level must be noted. Several supranational organisations in Europe, in fact, have adopted regional FoRB standards and set up human rights judicial bodies that made significant headway in furthering the rights and obligations of corporate religious entities.

The following begins by sketching the position of the OSCE. Because the status of religious institutions as corporate right-holders has found support also within the CoE, this legal order is analysed immediately afterward. Eventually, the position of the EU is considered. It is well-known that the latter navigates a complex terrain of national, cultural, and, consequently, religious traditions, while experimenting an unprecedented project of supranational legal integration. As will be shown, it was precisely because of the active engagement of Christian churches in the European integration discourse that the EU began in the early 1990s to seriously discuss the question of corporate religious freedom within its single-market project.

107 ibid paras 39–47.
108 ibid paras 49–51.
109 ibid para 3.
110 In this sense see Pamela Slotte and Helge Årsheim (n 51) 179.

The Organisation for Security and Co-operation in Europe

The OSCE (formerly Conference, CSCE) is a security-oriented intergovernmental organisation. Its origins can be traced back to a proposal by the Soviet Union in 1950 to set off a process of rapprochement between the East and West during the Cold War period.[111]

Despite initial scepticism, in the early 1970s, all European countries (also including the US and Canada) engaged in multilateral negotiations and discussions on human rights in connection with military security, economic/environmental cooperation, and humanitarian concerns. The so-called "Helsinki Process" culminated in the signing of the 1975 Helsinki Final Act. This is a politically binding document that laid down normative standards on security and human rights and, eventually, called for regular follow-up meetings for their progressive implementation. Thus, the CSCE worked as a continuous conference (as its name implies) until the 1990 Paris Summit Meeting. Here, the drafting of the Charter of Paris for a New Europe set the stage for the progressive move of the CSCE from its role as a forum for negotiation to an international organisation (OSCE) with its own operational structure.[112]

The "comprehensive security" approach

This brief analysis might help appreciate the political atmosphere in which the OCSE commitments were adopted. This background is important because the Cold War legacy deeply influenced the path along which the OSCE developed its approach to human rights in general and FoRB in particular.[113]

Overall, and following Malcolm Evans, the OSCE is "more than a human rights mechanism" because "the connection between human rights and security lies at the heart of its aims".[114] All things considered, this is reasonable given that the OSCE project was originally borne out of the commitment to soothe tensions between Soviet and Western blocs during the Cold War. In keeping with these security objectives, corporate FoRB rights were then accorded a central space in the prevention

111 For an account of the historical background of the OSCE see Urban Gibson and Karen S. Lord, 'Advancement in Standard Settings: Religious Liberty and OSCE Commitments' in Oslo Conference of Religious Freedom (n 20) 239–41.

112 For an extensive discussion on this point see generally Dominic McGoldrick, 'From "Process" to "Institution". The Development of the Conference on Security and Cooperation in Europe' in Dominic McGoldrick and Bernard S. Jackson (eds) *Legal Visions of the New Europe. Essays Celebrating the Centenary of The Faculty of Law, University of Liverpool* (Graham and Trotman 1993) 135.

113 In this sense see Malcolm D. Evans (n 2) 366–70.

114 ibid 369. See also the heading "*Questions relating to Security in Europe*" in Conference for Security and Co-operation in Europe (CSCE), *Helsinki Final Act*, 1 August 1975 1, 1–10; Conference for Security and Co-operation in Europe (CSCE), *Helsinki Concluding Document. The Challenges of Change*, 10 July 1992, para 21. For a more recent discussion on religion and security see 'Ensuring freedom of religion or belief and tolerance and non-discrimination for all is vital to security, say participants at OSCE meeting in Vienna' (OSCE, 22 June 2017) <https://www.osce.org/chairmanship/324851> accessed 25 October 2020.

and settlement of ethno-religious conflicts brought to light in the post-Cold War period.[115] This becomes even more evident when considering how the OSCE's promotion of international human rights standards was particularly active in countries of the former Soviet bloc. There, the social fragmentation caused by communism led to dangerous readings of religion as a surrogate for cultural identity and politics that, in turn, exacerbated violence against minorities on identarian grounds.[116]

All told, it is against this background that the OSCE has developed an approach to human rights and FoRB that diverges from that of the UN. The main difference is that from an OSCE perspective, couching religious freedom in a similar fashion to the UN's individualistic human-rights paradigm cannot provide an effective solution to settle a conflict's underlying causes. This is why the OSCE, instead, favours a holistic safeguard of religious or belief communities (also covering their corporate dimension) as the necessary groundwork toward security, societal harmony, and economic prosperity.[117] And to come full circle, the more the prosperity, the more the chances of developing peaceful relations within and among countries.[118]

Be that as it may, it must, however, be noted that the OSCE's positive attitude to FoRB in all its multifaceted dimensions (be they individual, group, or even corporate) is not due to security reasons alone. After all, the OSCE is an organisation founded on the combination between "security" and "cooperation" (as its name suggests). This mix, in turn, requires a commitment from all the OSCE participating states to "cooperate" not only in security activities (such as conflict prevention) but also in fostering economic development and, more relevant for this discussion, promoting the full respect of human rights and fundamental freedoms.[119] In this sense, and as clarified in the 2019 Policy Guidance docu-

115 See generally Giovanni Barberini, 'Religious Freedom in the Process of Democratisation of Central and European States' in Silvio Ferrari and Cole W. Durham, Jr. (eds), *Law and Religion in Post-Communist Europe* (Peeters 2003).

116 See Pasquale Annicchino (n 47) (describing the effort by the Orthodox Russian Church to reclaim a central role in politics and society after the end of communism) 81–88. For a discussion on the discriminatory treatment of religious minorities in post-communist European countries, see Giovanni Barberini (n 115).

117 In this sense, see OSCE/ODIHR 2019, *Freedom of Religion or Belief and Security: Policy Guidance* 1, 10 <https://www.osce.org/files/f/documents/e/2/429389.pdf> accessed 24 October 2020. In support of the link between FoRB and socio-economic prosperity, the OSCE/ODHIR Advisory Panel mentions the following studies: Brian J. Grim and Roger Finke, *The Price of Freedom Denied: Religious Persecution and Conflict in the Twenty-First Century* (Cambridge University Press 2011); Brian J. Grim, Greg Clark, and Robert Edward Snyder, 'Is Religious Freedom Good for Business?: A Conceptual and Empirical Analysis' (2014) 10(4) Interdisciplinary Journal of Research on Religion 2.

118 Giovanni Barberini (n 115) 11 (speaking of Kazakistan, the author argues that "deep down a state has a strong interest in protecting religious organisations because these also have contributed to the social rebirth of their country after a totalitarian regime").

119 More exactly, the OSCE "comprehensive" approach to security encompasses three dimensions: (1) the politico-military, (2) the economic and environmental, and (3) the human dimension. An introduction to these three complementary dimensions is available at: <https://www.osce.org/what-we-do> accessed 17 December 2020.

ment *Freedom of Religion of Belief and Security* launched by the OSCE/Office for Democratic Institutions and Human Rights(ODIHR) panel of experts on FoRB, the concepts of "security" and "freedom" (including religious freedom) should be thought of as closely related, if not even complementary.[120]

In other words, in the same way that the protection of FoRB is conducive, if not essential, to security, the Panel observed that greater security and social harmony, similarly, can lead to greater opportunities for individuals to be left alone in the enjoyment of their FoRB rights.[121] Seen in this way, the panel employed the concept of "comprehensive security" with a view not only to highlight the interrelatedness between security and FoRB but also to clarify how the promotion of the former should always go hand in hand with respect to human rights law standards.[122] Following this, it was recommended that FoRB claims vis-à-vis security need to be carefully balanced on a case-by-case basis,[123] thus avoiding an attitude that over stresses "security" at the expenses of FoRB in a post-9/11 language and fashion.[124]

Normative framework

Notwithstanding the above, it is, however, widely recognised that the early OSCE approaches to FoRB had mostly a strong security-oriented focus. To appreciate this, it suffices to note how, following some concerns over the status of national (and religious)[125] minorities during the 1992 Helsinki Summit, the OSCE confirmed and agreed that their protection would have been an optimal preemptive strategy against terrorism and other security threats.[126] Truth be told, however, this OSCE "securitisation approach" to FoRB should be traced back as early as to the 1975 Helsinki Final Act. Even more importantly, it was precisely in this con-

120 See OSCE/ODIHR 2019 (n 117) 7.

121 ibid 7; in this sense, see also Jeroen Temperman, '*Freedom of Religion or Belief and Security – Some Reflections*' (Talk About: Law and Religion Studies, 3 October 2019) <https://talkabout.iclrs.org/2019/10/03/freedom-of-religion-or-belief-and-security-some-reflections/> accessed 17 December 2020.

122 This concept is discussed in OSCE/ODIHR 2019 (n 117) 9–11.

123 ibid 6.

124 The risk that an excessive focus on security might be detrimental to FoRB protection is emphasised in Malcolm D. Evans (n 2) 370. On this connection, see also more generally Malcolm D. Evans 'Advancing Freedom of Religion or Belief: Agendas for Change' (2012) 1(1) Oxford Journal of Law and Religion 1, 5.

125 See Giovanni Barberini (n 115)10 (arguing that "the problems of national minorities, in many cases, signify problems of religious minorities" and taking the persecution of Hungarian Catholic minorities by the Romanian communist government as an example).

126 In support of this contention, see Malcolm D. Evans (n 2) 370. This approach is further confirmed by the establishment of an a High Commissioner on National Minorities to provide "early warning" and "early action" at the earliest possible stage of potential tensions involving national minorities. These tensions must 'have not yet developed beyond an early warning stage, but, in the judgement of the High Commissioner, have the potential to develop into a conflict within the CSCE area. See Title II of the the 'Helsinki Decisions' in *Helsinki Concluding Document* (n 114) para (3).

text that, for the very first time, the former CSCE also began to accord religion a central place in its agenda also from a human rights perspective. This is how the "security" and "cooperation" layers of this regional project started to intertwine.

To look more closely at this enmeshment between "security" and "cooperation", consider how a specific FoRB section entitled: *Respect for human rights and fundamental freedoms, including the freedom of thought, conscience, religion or belief* was integrated into the Helsinki Act.[127] Also, under the heading "*Cooperation under Humanitarian and Other Fields*", Section 1(d) of the Helsinki Act allowed "contacts and meetings" between "religious faiths, organisations and institutions".[128] For some, it was precisely this development that constituted the very first step toward protecting the corporate rights to worship and administration of faith-based institutions. While for others, this provision meant even more, as they praised it as the first real groundwork for more concrete recognition of corporate religious entities as right-bearers in their own standing.[129]

Moving swiftly on, subsequent noteworthy developments emerged from the 1983 Madrid Concluding Document under the section "*Questions Relating to Security in Europe*".[130] Within this text, governments agreed "to take the action necessary" to protect FoRB rights, thus, guaranteeing corporate entities a right to complain in case of a lack of positive measures adopted by a country.[131] Linked to this, governments also committed to "favourably consider" applications by religious groups for legal entity status.[132] This latter statement is, however, weak, as it does not contain a proper commitment to *concede* such status but only to "favourably consider" doing so.

That apart, it was within another text that the right to legal entity status was not just reaffirmed but also taken to a higher level of concreteness: the 1989 Vienna Concluding Document.[133]

Principle 16(3) of this document, in fact, shifts from the "favourably consider" formula toward a more outright commitment to "grant" such a status, provided, however, that religious groups are "prepared to practice their faith within the constitutional framework of their States".[134] Paragraph 16(4) turns then to elaborate on the legal benefits stemming from legal entity status. These

127 See *Helsinki Final Act* (n 114) 6.

128 ibid 40.

129 See Urban Gibson and Karen S. Lord (n 111) 246.

130 Conference for Security and Co-operation in Europe (CSCE), *Concluding Document — of the Madrid Meeting 1980 of Representatives of the Participating States of the Conference on Security and Co-operation in Europe, Held on the Basis of the Provisions of the Final Act Relating to the Follow-up to the Conference*, 6 September 1983 1, 6

131 ibid 7.

132 ibid 6.

133 In this sense, see Urban Gibson and Karen S. Lord (n 111) 249.

134 See Conference for Security and Co-operation in Europe (CSCE), *Concluding Document — of the Vienna Meeting 1986 of Representatives of the Participating States of the Conference on Security and Co-operation in Europe, Held on the Basis of the Provisions of the Final Act Relating to the Follow-up to the Conference*, 15 January 1989 1, 8.

include the rights (i) to maintain places of worship, (ii) to autonomy in internal structure and personnel, and (iii) to receive voluntary financial support and other contributions.[135] All things considered, the above cluster of rights makes up what German legal doctrine defines as the autonomy of a community "to regulate its *own affairs (eigene Angelegenheiten).*"[136] Such rights, in turn, gave some scholars a baseline to encourage an extensive reading of the wording "own affairs". More exactly, in their view, a broad understanding of this formula should have included not only strictly "internal" organisational matters but also a wider range of "external" activities relating to a community's religious mission as a whole.[137] In effect, the 1989 Vienna Concluding Document also covers the right to receive and dispense religious education (Principle 16(6)), to train religious personnel in appropriate institutions (Principle 16(8)), to respect individuals and communities in their right to acquire and possess material needed for religious practice (Principle 16(9)), and the right of religious institutions to produce, import, and disseminate religious publications and materials (Principle 16(10)).[138]

Based on this analysis, it is now easy to see how the OSCE pioneered some political consensus favouring a broad interpretation of the corporate dimension of FoRB.[139] By reference to Ronald Minnerath, the 1989 Vienna Concluding Document was, in fact, dubbed the first "manifesto of corporate rights of religious organizations."[140] This notwithstanding, and as a number of commentators recall, the OSCE commitments are political in nature and, therefore, not legally binding.[141] While this is certainly true, it has, however, been stressed that the normative strength of the OSCE lies precisely in its ability to combine "soft law" policymaking with concrete specifications of the content of human rights norms.[142] To dig into this, the mandate of the ODIHR is a case in point.

Based in Warsaw, this body is the OSCE institution for the furthering of human rights, democracy, and the rule of law.[143] At this stage, and just to have

135 ibid 8.
136 See Axel Freiherr Von Campenhausen, 'Church Autonomy in Germany' in Gerhard Robbers (n 16) 78, fn 1.
137 In this sense, see Ronald Minnerath (n 20) 292.
138 See *Concluding Document of the Vienna Meeting* (n 134) 9.
139 See Janne Haaland Matlary 'Implementing Freedom of Religion or Belief in the OSCE: Experiences From the Norwegian Chairmanship' in Oslo Conference of Religious Freedom (n 20) (discussing the OSCE diplomatic "co-optive powers" to reach consensus over the promotion of human and FoRB rights) 259–264.
140 Ronald Minnerath (n 20) 311.
141 Urban Gibson and Karen S. Lord (n 111) 252. Janne Haaland Matlary (n 139) (discussing the OSCE diplomatic "co-optive powers" to reach consensus over the promotion of human and FoRB rights) 256. Merilin Kiviorg, 'Collective Religious Autonomy under the European Convention on Human Rights: The UK Jewish Free School Case in International Perspective' (2010) Max Weber Programme 2010/40, 4 <https://cadmus.eui.eu/bitstream/handle/1814/15236/MWP_2010_40.pdf> accessed 25 October 2020.
142 See Janne Haaland Matlary (n 139) 259. See also Julian Rivers (n 15) 46.
143 For a brief overview of the tasks of the ODHIR, see: <https://www.osce.org/files/f/documents/b/b/13701.pdf> accessed 26 October 2020.

a small taste of the OSCE/ODHIR "soft power", one single example might suffice. The reader is then invited to go back as far as April 1996, the year in which the ODHIR organised a seminar in Warsaw on constitutional, legal, and administrative aspects of FoRB at the request of a number of non-governmental organisations (NGOs). Following this event, an Advisory Panel of Experts on Freedom of Religion or Belief, grappling with the task of reviewing domestic laws on FoRB as well as drafting new legislation, was established.[144] To that end, in 2004, the Advisory Panel issued the *Guidelines for Review of Legislation Pertaining to Religion or Belief*, later adopted by the Venice Commission (an independent Council of Europe consultive body) at its 59th Plenary Session.[145] This document elaborates on the potential legal obstacles to acquiring corporate legal personality and was further complemented by the 2014 *Guidelines on the Legal Personality of Religious or Belief Communities*.[146]

In sum, the OSCE has established itself as an influential actor capable not just of co-opting states but also of fostering them toward better compliance with well-articulated human rights norms.[147] More than this, it has provided, by far, the clearest delineation of religious institutions as corporate right-holders in their own capacity. However, not even at this level had explicit reference to religious exemptions from laws of general applicability been made. Allegedly, this is in line with the Advisory Panel of Experts' *Freedom of Religion or Belief and Security: Policy Guidance* (2019), which has called for a proportionality balance when determining the scope of FoRB claims.[148] Phrased differently, the Panel confirmed the need for a judicial "balancing approach", whereby the decision to carve out religious exemptions from a rule of general applicability should always follow a careful weighting of the competing rights at stake.[149] It follows, logically, that corporate autonomy claims must not categorically bar consideration of the merits of other competing rights at stake, such as those of ministers and lay personnel operating in a faith-based environment.

144 Urban Gibson and Karen S. Lord (n 111) 253.

145 See OSCE/ODIHR 2004, *Guidelines for Review of Legislation Pertaining to Religion or Belief* 1, 5 <https://www.osce.org/files/f/documents/d/b/13993.pdf> accessed 28 October 2020.

146 See OSCE/ODIHR 2014 (n 30).

147 In this sense, see Julian Rivers (n 16) 49.

148 OSCE/ODIHR 2019 (n 117). See also the limitation clauses under Principle 17 of the 1989 Vienna Concluding Document and Paragraph 9(4) of the 1990 Copenhagen Concluding Document. See *Concluding Document of the Vienna Meeting* (n 134) 9. Conference for Security and Co-operation in Europe (CSCE), *Document of the Copenhagen Meeting of the Conference on the Human Dimension of the CSCE*, 29 June 1990 1, 8.

149 OSCE/ODIHR 2019 (n 117) (discussing the principle of proportionality in relation to FoRB).

The Council of Europe

It has become clear from the previous section that the interplay between FoRB and security at the OSCE level has progressively facilitated the recognition of religious entities as subjects of rights under international law. It was, however, within another regional legal order that these OSCE political commitments finally obtained legal and judicial strength: the CoE. At this level, the main developments on the subject of corporate entities as FoRB claimant should be sought in the case law of the European Court and former Commission of Human Rights (ECtHR and ECommHR, respectively) for further elaboration in this section.

Overall, it is beyond the scope of this chapter to explore all the cases on this theme that have been brought to the attention of the "Strasbourg courts."[150] Nevertheless, some of them are notable and merit attention, especially in relation to the objective of this chapter to track the roadmap that the CoE followed toward the progressive recognition of religious autonomy rights. But before addressing the jurisprudence most relevant to this purpose, it might first be useful to briefly illustrate the basic features of the CoE and the human-rights based approach of its legal and judicial instruments.

The "human-rights based" approach

Formed in 1949, the CoE is a regional organisation of 46 sovereign states that develops legal and judicial standards on human rights, democracy, and the rule of law.[151] Briefly put, the origins of this body belong to a line of post-World War II commitments to protect European states both from gross human rights violations and communist subversion.[152] With this as the premise, there seems to be ample room for potential overlap between the CoE and the OSCE in their mandates. In effect, while the OSCE and the CoE differ in their nature[153] and composition,[154] they are both driven by a mutual interest in the promotion of human rights, alongside the building and strengthening of constitutional democracies in states in crisis or in transition.

150 A more exhaustive analysis of this case law can be found, for instance, in Jean-Pierre Schouppe, *La Dimension Institutionnelle De La Liberté de Religion Dans la Jurisprudence de La Cour Européenne Des Droits De L'homme* (Pedone, 2015) 277–312. See also Julian Rivers (n 16) 49–71; Ioana Cismas (n 29) 85–152, and Jeroen Temperman (n 25) 22–25.

151 Javier Martínez-Torrón and Rafael Navarro-Valls, 'The Protection of Religious Freedom in the System of the Council of Europe' in Oslo Conference of Religious Freedom (n 20) 210.

152 See Bernadette Rainey, Elizabeth Wicks, and Clare Ovey, *Jacobs, White, and Ovey: The European Convention on Human Rights* (Oxford University Press 2017) 3.

153 As noted, while the OSCE develops political standards, the CoE operates through legal and judicial mechanisms.

154 The CoE has 47 member states, while the OSCE is made up of 56 countries, including the US and Canada, and states in Central Asia.

Ample evidence of the various forms of OSCE/CoE consultation, liaison, and interplay in reaching overlapping human-rights-oriented objectives has emerged from the 2000 document *Relations between the OSCE and the CoE: Common Catalogue of Co-operation Modalities*.[155] Also, subsequent efforts to create synergies can be found in the 2005 *Joint Statement* signed by the chairmen of the two organisations, as well as in the *Declaration on Co-operation between the CoE and the OSCE* attached to it.[156] The latter states that OSCE/CoE cooperation should be "starting with" questions concerning the fight against terrorism and human trafficking, the protection of persons belonging to national minorities, and the promotion of tolerance and non-discrimination.[157] At first glance, this document seems to indicate that there might be an alignment between the CoE and the OSCE "comprehensive security" approach to human rights.

However, this is only partly true.[158] It has to be noted that, while for the OSCE, the protection of human freedoms is also seen as a means toward the achievement of greater security, it is an end in itself for the CoE.[159] In other words, and despite this overlap, the action of the CoE must be primarily read in light of the post-World War II "political philosophy and human rights agenda of the Allied Powers"[160] toward the advancement of human dignity, autonomy, and equality for everyone.

With these aims in mind, in 1950, the CoE's first 13 member states joined forces and drew up a treaty in Rome to protect basic rights that came into force in 1953: the European Convention on Human Rights (ECHR).[161] The Convention, in turn, established in 1954 the European Commission on Human Rights (ECommHR) that worked in tandem with the ECtHR since 1959, the

155 Geir Ulfstein, 'Relations between the Council of Europe and the OSCE: Common Catalogue of Co-operation Modalities', 26 April 2000, CM(2000)52.

156 Both documents are available at <https://rm.coe.int/CoERMPublicCommonSearchServices/DisplayDCTMContent?documentId=0900001680599dd5>

157 ibid.

158 For instance, the ECtHR itself described the Convention as "a constitutional instrument of European public order (*ordre public*)" See *Loizidou v Turkey*, App no 15318/89 (ECtHR, 23 February 1995) para 75. See also *Case of Refah Partisi (The Welfare Party) and Others v Turkey*, App nos 41340/98, 41342/98, 41343/98 and 41344/98 (ECtHR, 13 February 2003) (upholding the governmental banning of a Sunni Muslim political party to anticipate alleged Islamic threats to the Turkish constitutional order).

159 In this sense, see Directorate of Policy Planning (CoE), *The Council of Europe and tThe OSCE: Enhancing Co-operation and Complementarity through Greater Coherence. By Professor dr. juris Geir Ulfstein, University of Oslo*, 23 March 2012, DPP (2012)1, 3.

160 Bernadette Rainey, Elizabeth Wicks, and Clare Ovey (n 152) 3.

161 The first signatory countries were Belgium, Denmark, France, Germany, Iceland, Ireland, Italy, Luxembourg, the Netherlands, Norway, Sweden, Turkey, and the United Kingdom (UK). See ibid fn 4. See Council of Europe, 'Chart of Signatures and Ratifications of Treaty' 005 [1950] ETS No.005.

year the latter was created. The ECtHR, however, completely replaced the ECommHR in 1998.[162]

Taken together, the ECommHR was not a judicial body. Instead, it acted as a "filter" to preliminarily assess the compatibility of pending complaints with the ECtHR through a summary evaluation of the matters at stake.[163] Because the number of petitions kept growing, this "admissibility stage"[164] was necessary to weed out applications that would likely fail if taken to the merits phase at the ECtHR level.[165] Conversely, the ECtHR is an all-out international tribunal that ensures "the engagement undertaken by the High Contracting Parties in the Convention and the Protocols thereto".[166] It receives petitions from "any person, non-governmental organisation or group of individuals claiming to be the victim of a violation by one of the High Contracting Parties of the rights set forth in the Convention" and its Protocols.[167] Exhaustion of all domestic remedies is however needed before filing a complaint.[168] This latter principle sets out an obligation for the ECtHR to provide national authorities with an opportunity to address to the fullest extent possible an ECHR complaint before it could examine the issue under its jurisdiction.[169] This is what the Court itself described as its "subsidiary nature",[170] informed by the need for judicial review to be exercised, in preference, by those authorities that are closest to the citizens. This so-called "principle of subsidiarity", in turn, reveals three other major characteristics of the ECtHR.

First, this tribunal is not a court of "fourth instance", addressing mistakes of facts or laws made by domestic courts.[171] Rather, for some, its role is just one of

162 See Council of Europe (CoE), *Protocol No. 11 to the Convention for the Protection of Human Rights and Fundamental Freedoms Restructuring the Control Machinery Established Thereby*, 11 May 1994, European Treaty Series—No. 155. The Protocol entered into force on 1 November 1998. See Carolyn Evans, *Freedom of Religion under the European Convention on Human Rights* (Oxford University Press 2001) 8, fn 30.

163 See Carolyn Evans (n 162) 11.

164 For a detailed overview of the admissibility stage, see Council of Europe/European Court of Human Rights 2020, *Practical Guide on Admissibility Criteria*, 30 April 2020 <https://www.echr.coe.int/documents/admissibility_guide_eng.pdf> accessed 3 November 2020. See also European Convention on Human Rights (n 4) Article 27(2).

165 Carolyn Evans (n 163) 9.

166 See European Convention on Human Rights (n 4) article 19.

167 See ibid, article 34.

168 ibid, article 35(1).

169 See Julia Laffranque and others, 'Seminar to Mark the Official Opening of the Judicial Year Subsidiarity: A Two-sided Coin? 1. The Role of the Convention Mechanism. 2. The Role of the National Authorities' (2015) Background Paper, 1 <https://www.echr.coe.int/Documents/Seminar_background_paper_2015_ENG.pdf> accessed 5 February 2021.

170 Case *Relating to Certain Aspects of the Laws on the Use of Languages in Education in Belgium v Belgium (Merits)*, App Nos 1474/62; 1677/62; 1691/62; 1769/63; 1994/63; 2126/64 (ECtHR, 23 July 1968) para 10.

171 Steven Greer, 'The Margin of Appreciation: Interpretation and Discretion under the European Convention of Human Rights' (2000) Human rights files No. 17, 19 <https://www.echr.coe.int/librarydocs/dg2/hrfiles/dg2-en-hrfiles-17(2000).pdf> accessed 3 November 2020.

constitutional review of the member states' compliance to the Convention.[172] Whether or not the ECtHR has a constitutional nature is, nevertheless, still a much-debated issue[173] because, (and second) the Court produces rulings that "are not binding law per se" and "have only weak means of enforcement".[174] All this irrespective of how authoritative the ECtHR's jurisprudence actually is. In this connection, Andrea Pin and John Witte explain that, at bottom, the ECtHR has no power either to reverse a judgement rendered by domestic courts or to substantially affect a state's legislation and future case law.[175]

Third, and relatedly, the ECtHR's supplementary nature also implies that states enjoy ample leeway on how to interpret, implement, and fulfil their obligations under the Convention.

As a result, under this "margin of appreciation" doctrine,[176] the ECtHR gives a certain level of judicial deference to national tribunals and their principled criteria for determining the "democratic necessity" to restrict or not a particular right at stake.[177] In sum, because the ECtHR is centred, in a very real way, on this doctrine of judicial self-restraint, some would go so as far as to say that its functioning

172 For a discussion on the ECtHR as a constitutional court, see Alec Stone Sweet, 'Sur la constitutionalisation de la Convention Européenne des droits de l'homme: cinquante ans après son installation, la Cour Européenne conçue comme une Cour constitutionnelle' (2009) 80(1) Revue trimestrielle des droits de l'homme 923–937. For an English translation of this article, see: <https://digitalcommons.law.yale.edu/cgi/viewcontent.cgi?referer=&httpsredir=1&article=1070&context=fss_papers> See also Fiona de Londras and Kanstantsin Dzehtsiarou 'Managing Judicial Innovation in the European Court of Human Rights' (2015) 15(3) Human Rights Law Review 523, 526 (arguing that the ECtHR "is a key constitutionalist actor"). It also bears note that the ECtHR has occasionally described itself as a "constitutional instrument of European public order". See *Loizidou v. Turkey* (preliminary objections), App no 40/1993/435/514 (ECtHR, 23 February 1995).

173 For instance, see Giorgio Repetto, 'Introduction. The ECtHR and the European Constitutional Landscape. Reassessing Paradigms' in Giorgio Repetto (eds), *The Constitutional Relevance of the ECHR in Domestic and European Law* (Intersentia, 2013) (arguing that "the ECHR system has largely failed to maintain an autonomous constitutional role because of the progressive resistance shown by national public spheres to its case law and the unpredictability of its substantive interpretive criteria") 2.

174 Andrea Pin and John Witte, Jr., 'Meet the New Boss of Religious Freedom: The New Cases of the Court of Justice of the European Union' (2020) 55(2) Texas International Law Journal 223, 224. For a discussion on the issue of non-compliance by the member states with ECtHR's case law, see Veronika Fikfak, 'Changing State Behaviour: Damages before the European Court of Human Rights' (2019) 29(4) The European Journal of International Law 1091–1125.

175 ibid 228.

176 This doctrine is described in the CoE, *Protocol No. 15 Amending the Convention for the Protection of Human Rights and Fundamental Freedoms*, 24 June 2013, Council of Europe Treaty Series—no 213, Article 1.

177 Steven Greer (n 171) 25. In this sense, see also Dominic McGoldrick, 'A Defence of the Margin of Appreciation and an Argument For Its Application by the Human Rights Committee' (2016) 65(1) International & Comparative Law Quarterly 2, 27–8.

depends more on "the continuing cooperation of the Member States" and their domestic mechanisms than its effectiveness as an international tribunal.[178]

Be that as it may, the fact that the CoE has elaborated fully fledged mechanisms to protect citizens from potential abuses by national authorities explains why, in the words of some scholars, "the Council is the most developed regional system of human rights law".[179] In effect, the rights established under the ECHR drew inspiration directly from the 1948 UDHR without simply duplicating the provisions referred to there. The ECHR has been, thus, defined as a proper "living instrument",[180] meaning that its provisions undergo constant updating for present-day purposes by the ECtHR. For the scope of this discussion, it was precisely the interpretative action of this tribunal that finally enforced the corporate religious freedoms enunciated in OSCE documents. This will be discussed in the following paragraph.

Normative framework

Corporate religious freedom, though not articulated as such, is guaranteed under Article 9 of the ECHR, which is essentially similar in content to Article 18 of the UDHR and the ICCPR.

It reads:

1. Everyone has the right to freedom of thought, conscience and religion; this right includes freedom to change his religion or belief and freedom, either alone or in community with others and in public or private, to manifest his religion or belief, in worship, teaching, practice and observance.
2. Freedom to manifest one's religion or beliefs shall be subject only to such limitations as are prescribed by law and are necessary in a democratic society in the interests of public safety, for the protection of public order, health or morals, or for the protection of the rights and freedoms of others.

As it can be inferred from Paragraph I, FoRB rights belong to "everyone", thus suggesting that the very concept of religious freedom should also extend to cover corporate entities. In effect, in a similar way to Article 18(1) of the UDHR and the ICCPR, this provision restates the right to "manifest" religion "either alone or in community with others". And, as already noted for the UN, it is precisely this "communal dimension" of FoRB that provides implicit authority for recognition

178 In this sense, see Andrea Pin and John Witte, Jr (n 174) 228.

179 Sylvie Langlaude, 'The Rights of Religious Associations to External Relations: A Comparative Study of the OSCE and the Council of Europe' (2010) 32(3) Human Rights Quarterly 502, 504. See also Carolyn Evans (n 163) 10.

180 See, for instance, *Tyrer v UK*, App No 5856/72 (ECtHR, 25 April 1978) para 31; *Kress v France*, App No 39594/98 (ECtHR, 7 June 2001) para 70; *Christine Goodwin v UK*, App No 28957/95 (ECtHR, 11 July 2002) para 75; *Bayatyan v Armenia*, App No 23459/03 (ECtHR, 7 July 2011) para 102.

of corporate autonomy rights. However, as is evident, the Convention does not explicitly enumerate such rights, while Article 9(2) only stipulates the potentially applicable restrictions to FoRB. Against this background, and as already suggested, specific indications over the corporate freedom of religious institutions are best found in secondary ECHR sources, such as the ECommHR and ECtHR's case law. The latter are analysed below.

ECommHR case law (late 1960s to late 1990s)

In the first strand of case law, the CoE's judicial bodies were challenged with the question of whether corporate religious entities could stand trial under the Convention. This was initially a matter of controversy and circumspection.

To begin with, in 1968, the former ECommHR ruled in *C. of S. v. United Kingdom.*[181] In that case, the Church of Scientology in the UK complained against an openly hostile governmental campaign aimed at curbing the growth of Scientology in the UK. It alleged that governmental actions violated its rights under Article 9 of the ECHR in conjunction with Article 14 (prohibition of discrimination), Article 6 (right to a fair trial), and Article 13 of the ECHR (right to an effective remedy). No natural person was mentioned as party to the action. The Court, therefore, decided that "a corporation, being a legal and not a natural person, is incapable of having or exercising the rights mentioned in Article 9, paragraph (1) of the Convention".[182] It then declared the application inadmissible *ratione personae*, as the plaintiff-corporation lacked standing under Article 34 ECHR (at the time Article 25).[183] Now, because of that, and since because this provision allows, among others, "non-governmental organisations" to lodge complaints under the ECHR, the Court's ruling appeared in some ways contradictory. For if religious institutions should also be considered "non-governmental organisations",[184] it follows that they might be entitled to lodge legal action under the Convention as well.[185] Further, this decision is "all the more striking"[186] because, on that same occasion, the ECommHR reiterated that fair trial rights (Article 6 ECHR) can be exercised by "a legal as well a natural

181 App no 3798/68 (ECommHR, 17 December 1968) 29 CD 70.
182 ibid 6.
183 ibid 6. More exactly, the ECommHR declared the inadmissibility under Article 27 (competence of single judges), which, in turn, defers to the criteria under Article 34. See European Convention on Human Rights (n 4) article 27.
184 Churches with established constitutional ties to the state represent a potential challenge to this assertion. However, as will be discussed below, because of the ecclesiastical and spiritual nature of official churches, the EctHR clarified that they do not participate in the exercise of governmental powers *stricto sensu*. Thus, they qualify as "non-governmental" organisations.
185 In this sense, see also Julian Rivers (n 16) 54.
186 Jeroen Temperman (n 25) 23.

person".[187] Interestingly enough, it was in another case involving scientologists that the ECommHR changed course from its previous decision.

In 1979, the Commission heard *X and Church of Scientology v. Sweden*.[188] This case presented the question of whether Article 9 ECHR also covers statements of purported religious belief appearing in advertisements of a purely commercial nature. The dispute arose, in fact, from the objections raised by the Church of Scientology against an administrative injunction to amend certain passages of an advertisement marketing "religious artefacts" (so-called E-Meters). Overall, the ECommHR attached particular importance to the fact that, unlike the previous case, the claim was not brought just by the Church of Scientology itself but also by one of its ministers (Pastor X). On these grounds, the ECommHR reversed its previous case law, concluding that "the distinction between a church and its members under article 9.1 of the Convention was artificial".[189] It, thus, held that the Church of Scientology, as an NGO, had standing under Article 25 of the ECHR "in its own capacity and as a representative of its members".[190] This latter statement is, however, confusing. The ECommHR did not clarify whether this means that churches hold corporate rights per se (in their own capacity) or, instead, whether they acquire them derivatively from the FoRB rights of their adherents (as corporate representatives of their members).[191] This is important because the ECommHR's reasoning seems to imply that, for churches to be proper rights-holders, a perfect overlapping (i.e., representation nexus)[192] between their interests and those of their members is needed. With the end result being a church's capacity to stand trial would be frustrated in case of internal dissents among the clergy (or schisms in the worst-case scenario).[193] However, it is evident from this decision that, for the Commission, corporate religious freedom should have been understood as a right of the institution *as such* that, in turn, finds its roots in the "aggregating of the rights"[194] of its individual members.[195] This, in turn, gave additional reason to think that, for churches to claim FoRB rights, a perfect overlapping between their interest and those of their members is not necessarily needed.[196]

187 ibid 7.
188 App no 7805/77 (ECommHR, 17 December 1979) 16 DR 68.
189 ibid 70.
190 ibid.
191 In this sense, see Julian Rivers (n 16) 100.
192 This term can be traced back to: Ioana Cismas (n 29) 82.
193 ibid 100–01.
194 Carolyn Evans (n 163) 14.
195 Ioana Cismas (n 29) 100. In this sense, see also Pieter Van Dijk and Fried Van Hoof, *Theory and Practice of the European Convention on Human Rights* (Kluwer Law International 1998) 552.
196 The ECommHR had already accepted three years before the Church of Sweden's right to manifest religion despite the dissent by a member of the clergy from the general practice of the church. See *X v Denmark*, App No. 7374/76 (ECommHR, 8 March 1976) 5 DR 157.

Later developments in the 1990s Strasbourg's case law confirmed this approach. In a string of religious property disputes, the ECommHR accepted that churches *as such* are the primary victims of FoRB rights violations and not the individuals applying on their behalf.[197]

This view was also reiterated by the ECtHR in *Holy Monasteries v Greece* (1994), in which it held that eight Greek monasteries (organically integrated in the hierarchy of the state Greek Orthodox Church) were NGOs that could stand trial under the Convention.[198] Interestingly, this case turned into an important occasion to clarify whether churches with constitutional ties with the state also satisfy the "non-governmental" requirement under Article 25 of the ECHR. In answering the question in the affirmative, the Court gave a "narrow"[199] interpretation of this requirement. To wit, despite state–church entanglements, the Court considered that the objectives of the monasteries were "essentially ecclesiastical and spiritual ones".[200] Also, and because of their corporate personhood, the Court noted that they were separate legal entities from the state-favoured Greek Orthodox Church.[201] Unifying these two observations, the Court concluded that the applicant monasteries did not participate in any exercise of governmental power. Thus, they could not "be classed with governmental organisations established for public administration purposes".[202] Additionally, this case reveals that various forms of state religion (or "prevailing religion" in the case of Greece)[203] and state churches (as in England or in some Scandinavian countries) are generally compatible with the ECHR.[204] In reality, the ECommHR already made this argument in its 1989 decision in *Darby v. Sweden*. On that occasion, however, it also clarified that membership in an official church must never be made compulsory.[205]

ECtHR case law (2000–2010)

Having established that churches can stand trial to claim FoRB rights, the Strasbourg organs, thus, acknowledged that corporate religious freedom is not

197 *Serbo-Greek Orthodox Church in Vienna v Austria* (ECommHR, 2 April 1990); *ISKCON v United Kingdom* (ECommHR, 8 March 1994).

198 *Case of Holy Monasteries v Greece* Apps no 13092/87 and 13984/88 (ECtHR, 9 December 1994) para 49.

199 In this sense, see: Ioana Cismas (n 29) 89.

200 *Holy Monasteries* (n 198) para 49.

201 Ioana Cismas (n 29) 89.

202 ibid.

203 Constitution of Greece, article 3.

204 The distinction between state religions and state churches is, however, subtle. In effect, when a religion is officially endorsed by the state through the constitution (state religion) its church will almost automatically obtain a privileged position among the others, regardless of the specific constitutional recognition of the latter. See Jeroen Temperman (n 84) 33 (arguing that the distinction between state churches and state religions is often "belied by reality").

205 *Darby v. Sweden*, App no 11581/85 (EComHR, 9 May 1989), para. 45.

just a bundle of individual rights. Rather, it is a right of the institution *itself* that is very much tied to the group to which the individual belongs. This outcome shines a light on the fact that, as a matter of inverse logic, without protection of a religious institution *as such*, its adherents (*as such*) would be frustrated in their FoRB rights.

As will be shown, it was following this logic that, in the second strand of case law between 2000 and 2010, the ECtHR finally inferred church autonomy rights from the text of Article 9 of the ECHR. In other words, despite the silence of the Convention on this right, religious autonomy was progressively understood through the value which it had for individual believers. As such, in Merilin Kiviorg's terms, "[I]nstitutional autonomy for the sake of institutional autonomy makes no sense in the context of human-rights protection".[206]

As a preliminary note, there is an interesting coincidence between the ECtHR's greater openness for corporate religious autonomy since the early 2000s and the progressive incorporation of countries from the former Soviet bloc to the CoE in the same period.[207] Taken together, it is said that, within these states, governmental restrictions on religious minorities have become a particularly visible trend.[208]

This explains growing concerns at the CoE level that eventually developed into a combined action with the Venice Commission, the EU, and the OSCE to facilitate the alignment of these countries with international standards of human rights and FoRB protection.[209] In support of this contention, perhaps a more comprehensive articulation of religious autonomy can be found in *Hasan and Chaush v. Bulgaria* (2000), a case involving precisely one of the most restrictive post-communist countries in terms of religious association laws.[210]

This controversy arose from the interference of government authorities in the election and appointment of a Muslim religious leader. In finding against the government, for the first time ever, the ECtHR acknowledged the existence of a right to "organisational autonomy" under Article 9 of the ECHR to protect the applicant Muslim community.[211] The grounds for its finding was the absence of a legal basis to justify interference by state authorities. In particular, because governmental intervention in an internal leadership dispute was not "prescribed by law" under Article 9(2) of the ECHR, it was deemed to be grounded on unduly arbitrariness and "unfettered discretion".[212] In this connection, the ECtHR remarkably held that "religious communities traditionally and universally exist in

206 Merilin Kiviorg (n 141) 321.
207 In this sense, see Javier Martínez-Torrón and Rafael Navarro-Valls (n 151) 215.
208 Jeroen Temperman (n 84) 254.
209 See Giovanni Barberini (n 115) 12–13.
210 ibid, 16.
211 *Hasan and Chaush v. Bulgaria*, App no 30985/96 (ECtHR, 26 October 2000) para 104. Famously, the Court held: "[w]ere the organisational life of the community not protected by Article 9 of the Convention, all other aspects of the individual's freedom of religion would become vulnerable". ibid para 62.
212 ibid para 86.

the form of organised structures".[213] Thus, where their organisational rights are at issue "Article 9 of the Convention must be interpreted in the light of Article 11, which safeguards associative life against unjustified State interference".[214] This latter statement represented an important quantum leap. By interpreting Article 9 in light of Article 11 of the ECHR (freedom of assembly), the ECtHR has been, in fact, in a position to extend autonomy rights to all religious entities, whether they belong to official majority faiths or not.[215]

But more than this, in upholding and linking Articles 9 and 11 of the ECHR, the ECtHR went even further in its 2001 ruling in *Metropolitan Church of Bessarabia v Moldova.* In this case, the Court added that Article 9 must be seen not only in the light of Article 11 but also in the light of Article 6 of the ECHR (right to a fair trial).[216] In sum, it is now easy to see how the ECtHR recognised the right to church autonomy, especially with a view of protecting newer or non-dominant religions. This trend was followed for the entire decade. In particular, between 2000 and 2010, the ECtHR held several state authorities to be in violation of religious autonomy for denying legal entity status to the Moscow Branch of the Salvation Army and the Church of Scientology of Moscow (2007);[217] interfering in an internal leadership dispute within the Bulgarian Orthodox Church (2009);[218] and dissolving the Moscow's Jehovah Witness community and refusing its re-registration (2010).[219]Clearly, what is notable of all these judgements is the narrow discretion afforded to governmental regulatory power in the area of church autonomy.

This would appear that, for the ECtHR, it is the autonomous existence of plural religious or belief communities, rather than their control or suppression, to be a foundational bloc of democratic societies.[220] Perhaps more significantly for

213 ibid para 62.
214 ibid.
215 Commenting on this jurisprudential approach, Ioana Cismas observes that "the privilege of self-administration, traditionally granted to a specific church by virtue of historic affinities with the state, has become the right of all religious organizations." Ioana Cismas (n 29) 123. As early as 1997, the ECtHR gave an extensive interpretation of the equality principle vis-à-vis religious institutions in *Canea Catholic Church v Greece.* On that occasion, it held that any church, of whatever denomination, has the right to obtain legal personality at the same conditions as those applied to other religious communities. See App no 143/1996/762/963 (ECtHR, 16 December 1997) (finding a violation of Article 9 in conjunction with Article 14 of the ECHR (prohibition of discrimination).
216 *Metropolitan Church of Bessarabia and Others v Moldova*, App no 45701/99 (ECtHR, 13 December 2001) para 118.
217 *Case of the Moscow Branch of the Salvation Army v Russia*, App no 72881/01 (ECtHR, 5 January 2007); *Church of Scientology Moscow v. Russia*, App no 18147/02 (ECtHR, 5 April 2007).
218 *Holy Synod of the Bulgarian Orthodox Church (Metropolitan Inokentiy) et al. v. Bulgaria*, App nos 412/03 and 35677/04 (ECtHR, 22 January 2009).
219 *Jehovah's Witnesses of Moscow v. Russia*, App no 302/02 (ECtHR, 10 June 2010).
220 See *Hasan and Chaush* (n 211) para 62. The ECtHR famously spelled out the significance of FoRB to democratic society and democratic pluralism in its first 1993 decision on religious matters in *Kokkinakis v Greece*, App no 14307/88 (25 May 1993) para 31.

the purpose of this investigation, the ECtHR also clarified that religious institutions, in view of their autonomy rights, must be "free to determine at their own discretion the manner in which new members are admitted and existing members excluded".[221] It is, therefore, no coincidence that, in some subsequent jurisprudential developments, the Court finally welcomed their entitlement to religious exemptions in employment. This discourse is, however, more complex and cannot be addressed in a few sentences. Chapter II will revert to this issue in greater detail. For now, it suffices it to conclude by considering a third and final area of European regional jurisdiction: the EU.

The European Union

The EU is a supranational "coalition"[222] between 27 member states. What makes it particularly different from the European projects analysed so far is that, for the first time ever, its participating states accepted to transfer part of their sovereign powers to a supranational polity to attain objectives of political unity, peace, stability, and prosperity. The war-torn founding countries saw in this project an opportunity for recovery and reconstruction that, in the aftermath of World War II, should have started from interstate economic cooperation. This was because, for longstanding unity and peace to be achievable, the facilitation of international trade and commerce as a means to rehabilitate domestic industries was seen as a first and crucial step. The underlying logic being that, by making states economically interdependent, they would have been less prone to conflict.[223]

For this purpose, in the period 1950–57 three legally distinct communities were created: the European Community on Steel and Coal (ECSC—1951); the European Atomic Energy Community (EURATOM—1957), and the European Economic Community (EEC—1957).[224] Starting with coal and steel in 1951, the goal was to progressively develop a "common market"[225] for virtually "all goods and services"[226] under the checks and balances of a competition authority:

221 *Svyato-Mykhaylivska Parafiya v. Ukraine*, App no 77703/01 (ECtHR, 14 September 2007).

222 The term "coalition" is preferred here because, while EU member states remain "sovereign" in their decisions, the EU "is not, strictly speaking, an international organisation". In this sense, see Philip McDonagh and others, *On the Significance of Religion for Global Diplomacy* (Routledge, 2021) 43.

223 In this sense, see: <https://europa.eu/european-union/about-eu/eu-in-brief_en> (accessed 8 March 2021).

224 See respectively, Treaty Establishing the European Coal and Steel Community, ECSC Treaty, 18 April 1951 (unreported); Treaty Establishing the European Atomic Energy Community (Euratom) 25 March 1957 (unreported); Treaty Establishing the European Economic Community, 25 March 1957 (unreported).

225 ibid art 1–4; ibid art 92; ibid art 117.

226 Marise Cremona, 'The Treaties that Created Europe' in Giuliano Amato and others (eds), *The History of the European Union. Constructing Utopia* (Hart, 2019) 136.

the European Commission.[227] The project of establishing a unified and tariff-free trading territory was to be completed by 1992 with the transition to an "internal" (or "single") market.[228] The latter should have, in fact, complemented the free market for goods, capital, and services with the removal of barriers of all kinds: from physical barriers limiting the free circulation of people (i.e., internal frontier controls) to non-tariff barriers (e.g., different national products standards and regulations) that could frustrate interstate business cooperation.[229] Also, in 1992, by instituting the EU as a three-pillar governance system, the Maastricht Treaty turned the communities into its "first pillar", alongside the Common Foreign and Security Policy (second pillar) and the Cooperation in Justice and Home Affairs (third pillar). Eventually, in 2007, the Lisbon Treaty amended the Treaty of Maastricht and the Treaty Establishing the European Economic Community (now Treaty on the Functioning of the European Union (TFEU)), thereby setting up the current EU two-pillar constitutional structure. Based on this analysis, the reader might now logically assume that religion would appear to be remote from the discussions that took place during the first decades of European integration. Yet, this is only partly true.

In reality, religion was deeply embedded in the political philosophy of the European founding fathers. All of them were, in fact, men of faith (coming from the top echelons of Christian Democratic parties) and mostly committed to the values of human dignity, forgiveness, and reconciliation.[230] Thus, in their view, closer economic cooperation should have been framed into a broader effort to achieve a political (and possibly federal) integration grounded on peace, human rights, democracy, and the rule of law.[231] Perhaps this religiously oriented reading of the European process might help explain why the disgraceful war-time experience impressed on the Christian founders the importance of blending market and

227 With the sole exception of the coal and steel industries that remained under the competence of the ECSC's High Authority until it was merged into the European Commission in 1967. See ibid 92. See also Treaty Establishing a Single Council and a Single Commission of the European Communities, 8 April 1965 (unreported) art 9.

228 This deadline was set in 1985 by Jacques Delors, President of the European Commission, who "convinced the Member States to launch a process of completing the single market by 1992, and to sign the Single European Act (SEA) which underpinned it". See Christian Salm and Wilhelm Lehmann, 'Jacques Delors. Architect of the Modern European Union' (2020) European Union History Series, 2 <https://www.europarl.europa.eu/RegData/etudes/BRIE/2020/652009/EPRS_BRI(2020)652009_EN.pdf> accessed 16 January 2021.

229 See Commission of the European Communities, 'Completing the Internal Market. White Paper from the Commission to the European Council' COM (85).

230 See Gary Wilton, 'Christianity at the Founding. The Legacy of Robert Schuman' in Jonathan Chaplin and Gary Wilton (eds), *God and the EU. Faith in the European Project* (Routledge, 2017) 13–33.

231 See Robert Schuman, 'The Schuman Declaration — 9 May 1950' <https://europa.eu/european-union/about-eu/symbols/europe-day/schuman-declaration_en> accessed 22 January 2020.

human freedoms. In a word, the goal was to attain not just economic efficiency but also social justice.

Interestingly, this view found an echo in their choice of a "social market economy'"(SME) as the model for the future design of the European economic framework.[232] But Christian inspiration aside, the need for fusing liberal and socialist values was also a matter of efficiency-related reasons.[233] Mario Monti considers, for instance, the pivotal role that the German SME policy programme played in the country's rapid economic rebirth after World War II. Linked to this, he explains that it was precisely because of this "economic miracle" that the connection between financial and social performance started to be seen concretely as the new (and European) way forward.[234] Against that, one could now easily see why, beginning in the 1970s, the European integration process gradually criss-crossed with legal[235] and jurisprudential[236] developments on human rights protection, FoRB included. As to the latter, it is submitted here that the relationship between the EU and FoRB has walked along two interrelated paths informed by two distinct approaches to religion.[237] In what follows, such approaches are addressed in turn.

The "protectionist" approach

As can be seen from the above, what were originally three distinct economic communities gradually fused into a unique supranational regional order: the EU. In

232 Consolidated Version of the Treaty on European Union [2012] OJ C 326/13, art 3(3) (stating that the EU "shall establish an internal market (…) based on (…) an highly competitive social market economy"). For a discussion on the relationship between religion and the SME in the EU, see Werner Lachmann, 'The German Social Market Economy: Its Theological Justification and Role in European Integration' in Jonathan Chaplin and Gary Wilton (n 225) 89–108.

233 Sionaidh Douglas-Scott, 'The Problem of Justice in the European Union Values, Pluralism, and Critical Legal Justice' in Julie Dickson and Pavlos Eleftheriadis (eds), *Philosophical Foundations of European Union Law* (Oxford University Press, 2012) 416 (introducing the formula 'output legitimacy' to describe the EU's efficiency-oriented line of action).

234 Mario Monti 'Competition and Solidarity in the European Construct' in Giuliano Amato (n 226) 91.

235 The EU witnessed a season of human rights codification that gradually unfolded through the the Single European Act (1986); the Treaties of Maastricht (1992), Amsterdam (1997), Nice (2001), the failed Constitutional Treaty (2004), and the Lisbon Treaty (2007).

It is impossible here to relate in full with these developments. For a concise account, see Pasquale Annicchino (n 47) 45–46. For a more detailed discussion, see Giuliano Amato and Nicola Verola, 'Freedom, Democracy, Rule of Law' in Giuliano Amato (n 226) 57–88.

236 For an early stage case law, see Case 29/69 *Erich Stauder v City of Ulm-Sozialamt* (1969) ECR 419; Case 11/70, *Internationale Handelsgesellschaft* (1970) ECR 1125, 1134. In 1976, the Court of Justice also issued an important judgement recognising, for the first time ever, that human rights standards should extend to cover FoRB. See Case 130/75, *Vivien Prais v Council of the European Communities* (unreported) 27 October 1976.

237 For an introduction to this topic, see Ronan McCrea, *Religion and the Public Order of the European Union* (Oxford Scholarship Online 2011) 143–196.

its current form, the EU is best thought as an effort toward "unity in diversity".[238] That is to say, from the start, the EU has strived to condense the instances of a multiplicity of national actors (culturally diverse but united under the same supranational system) into a pattern of European shared values.[239]

Overall, in its effort to reconcile 27 countries diverging in their moralities, the EU has been unavoidably beset by questions of ethical inheritance that, so it was felt, domestic (and mostly Christian) churches might help to answer.[240] This is why the participation of churches in the European integration discourse progressively informed a dialogue between religious leaders and EU policymakers on topics of common interest from social welfare issues to overall questions on EU enlargement.[241] As these developments increasingly drew churches into European debates, an important quantum leap in their relations with Europe took place in the years of Jacques Delors's mandate. The latter served as president of the European Commission from 1985 to 1995.[242] Because of Delors's personal commitment to ethical and religious issues, in 1990, a programme titled *A Soul for Europe: Ethics and Spirituality* was launched. This is how, for the first time ever, the EU formally recognised the social importance of religion in giving spiritual assistance to the European project.[243] But even more importantly, this

238 Treaty Establishing a Constitution for Europe (unreported) 13 January 2005, article I-8 ("[t]he motto of the Union shall be: 'United in diversity'"). As early as 1986, the Single European Act clarified its ultimate aim to make "concrete progress towards European unity". European Single Act [1987] OJ No L 169/1, article 1. This was formally achieved by the 1992 Maastricht Treaty. In article F(2), it stressed that the protection of the fundamental rights of (*diverse*) EU citizens shall pass through the respect of each member state's social *unity* within their common constitutional traditions. Treaty on European Union (unreported) 7 February 1992, article F(2) (now Consolidated Version of the Treaty on European Union (n 231) article 6(3)). Eventually, see Charter of Fundamental Rights of the European Union (n 4) art 22 (stating that "[t]he Union shall respect cultural, religious and linguistic diversity.")

239 Consolidated Version of the Treaty on the Functioning of the European Union [2012] [2008] OJ C 326/47, art 167(4) ("[t]he Union shall take cultural aspects into account in its action under other provisions of the Treaties, in particular in order to respect and to promote the diversity of its cultures.")

240 Guy Milton, 'God and the Constitution' in Jonathan Chaplin and Gary Wilton (n 230) 193.

241 Beginning with the establishment of the Jesuit office *Catholic European Study Information Centre* in Brussels in 1963, several Christian actors started to engage in formal discussions with European policymakers. For a discussion on Catholic, Protestant, and Orthodox contributions to the EU see, respectively John Loughlin, 'European Integration. A Catholic Perspective' in Jonathan Chaplin and Gary Wilton (n 230) 33–48; Sandler Luitwieler, 'The EU: Protestant Contributions, Then and Now' in Jonathan Chaplin and Gary Wilton ibid; Peter Petkoff, 'New Worlds and New Churches: The Orthodox Church(es) and the European Union' in ibid 70–88.

242 See Christian Salm and Wilhelm Lehmann (n 228).

243 Michał Matlak, 'Jacques Delors, the Single Market and the Failed Attempt to Give *a Soul to Europe*' (2018) Robert Schuman Centre for Advanced Studies Research Paper 2018/06, 6 <https://papers.ssrn.com/sol3/papers.cfm?abstract_id=3157116> accessed 10 March 2021 (explaining that underpinning this programme was the idea that the future EU could not "be based solely on market and supranational bureaucracy").

programme also gave churches a more direct voice and an opportunity to lobby for some kind of recognition and protection at the EU level of their status and autonomy rights under national laws.[244] As will be shown, it was precisely against this background that the EU progressively developed what will be called a "protectionist" approach to corporate religion.[245]

In order to get a better sense of this, the position of European churches vis-à-vis the EU should first be framed into the broader issue of their "struggle for recognition"[246] (to parse Francis Fukuyama) of their interests, aspirations, and concerns under the single market project. As the latter accelerated its pace (thanks to Delors's initiative to complete the single market by 1992), religious leaders feared that the spread of capitalist economy could jeopardise their cultural influence and authority in the public domain. This kind of thinking characterised, for instance, many post-war Protestant theologians who, in supporting Christian social teachings, took a stand against the European SME model. And this was because of the alleged affinity of the latter with neoliberal capitalism (thus, regardless of SME's social corrections to free market principles).[247] This opposition could be read also as an effort to slow down the advance of minority (and sometimes newer) faiths as a natural concomitant of modern market economies and their expanding flows of financial and (religiously diverse) human capital. In other words, and borrowing from Marco Ventura, "[t]traditional dominant churches accepted the capitalist economy and European integration, only insofar as these did not imply a religious market encouraging new highly competitive actors."[248] Such acceptance was conditional on European lawmakers, including in the Treaties the guarantee that churches would be sheltered in their status and autonomy rights from the economic processes of the market. In light of this, it

244 ibid (drawing a casual connection between *A Soul for Europe* and further developments in the constitutional protection of churches under EU Law).

245 The text that first introduced this concept into the literature is Marco Ventura, *La Laicità dell'Unione Europea. Diritti, Mercato e Religione* (Giappichelli Editore 2001) 155–63. The author further elaborated on this idea in Marco Ventura, 'Protectionnisme et libre-échangisme. La nouvelle gestion juridique de la religion en Europe' (2003) 64(1) Conscience et liberté 122–132.

246 See Francis Fukuyama (n 48) (drawing on Hegel's idea of a "struggle for recognition" to suggest that the human desire for public acknowledgment of his own status is the motor driving human history) 135.

247 Werner Lachmann (n 232) 94. For a Catholic analysis of capitalism urging to reorient economic activities toward the common good, with the ultimate goal of eradicating poverty, exploitation, and alienation, see Pope John Paul II's encyclical *Centesimus Annus* (1991) available at: <https://www.vatican.va/content/john-paul-ii/en/encyclicals/documents/hf_jp-ii_enc_01051991_centesimus-annus.html#%247> accessed 13 July 2021.

248 Marco Ventura, 'Dynamic Law and Religion in Europe. Acknowledging Change. Choosing Change' (2013) Robert Schuman Centre for Advanced Studies Research Paper 2013/91, 18 <https://papers.ssrn.com/sol3/papers.cfm?abstract_id.2376194> accessed 16 January 2021

is no surprise that the first developments in EU law and religion represented a compromise solution resulting from policy negotiations.[249]

The 1997 *Declaration on the Status of Churches* appended to the Amsterdam Treaty is a case in point. Paragraph I of the Declaration reads, "The European Union respects and does not prejudice the status under national law of churches and religious associations or communities in the Member States".

On the face of it, this provision sketched, for the first time, an area of non-interference in the internal affairs of churches that elevated them to "sovereign" status.[250] But what is notable is that, in a similar way to churches, this principle of non-interference also covered humanist influences in EU moral matters. Paragraph II of the Declaration states that "The European Union equally respects the status of philosophical and non-confessional organisations."[251] Importantly, this was a clear recognition that, Christianity aside, Europe is also rooted in a humanist tradition that has progressively reduced religious influence over law and politics in certain countries.[252]

In any case, later on, on 18 June 2004, these political statements were repeated and included in two distinct paragraphs of Article I-52 of the 2004 Treaty establishing a Constitution for Europe.[253] Additionally, this text introduced a third paragraph that finally formalised the dialogue between the EU and religions. Paragraph III holds that "Recognising their identity and their specific contribution, the Union shall maintain an open, transparent and regular dialogue with these churches and organisations."[254] Eventually, and to complete this picture, all three paragraphs were transposed into the 2007 Lisbon Treaty (that replaced the 2000 draft Constitutional Treaty) and, thus, encapsulated in the hard letter of Article 17 of the Treaty on the Functioning of the European Union (TFEU). The latter finally gave legally binding and constitutional strength to President Delors's commitment to enter into a dialogue with religious/humanist partners. Despite this effort to systematically organise EU relations with manifold faiths (and, remarkably, to put religious and non-religious instances on the same footing), the scope of this norm has, however, not been without controversy.

249 In this sense, see Pasquale Annicchino (n 47) 48.

250 In this sense, see Francesco Margiotta Broglio, 'Il Fenomeno Religioso nel Sistema Giuridico dell'Unione Europea' in Francesco Margiotta Broglio, Cesare Mirabelli and Francesco Onida (eds), *Religioni e Sistemi Giuridici* (Il Mulino 2000); Marco Ventura (n 247) 19.

251 ibid.

252 In this sense, see Ronan McCrea (n 237) 16. See also Consolidated Version of the Treaty on European Union (n 226) preamble (making reference to both the "religious" and the "humanist" inheritance of Europe). France and the Netherlands are illustrative examples. They both rejected the premature 2002–2003 process toward a Constitution for Europe by calling into question any potential reference to a creator God or to Europe's Christian heritage in the constitutional preamble. See Guy Milton (n 240), 205.

253 For a discussion on this provision, see Michal Rynkowski, 'Remarks on Art. 1–52 of the Constitutional Treaty: New Aspects of the European Ecclesiastical Law' (2005) 6(11) German Law Journal 1720–29.

254 Treaty Establishing a Constitution For Europe (n 238) art I-52(3).

Simply put, under Article 17 of the TFEU, religions lacking deep cultural roots in Europe (or unable to harmonise themselves with EU humanist elements, e.g., Islam) have been said to be at risk of being treated as "outsiders" of inferior status to "insider" state-favoured religions.[255] Seen in this way, for instance, Marco Ventura described this outsider/insider dichotomy in terms of a "selective dialogue" between the EU and monopolistic religious/humanist traditions at the expense of competitive minority (or newer) faiths.[256] More than this, in introducing and unpacking the idea of this EU "protectionist approach" to religion, the author also pointed out its most evident contradiction: on the one hand, an EU system protecting (and privileging) culturally established faiths has progressively emerged, while on the other, EU law has developed a second and countervailing approach to religion that aims precisely to challenge such national religious monopolies.[257]

By and large, and as will be discussed below, at the heart of this contradiction lies the need to mediate conflicts between element of national culture (including traditional religions) vis-à-vis the economic needs and goals of the EU single market. In this connection, and perhaps counterintuitively, the realisation of these EU objectives also involves the promotion of the equal treatment of all religions, most notably through the prohibition of direct and indirect discrimination in employment. It is against this background that the EU has begun to facilitate even the newest and most marginalised faith-based actors together with their demands for greater protection (and, thus, a more competitive position) under the EU single market. This parallel and "competitive"[258] EU approach to religion is discussed below.

The "competitive" approach

So far, it has been shown that the EU's relationship with FoRB has been mostly wedded to the Christian and secular heritage of its member states. Religion, however, has not always been seen as a historical matter of identity. This is all the more true when looking at the EU commitment to uphold "fundamental rights"[259] (FoRB included) as basic European common values and, thus, regardless of their

255 This outsider/insider dichotomy can be traced back to Ronan McCrea, 'EU Law and Religion: Protecting a Privileged Position for Majority Faiths?' in Hedvig Bernitz and Victoria Enkvist (eds) *Freedom of Religion. An Ambiguous Right in the Contemporary European Legal Order* (Hart Publishing, 2020).

256 Marco Ventura (n 248) 20–22.

257 Marco Ventura, 'L'articolo 17 TFUE come fondamento del diritto e della politica ecclesiastica dell'Unione Europea' (2014) 22(2) Quaderni di Diritto e Politica Ecclesiastica 293, 294.

258 This term could be traced back to Marco Ventura (n 245) 149–155.

259 Consolidated Version of the Treaty on European Union (n 232) art 6(3). See also ibid art 7 (introducing a sanction procedure that suspends the Treaty rights of the member states that are found to be in a gross violation of human rights standards).

genealogy and normative foundations, "transcendent or otherwise".[260] In order to ensure that such values are respected, an EU human rights document was approved by the Nice European Council in 2000: the Charter of Fundamental Rights of the European Union (CFREU). Originally drafted as a political bill of rights, it was only with the entry into force of the Lisbon Treaty in 2009 that the Charter finally became a binding source of EU law, as provided by Article 6(1) of the Maastricht Treaty. Also, through Article 6(3) of this latter treaty, the scope of the CFREU has been connected to the ECHR and its case law, both constituting general principles of EU law and standards for judicial review of EU provisions.

Against this background, the CFREU established a minimum degree of human rights protection that, as far as FoRB is concerned, largely corresponds in scope and application to Article 9 of the ECHR.[261] Religion, both in its individual and collective dimensions, is, in fact, protected under Article 10 of the CFREU along with a general guarantee of non-discrimination (Article 21 CFREU) and respect for religious diversity (Article 22 CFREU). All things considered, however, "[t]he adoption of the Charter did not transform the European Union into a human rights organisation."[262]

Therefore, here it is a question of looking at which rationale has informed the protection of fundamental rights in general, and FoRB in particular, at the EU level. In this connection, it might be useful to recall that the EU is a "functional legal order"[263] created to integrate the national economies of its member states. Thus, it follows that the safeguard of human rights is generally justified in light of an assessment of their suitability to meet and facilitate the economic goals of the Union.[264] In relation to FoRB then, religion is accommodated only to the extent it can be subsumed into the economic framework of the four freedoms of movement of people, capital, goods and services that the EU aims to achieve.[265] This is what Marco Ventura has termed a "competitive" approach to FoRB, in which religion is balanced against the needs of the market.

In sum, if the goal of the single market is to facilitate free movement, then in the same way a French stylist could work at Prada in Italy, or a Greek pilot fly for

260 Guy Milton (n 240)193. See also José Casanova, 'Religion, European Secular Identities, and European Integration' in Timothy A. Byrnes and Peter J. Katzenstein (eds), *Religion in an Expanding Europe* (Cambridge University Press, 2006) 81 (describing the proclamation of human rights as "a basic social fact" common to all Europeans).

261 It is worth recalling here that human rights protection under EU law has had a long history that, since the 1970s, was initially CJEU-driven. For early case law, see Chapter I, 34, (fn 235).

262 Marta Cartabia, 'The Charter of Fundamental Rights of the European Union' in Giuliano Amato (n 226) 117.

263 Armin Von Bogdandy, 'The European Union as a Human Right Organisation? Human Rights and the Core of the European Union' (2000) 37(6) Common Market Law Review 1307, 1308.

264 In this sense, see Eleanor Spaventa, 'Should We "Harmonize" Fundamental Rights in the EU? Some Reflections about Minimum Standards and Fundamental Rights Protection in the EU Composite Constitutional System' (2018) 55(4) Common Market Law Review 997, 1000.

265 In this sense, see Ronan McCrea (n 237) (describing this EU approach as one that addresses religion as an "economic choice within the market.") 143.

German Lufthansa, a Dutch national can (or better, could)[266] similarly take employment with the British branch of the Church of Scientology. The latter example is worthy of attention because it is actually based on a real-life freedom of movement case that the Court of Justice of the European Communities (CJEC) (now Court of Justice of the European Union (CJEU)) took up in 1974. Briefly put, the dispute arose from a claim by Ms. Yvonne Van Duyn, a member of the Church of Scientology in the Netherlands, against the British government.[267] She alleged that the UK Home Office, the lead government department for immigration, had violated the principle of free circulation of workers by denying her entry permit as a ministerial employee at the Church of Scientology in the UK. In effect, the British government took the view that Scientology was socially harmful. It, thus, discouraged its practice, although no domestic law could substantially prohibit it.

Without detailing the reasoning of the CJEC, it suffices to note that the Court found against the applicant. In fact, the Court interpreted the notion of "public policy" as a justification for derogating from the principle of freedom of movement of workers.[268] Despite this outcome, it is of note that a court usually focused on economic affairs went on to hold that it had jurisdiction to hear a case involving a FoRB issue. This was because the CJEC saw Ms Van Duyn's right to carry out pastoral work in another EU country as an economic matter of freedom of movement rather than a matter of religious freedom per se.[269] In practice, this is how, as early as 1974, religion began to be seen as an integral part of a market area consisting of four freedoms of movement that would henceforth include a fifth one: the free circulation of faiths.

Taken together, the *Van Duyn* case has proven wrong the general assumption that the EU has no competence on religion because of the (prima facie) non-economic nature of the latter.[270] Rather, further EU case law followed the lead

266 In fact, following the expiration of the Brexit "transition period" on 31 December 2020 (which started immediately after the UK left the EU on 31 January 2020), EU rules on freedom of movement have now ceased to apply to the UK. See Roger Casale, 'Hello, Brexit. Farewell, Freedom of Movement' (The New European, 31 December 2020) <https://www.theneweuropean.co.uk/brexit-news/roger-casale-on-the-end-of-free-movement-6872798> accessed 15 January 2021.

267 Case 41/74, *Yvonne Van Duyn v Home Office* (1974) ECR 1337.

268 ibid 1350–1351.

269 In this sense see: Marco Ventura (n 248) 8.

270 In line with the principles of conferral and subsidiarity under Article 5 of the TEU, the EU retains exclusive jurisdiction only in a few and economic-related areas, whilst, in others, its competences are shared with the member states. See Consolidated Version of the Treaty on European Union (n 232) art 5(2) and (3). EU exclusive and non-exclusive competences are enumerated respectively in Consolidated Version of the Treaty on the Functioning of the European Union (n 239) art 3 and 4. From here, it follows that it remains for member states to take decisions on state-religion relationships together with their respective ecclesiastical authorities. See Marie Claire Foblets, 'Freedom of Religion and Belief in the European Workplace: Which Way Forward and What Role for the European Union?'(2013) 13(1) International Journal of Discrimination and the Law 240, 247.

of this "competitive" approach to FoRB,[271] thereby suggesting (in the words of Marco Ventura) that "it is unrealistic to continue to argue that EU is relegated to the margins in the debate on the regulation of religion."[272]

With this in mind, it is now easy to see how this protectionist/competitive dichotomy indicates an ambivalent position of the EU to religion. It was in 2000 that such an ambivalence eventually took concrete form with the adoption of one of the first EU pieces of anti-discrimination legislation in employment: Directive 2000/78/EC.[273] For the scope of this chapter, suffice it to say that this has been the first provision under the international FoRB framework to introduce a statutory religious exemption for churches and "public or private organisations the ethos of which is based on religion or belief"[274] from anti-discrimination rules. This exceptional treatment for churches clearly resonates with a "protectionist" approach to FoRB. For that very reason, at the same time, Directive 2000/78/ EC risks frustrating the "competitive" goal of removing discriminatory "entry barriers'" to employment so as to maximise economic growth via the inclusion of as many individuals as possible in the processes of wealth creation and income distribution. The scope of this exception and the position that the CJEU took on this issue will be unpacked in greater detail in Chapter II.

Conclusion

In this chapter, four jurisdictions and their relationship with corporate religious freedom have been considered: the UN, the OSCE, the CoE, and the EU.

Overall, all of them differ in their approach to institutional religion in a number of ways. In brief summary, at the universal level, the UN follows an "individualistic approach" to FoRB that emphasises the conscience and autonomy rights of people *qua* physical persons. Compared with the other jurisdictions, this is the

271 See Case 300/84 *Van Rosmaalen v Bestuir van de Betrijfsvereinigingen* [1986] ECR 3097; Case 196/87 *Udo Steymann v Staatssecretaris van Justitie* [1988] ECR 6159. These cases are discussed in Ronan McCrea (n 236) 145–47. In deciding two major cases in 2018 on religious discrimination in church employment, the CJEU found in favour of the right of employees to be free from the discriminatory occupational requirements imposed by their church employers. Thus, the Court seems to be currently following a "protectionist" approach to FoRB. These decisions will be discussed in Chapter II. See Case C-414/16, *Vera Egenberger v Evangelisches Werk für Diakonie und Entwicklung e.V.* [2018] EU:C:2018:257; Case C-68/17, *IR v JQ* [2018] EU:C:2018:696.

272 Pasquale Annicchino (n 47) 49. By reference to Marco Ventura, the author also indicates that Article 17 of the TFEU "represented a fundamental contribution to the birth of a true religious law of the European Union". Marco Ventura (n 245) 302.

273 In this sense, see Marco Ventura, 'Non-Discrimination and Protection of Diversity and Minorities' in Giuliano Amato (n 226) 252.

274 See Council Regulation (EC) 2000/78 establishing a general framework for equal treatment in employment and occupation (EC Employment Equality Directive) [2000] L 303/16, art 4(2).

level in which the protection of religious institutions as holders of FoRB rights and exceptions is the lowest if not nil.

By contrast, the regional levels of the OSCE and the CoE opened up to religious institutions *qua* juridical persons as FoRB claimants. These organisations, however, differ in the way they address corporate religious freedom. They follow what have been dubbed a "comprehensive security" and "human-rights based" approach to FoRB, respectively. In practice, while the protection of institutional expressions of religion is a means to prevent conflicts for the OSCE, it is an end in itself for the CoE (or at least in principle).[275] Further, another difference is that the OSCE is a political and monitoring body, while the CoE is a legal organisation accompanied by the interpretative and adjudicative action of an all-out interstate court: the ECtHR. In sum, the CoE's favourable stance on corporate religious freedom, combined with a proper system of judicial review, denotes a potential for treating religion as positive and special. In a strand of church employment cases, the ECtHR has recognised the special weight of church autonomy rights, thus, creating religious exceptions by interpretation from Article 9 of the ECHR. This will be revisited in Chapter II.

Similarly, the EU has crafted its own religious exceptions, although not judicially, but legally, and in the form of an employment anti-discrimination directive. This came as a result of an EU "protectionist" approach that accommodates mainstream Christian churches and secular organisations with strong cultural roots in the member states. In any case, it has also been noted that the relationship between the EU and religion could not be linked solely and exclusively to sensitive matters of each member state's culture and identity. The EU has also developed a "competitive" approach to FoRB that balances religion with its market-oriented goals, thus, facilitating, empowering, if not even encouraging competitive religious actors. Because this approach assumes the possibility of limiting religious autonomy rights for economic-related reasons, it now remains to be seen how the CJEU has effectively handled religious exemptions and how it differs from the ECtHR.

Reference list

Ahdar R. and Leigh I., *Religious Freedom in the Liberal State* (Oxford University Press, 2013) (DOI: 10.1093/acprof:oso/9780199253623.001.0001).

Alston P. and Mégret F., 'Introduction. Appraising the United Nations Human Rights Regime' in Mégret Fréderic and Alston Philip (eds), *The United Nations and Human Rights. A Critical Appraisal* (Oxford University Press, 2020), 1–36.

Amato G. and others (eds), *The History of the European Union. Constructing Utopia* (Hart, 2019) (DOI: 10.5040/9781509917440).

275 It was noted in fact how the approaches of the OSCE and the CoE sometimes might *de facto* overlap.

——— and Verola N., 'Freedom, Democracy, Rule of Law' in Giuliano Amato and others (eds), *The History of the European Union. Constructing Utopia* (Hart, 2019), 57–88.

Annicchino P., *Law and International Religious Freedom. The Rise and Decline of the American Model* (Routledge, 2017).

Barberini G., 'Religious Freedom in the Process of Democratisation of Central and European States' in Silvio Ferrari and Cole W. Durham, Jr. (eds), *Law and Religion in Post-Communist Europe* (Peeters, 2003), 8–21.

Berkmann J. B., 'Catholic Church Law: Challenges by Secular Law and Religious Pluralism' (2021) 7(1) Interdisciplinary Journal for Religion and Transformation in Contemporary Society, 95–124.

Bielefeldt H., Ghanea N. and Wiener M., *Freedom of Religion or Belief. An International Law Commentary* (Oxford University Press, 2016) (DOI: 10.1093/law/9780198703983.001.0001).

Boyle A., 'Soft Law in International Law Making' in Malcolm D. Evans (eds), *International Law* (Oxford University Press, 2006), 118–136.

Broglio M. F., 'Il Fenomeno Religioso nel Sistema Giuridico dell'Unione Europea' in Francesco Margiotta Broglio, Cesare Mirabelli and Francesco Onida (eds), *Religioni e Sistemi Giuridici* (Il Mulino, 2000).

———, Mirabelli C. and Onida F. (eds), *Religioni e Sistemi Giuridici* (Il Mulino, 2000).

Byrnes A. T. and Katzenstein P. J. (eds), *Religion in an Expanding Europe* (Cambridge University Press, 2006).

Cartabia M., 'The Charter of Fundamental Rights of the European Union' in Giuliano Amato and others (eds), *The History of the European Union. Constructing Utopia* (Hart, 2019), 113–130.

Casale R., 'Hello, Brexit. Farewell, Freedom of Movement' (*The New European*, 31 December 2020).

Casanova J., 'Religion, European Secular Identities, and European Integration' in Timothy A. Byrnes and Peter J. Katzenstein (eds), *Religion in an Expanding Europe* (Cambridge University Press, 2006), 69–92.

Chaplin J. and Wilton G. (eds), *God and the EU. Faith in the European Project* (Routledge, 2017).

Cismas I., *Religious Actors and International Law* (Oxford University Press, 2014) (DOI: 10.1093/acprof:oso/9780198712824.001.0001).

Clapham A., *Human Rights Obligations of Non-State Actors* (Oxford University Press, 2006) (DOI: 10.1093/acprof:oso/9780199288465.001.0001).

Cremona M., 'The Treaties that Created Europe' in Giuliano Amato and others (eds), *The History of the European Union. Constructing Utopia* (Hart, 2019), 133–149.

Dalla Torre G., *La Città Sul Monte. Contributo ad Una Teoria Canonistica Delle Relazioni Fra Chiesa e Comunità Politica* (Ave, 2007).

De Londras F. and Dzehtsiarou K., 'Managing Judicial Innovation in the European Court of Human Rights' (2015) 15(3) Human Rights Law Review, 523–547 (DOI: 10.1093/hrlr/ ngv020).

Dickson B., 'The United Nations and Freedom of Religion' (1995) 44(2) International and Comparative Law Quarterly, 327–357.

Dickson J. and Eleftheriadis P. (eds), *Philosophical Foundations of European Union Law* (Oxford University Press, 2012) (DOI: 10.1093/acprof:oso/97801995887 70.001.0001).

Doe N., *Law and Religion in Europe: A Comparative Introduction* (Oxford University Press, 2011) (DOI: 10.1093/acprof:oso/9780199604005.001.0001).

Douglas-Scott S., 'The Problem of Justice in the European Union Values, Pluralism, and Critical Legal Justice' in Julie Dickson and Pavlos Eleftheriadis (eds), *Philosophical Foundations of European Union Law* (Oxford University Press, 2012), 412–447 (DOI: 10.1093/ acprof:oso/9780199588770.003.0016).

Durham Jr. W. C., 'The Right to Autonomy in Religious Affairs: A Comparative View' in Robbers Gerhard (ed), *Church Autonomy: A Comparative Survey* (Peter Lang, 2001), 683–714.

———, 'Facilitating Freedom of Religion or Belief Through Religious Associations Law' in Oslo Conference of Religious Freedom and others (eds), *Facilitating Freedom of Religion or Belief: A Deskbook* (Martinus Nijhoff Publishers, 2004).

Evans C., *Freedom of Religion Under the European Convention on Human Rights* (Oxford University Press, 2001).

Evans D. M., *Religious Liberty and International Law in Europe* (Cambridge University Press, 1997).

——— (ed), *International Law* (Oxford University Press, 2006).

———, 'Advancing Freedom of Religion or Belief: Agendas for Change' (2012) 1(1) Oxford Journal of Law and Religion, 5–14.

Ferrari S. and Durham Jr. W. C. (eds), *Law and Religion in Post-Communist Europe* (Peeters, 2003).

Fikfak V., 'Changing State Behaviour: Damages before the European Court of Human Rights' (2019) 29(4) The European Journal of International Law, 1091–1125 (DOI: 10.1093/ejil/chy064).

Foblets M. C., 'Freedom of Religion and Belief in the European Workplace: Which Way Forward and What Role for the European Union?' (2013) 13(1) International Journal of Discrimination and the Law, 241–255.

Freedman R., 'The Human Rights Council' in Fréderic Mégret and Philip Alston (eds), *The United Nations and Human Rights. A Critical Appraisal* (Oxford University Press, 2020), 181–238.

Fukuyama F., *The End of History and the Last Man* (The Free Press, 1992).

Gedicks F. M., 'The Recurring Paradox of Groups in The Liberal State' (2010) 1(1) Utah Law Review.

Ghanea N., 'Religion, Equality and Non-Discrimination' in John Witte and M. Christian Green (eds), *Religion and Human Rights: An Introduction* (Oxford University Press, 2011), 204–217 (DOI: 10.1093/acprof:osobl/9780199733453.003.0012).

Gibson U. and Lord K. S., 'Advancement in Standard Settings: Religious Liberty and OSCE Commitments' in Oslo Conference of Religious Freedom and others (eds), *Facilitating Freedom of Religion or Belief: A Deskbook* (Martinus Nijhoff Publishers, 2004), 239–254.

Greer S., 'The Margin of Appreciation: Interpretation and Discretion Under the European Convention of Human Rights' (2000) Human Rights Files 17, 5–58.

Grim B. J. and Finke R., *The Price of Freedom Denied: Religious Persecution and Conflict in the Twenty-First Century* (Cambridge University Press, 2011).

———, Clark G. and Snyder R. E., 'Is Religious Freedom Good for Business?: A Conceptual and Empirical Analysis' (2014) 10(4) Interdisciplinary Journal of Research on Religion, 1–19.

Gunner G., Slotte P. and Kitanović E. (eds), *Human Rights, Religious Freedom and Faces of Faith* (Globethics.net, 2019).

———, 'Introduction. Human Rights, Freedom of Religion or Belief and the Church' in Göran Gunner, Pamela Slotte and Elizabeta Kitanović (eds), *Human Rights, Religious Freedom and Faces of Faith* (Globethics.net, 2019), 13–28.

Hennebel L., 'The Human Rights Committee' in Mégret Fréderic and Alston Philip (eds), *The United Nations and Human Rights. A Critical Appraisal* (Oxford University Press, 2020), 339–391.

Jurgens E., 'Are Freedom of Religion and a Special Legal Position for Churches, Necessary or Even to be Desired in a Liberal Democracy under the Rule of Law?' in Hidegard Warnink (ed), *Legal Position of Churches and Church Autonomy* (Peeters, 2001), 239–244.

Keller H. and Ulfstein G. (eds), *UN Human Rights Treaty Bodies: Law and Legitimacy* (Cambridge University Press, 2012) (DOI: 10.1017/CBO9781139047593).

——— and Ieena G., 'General Comments of the Human Rights Committee and Their Legitimacy' in Helen Keller and Geir Ulfstein (eds), *UN Human Rights Treaty Bodies : Law and Legitimacy* (Cambridge University Press, 2012), 116–198.

Kiviorg M., *Freedom of Religion or Belief—The Quest for Religious Autonomy* (DPhil thesis, Wolfson College, 2011).

———, 'Collective Religious Autonomy versus Individual Rights: A Challenge for the ECtHR?' (2014) 39(1) Review of Central and East European Law, 315–341.

———, 'Collective Religious Autonomy Under the European Convention on Human Rights: The UK Jewish Free School Case in International Perspective' (2010) Max Weber Programme 2010/40, 1–14.

Lachmann W., 'The German Social Market Economy: Its Theological Justification and Role in European Integration' in Chaplin Jonathan and Wilton Gary (eds), *God and the EU. Faith in the European Project* (Routledge, 2017), 89–108.

Laffranque J. and others, 'Seminar to Mark the Official Opening of the Judicial Year Subsidiarity: A Two-Sided Coin? 1. The Role of the Convention Mechanism. 2. The Role of the National Authorities' (2015) Background Paper, 1–12.

Langlaude S., 'The Rights of Religious Associations to External Relations: A Comparative Study of the OSCE and the Council of Europe' (2010) 32(3) Human Rights Quarterly, 502–529.

Lerner N., *Religion, Secular Beliefs and Human Rights: 25 Years After the 1981 Declaration* (Brill, 2006).

———, 'The Nature and Minimum Standards of Freedom of Religion or Belief' (2000) 2000(3) Brigham Young University Law Review, 905–932.

Loughlin J., 'European Integration. A Catholic Perspective' in Chaplin Jonathan and Wilton Gary (eds), *God and the EU. Faith in the European Project* (Routledge, 2017).

Luitwieler S., 'The EU: Protestant Contributions, Then and Now' in Chaplin Jonathan and Wilton Gary (eds), *God and the EU. Faith in the European Project* (Routledge, 2017).

Martínez J. T. and Navarro-Valls R., 'The Protection of Religious Freedom in the System of the Council of Europe' in Oslo Conference of Religious Freedom and others (eds), *Facilitating Freedom of Religion or Belief: A Deskbook* (Martinus Nijhoff Publishers, 2004), 50–69.

Matlak M., 'Jacques Delors, the Single Market and the Failed Attempt to Give *a Soul to Europe*' (2018) Robert Schuman Centre for Advanced Studies Research Paper 2018/06, 1–11.

Matlary J. H., 'Implementing Freedom of Religion or Belief in The OSCE: Experiences from the Norwegian Chairmanship' in Oslo Conference of Religious Freedom and others (eds), *Facilitating Freedom of Religion or Belief: A Deskbook* (Martinus Nijhoff Publishers, 2004), 255–272.

McCrea R., 'EU Law and Religion: Protecting a Privileged Position for Majority Faiths?' in Hedvig Bernitz and Victoria Enkvist (eds), *Freedom of Religion. An Ambiguous Right in the Contemporary European Legal Order* (Hart Publishing, 2020), 51–60 (DOI: 10.5040/9781509935895).

———, *Religion and the Public Order of the European Union* (Oxford Scholarship Online, 2011) (DOI: 10.1093/acprof:oso/9780199595358.001.0001).

McDonagh P. and others, *On the Significance of Religion for Global Diplomacy* (Routledge, 2021).

McGoldrick D., 'A Defence of the Margin of Appreciation and an Argument for its Application by the Human Rights Committee' (2016) 65(1) International & Comparative Law Quarterly, 21–60.

———, 'From "Process" to "Institution". The Development of the Conference on Security and Cooperation in Europe' in Dominic McGoldrick and Bernard S. Jackson (eds), *Legal Visions of the New Europe. Essays Celebrating the Centenary of the Faculty of Law, University of Liverpool* (Graham and Trotman, 1993).

———, McGoldrick D. and Jackson B. S. (eds), *Legal Visions of the New Europe. Essays Celebrating the Centenary of the Faculty of Law, University of Liverpool* (Graham and Trotman, 1993).

Mégret F. and Alston P., *The United Nations and Human Rights. A Critical Appraisal* (Oxford University Press, 2020).

Milton G., 'God and the Constitution' in Jonathan Chaplin and Gary Wilton (eds), *God and the EU. Faith in the European Project* (Routledge, 2017), 191–207.

Minnerath R., 'The Right to Autonomy in Religious Affairs' in Oslo Conference of Religious Freedom and others (eds), *Facilitating Freedom of Religion or Belief: A Deskbook* (Martinus Nijhoff Publishers, 2004), 291–320.

Monti M., 'Competition and Solidarity in the European Construct' in Giuliano Amato and others (eds), *The History of the European Union. Constructing Utopia* (Hart, 2019), 89–112.

Moyn S., 'From Communist to Muslim: European Human Rights, the Cold War, and Religious Liberty' (2014) 113(1) The South Atlantic Quarterly, 63–86.

Oslo Conference of Religious Freedom and others (eds), *Facilitating Freedom of Religion or Belief: A Deskbook* (Martinus Nijhoff Publishers, 2004).

Pacillo V., *Buon Costume e Libertà Religiosa. Contributo all'Interpretazione dell'Art. 19 della Costituzione Italiana* (Giuffrè Editore, 2012).

Pin A. and Witte Jr. J., 'Meet the New Boss of Religious Freedom: The New Cases of the Court of Justice of the European Union' (2020) 55(2) Texas International Law Journal, 1–57.

Rainey B., Wicks E. and Ovey C., *Jacobs, White, and Ovey: The European Convention on Human Rights* (Oxford University Press, 2017).

Repetto G. (ed), *The Constitutional Relevance of the ECHR in Domestic and European Law* (Intersentia, 2013).

———, 'Introduction. The ECtHR and the European Constitutional Landscape. Reassessing Paradigms' in Giorgio Repetto (ed), *The Constitutional Relevance of the ECHR in Domestic and European Law* (Intersentia, 2013), 1–20.

Rivers J., *The Law of Organized Religions. Between Establishment and Secularism* (Oxford University Press, 2010).

Robbers G. (eds), *Church Autonomy: A Comparative Survey* (Peter Lang, 2001).

Ruffini F., *La Libertà Religiosa. Storia dell'idea* (Feltrinelli,1967).

Rynkowski M., 'Remarks on Art. 1–52 of the Constitutional Treaty: New Aspects of the European Ecclesiastical Law' (2005) 6(11) German Law Journal, 1720–1730.

Salm C. and Lehmann W., 'Jacques Delors. Architect of the Modern European Union' (2020) European Union History Series, 2–12.

Scharffs B. G, The Autonomy of Church and State' (2004) 1(4) Brigham University Law Review, 1219–1347.

———, Maoz A. and Isaacson Woolley A., 'Introduction. Freedom of/for/from Within Religion: Conceptually Inseparable Rights' in Brett G. Scharffs, Asher Maoz and Ashley Isaacson Woolley (eds), *Religious Freedom and the Law. Emerging Contexts for Freedom for and from Religion* (Routledge, 2019).

——— (eds), *Religious Freedom and the Law. Emerging Contexts for Freedom for and from Religion* (Routledge, 2019).

Scheinin M., 'The Human Rights Committee and Freedom of Religion or Belief' in Oslo Conference of Religious Freedom and others (eds), *Facilitating Freedom of Religion or Belief: A Deskbook* (Martinus Nijhoff Publishers, 2004), 189–202.

Schouppe J. P., *La Dimension Institutionnelle De La Liberté de Religion Dans la Jurisprudence de La Cour Européenne Des Droits De L'homme* (Pedone, 2015).

Slotte P. and Årsheim H., 'The Ministerial Exception — Comparative Perspectives' (2015 4(2) Oxford Journal of Law and Religion, 171–198 (DOI: 10.1093/ojlr/rwv008).

Spaventa E., 'Should We "Harmonize" Fundamental Rights in the EU? Some Reflections About Minimum Standards and Fundamental Rights Protection in the EU Composite Constitutional System' (2018) 55(4) Common Market Law Review, 997–1023.

Stone S. A., 'Sur la constitutionalisation de la Convention Européenne des droits de l'homme: cinquante ans après son installation, la Cour Européenne conçue comme une Cour constitutionnelle' (2009) 80(1) Revue trimestrielle des droits de l'homme.

Sullivan D. J., 'Advancing the Freedom of Religion or Belief Through the UN Declaration on the Elimination of Religious Intolerance and Discrimination' (1988) 82(3) The American Journal of International Law, 487–520.

Tahzib B. G., *Freedom of Religion or Belief: Ensuring Effective International Protection* (Martinus Nijhoff Publishers, 1996).

Temperman J., *Corporate Religious Freedom and the Rights of Others* (Eleven, 2019).

———, 'Freedom of Religion or Belief and Security – Some Reflections' (*Talk About: Law and Religion Studies*, 3 October 2019).

———, *State-Religion Relationships and Human Rights Law: Towards a Right to Religiously Neutral Governance* (Brill, 2010).

Ulfstein G., 'Relations Between the Council of Europe and the OSCE: Common Catalogue of Co-operation Modalities', 26 April 2000, CM(2000), 1–11.

Van Dijk P. and Van H. F., *Theory and Practice of the European Convention on Human Rights* (Kluwer Law International, 1998).

Ventura M.,'Dynamic Law and Religion in Europe. Acknowledging Change. Choosing Change' (2013) Robert Schuman Centre For Advanced Studies Research Paper 2013/91, 1–38.

———, *La Laicità dell'Unione Europea. Diritti, Mercato e Religione* (Giappichelli Editore, 2001).

———, 'L'articolo 17 TFUE come fondamento del diritto e della politica ecclesiastica dell'Unione Europea' (2014) 22(2) Quaderni di Diritto e Politica Ecclesiastica 293–304.

———, 'Non-Discrimination and Protection of Diversity and Minorities' in Giuliano Amato and others (eds), *The History of the European Union. Constructing Utopia* (Hart, 2019), 239–256.

———, 'Protectionnisme et libre-échangisme. La nouvelle gestion juridique de la religion en Europe' (2003) 64(1) Conscience et liberté, 122–132.

———, 'The Formula "Freedom of Religion or Belief" in the Laboratory of the European Union' (2020) 23(1) Studia z Prawa Wyznaniowego, 7–53 (DOI: 10.31743/spw.9833).

Von Bogdandy A., 'The European Union as a Human Right Organisation? Human Rights and the Core of the European Union' (2000) 37(6) Common Market Law Review, 1307–1338.

Von Campenhausen A. F., 'Church Autonomy in Germany' in Gerhard Robbers (ed), *Church Autonomy: A Comparative Survey* (Peter Lang, 2001).

Warnink H. (ed), *Legal Position of Churches and Church Autonomy* (Peeters, 2001).

Wilton G., 'Christianity at the Founding. The Legacy of Robert Schuman' in Jonathan Chaplin and Gary Wilton (eds), *God and the EU. Faith in the European Project* (Routledge, 2017), 30–32.

Witte J. and Green M. C. (eds), *Religion and Human Rights: An Introduction* (Oxford University Press, 2011) (DOI: 10.1093/acprof:osobl/9780199733453.001.0001).

2 Employment

Matteo Corsalini

The previous chapter examined corporate religious freedom from the perspective of four international legal orders: the UN, the OSCE, the CoE, and the EU. By appraising how they addressed the question of whether religious institutions should enjoy FoRB rights under international law, the goal was to establish which of these legal orders has taken a more favourable stance toward religious entities as corporate FoRB claimants.

This preliminary evaluation now allows this book to restrict the field of inquiry to two of the four models considered, the CoE and the EU, as the latter's favourable position on corporate religious freedom, combined with their legal and judicial strength, makes them ideally suited for accommodating requests for religious exemptions from otherwise applicable laws by religious institutions. It is precisely this sub-issue of how different European legal orders deal in practice with calls for corporate religious exemptions that constitutes the fulcrum of this chapter.

As discussed in Chapter 1, religious exemptions are often invoked to challenge the general prohibition of discrimination in faith-based employment. This is because the freedom to appoint spiritually qualified personnel is most important for religious employers to freely engage in their own forms of moral expression and maximise their religious autonomy rights. Thus, in principle, a church's ability to make choices about its ministers deserves protection under its right to corporate religious freedom. This explains, for instance, why the Catholic Church's traditional recruitment of only males as leaders within its hierarchy stands outside the reach of states' regulations on equality between men and women.

On the flip side, however, a recognition of these exemptions sometimes corresponds to a limitation of the rights of individuals operating in church employment. To take a few examples, a minister dismissed for having taught a doctrine disapproved by the official church might claim to be exercising an individual FoRB right of his own. Again, the religiously motivated termination of an African American minister can be challenged as an unfair dismissal on grounds of race.

Most notably, further tensions in workplace dynamics occur when exceptions radiate into adjacent secular domains. This problem can be posed with a question: could a church advance religious reasons for dismissing lay employees/volunteers (e.g., administrative staff, musicians, gardeners, bus drivers) whose duties are not a "core religious activity" (such as conducting worship services, rituals,

DOI: 10.4324/9781003340829-4

liturgies, confession, teaching the faith)? The same query goes for anti-discrimination claims by qualified ministers engaging in "non-core activities" (e.g., the teaching of completely secular subjects) contractually regulated by civil law.[1]

Also, a new line of research is now considering the question of whether religious exemptions could be invoked by other secular organisational structures, such as faith-based hospitals, schools, and for-profit corporations in particular.[2] Tellingly, the FoRB claims of the latter are signalling an interesting turn of events, in which corporate religious freedom is gradually moving from protecting churches in the organisation of their internal affairs (read: business) to considering the FoRB rights of commercial *businesses* as such. Part II of this book will deal with this "business turn" in law and religion in greater detail. That aside, for now, the analysis in this chapter is limited to considering requests for religious exemptions invoked by church bodies to protect the organisation of their internal *business*.

In this connection, an important premise is as follows: analysing how different legal orders address the subject of corporate religious exemptions is particularly important to acknowledge different conceptions of what constitutes "the religious" and "the secular" under the law.[3] To appreciate this argument, an illustrative example is the case of a church claiming that, in a similar way to ordained ministers, secular staff should also abide by specific religious lifestyle norms because of their spiritual involvement in its religious mission. Thus, as a matter of doctrine, in the church's eyes, there is actually no distinction between "religious" or "secular" work because all employees are seen as part of an integrated whole.[4] If courts were inclined to accept this "organic view"[5] of employment and extend religious exemptions to also cover secular employees and activities, then, as a matter of logic, the latter themselves would become "religious" (in a legal sense, at least). As will be discussed, not only did such a broad interpretation of religious exemptions actually happened, but, interestingly, it also signalled a challenging blurring of the religious/secular divide under the law.

1 For a discussion over the divide between "core" and "non-core" religious activities, see W. Cole Durham, Jr., 'The Right to Autonomy in Religious Affairs: A Comparative View' in Gerhard Robbers (eds), *Church Autonomy: A Comparative Survey* (Peter Lang 2001) 692–95.

2 For a discussion on the FoRB rights of commercial businesses, see Chapters III and IV of this book.

3 This view is supported in Pamela Slotte and Helge Årsheim, 'The Ministerial Exception — Comparative Perspectives' (2015) 4(2) Oxford Journal of Law and Religion 171, 176.

4 This scenario is discussed in Alvin J. Esau,'Islands of Exclusivity: Religious Organizations and Employment Discrimination' (2000) 33(3) British Columbia Law Review 719, 734–735. A recent sociological study explored how a number of Christian conservative CEOs in the US see money-making as a religious duty per se that is anchored in biblical scriptures. See the interviews collected in Bradley C. Smith, *Baptizing Business. Evangelical Executives & the Sacred Pursuit of Profits* (Oxford University Press 2020).

5 Alvin J. Esau (n 4) 734.

In other words, the enforcement of religious lifestyle norms within faith-based institutions is as much a social as a legal phenomenon that is amplified by the fact-finding and decision-making processes of the courts. After all, the decision to extend a church's ability to make autonomous employment decisions (or to extend it in a way that might fly in the face of anti-discrimination laws) "involves a test that at the bottom is subject to the value choices of the adjudicator".[6] Linked to this, and perhaps more worryingly from a civil law perspective, it bears note that an expansive understanding of religious exemptions to justify the dismissal of allegedly "dissident" workforce sometimes portends detrimental outcomes for church employees. To state the obvious, termination processes might be demeaning to the emotional, physical, and economic well-being of those who face the prospect of losing their jobs. As is evident, the subject of religious exemptions in employment is, thus, closely linked to the sensitive issue of unfair employment dismissals. It is, therefore, worthy of attention and discussion.

With this in mind, this chapter begins by exploring how the CoE progressively developed broad religious exemptions for churches by giving their FoRB rights under the Convention special weight when balanced against employees' rights. For reasons that will become evident, the approach and the case law of the US Supreme Court (USSC) should necessarily be included in this discussion. This chapter concludes by considering the approach of the CJEU, which provided a marked contrast to the ECtHR by narrowly interpreting the religious exemptions under its anti-discrimination legislation.

Having come this far, a clarification is needed because the reader could easily get the impression that it might be odd to have a sub-section on the USSC in between the two paragraphs on the ECtHR and the CJEU; however, this structure is only meant to reflect the chronological order of the selected case law as well as to emphasise the judicial dialogue that, as will be seen, has developed between courts across the Atlantic.

The European Court of Human Rights

As noted in Chapter I, in the period 2000–10, the ECtHR progressively recognised that religious organisations have autonomy rights that can be opposed to the interference of state authorities in internal ecclesiastical matters. In particular, a church's self-determination in the hiring or firing of ministers was said to be at the heart of corporate religious freedom.[7]

However, because it is also true that a church's membership control might sometimes result in discriminatory employment practices, between 2009 and 2011, the ECtHR began to introduce procedural and substantial limitations to overly discretionary religious powers. As it is shown in this chapter, such restrictions were achieved through what scholars have dubbed an "ad hoc

6 ibid 719.
7 *Svyato-Mykhaylivska Parafiya v. Ukraine*, App no 77703/01 (ECtHR, 14 September 2007).

balancing approach": a case-by-case assessment of the conflicts at hand via a proportional balancing of the competing human rights at stake.[8] Subsequent case law, however, indicated a change of course. Since 2012, the ECtHR has, in fact, edged toward a "one-sided approach"[9] to church employment disputes. In a word, this is an approach that gives special weight to church autonomy instead of properly balancing employer/employee rights on an equal footing. As will be seen, by shifting its view toward such a "one-sided" paradigm, the ECtHR de facto began to create its own religious exemptions for churches.[10]

In the following, this chapter offers an account of how this change in the Court's approach happened and how it is somehow connected to discourses in the US about the so-called "ministerial exception" doctrine. At its core, this exemption shields a religious institution's hiring and firing practices of ministers, even when other important claims, such as employment discrimination complaints, come into play. Here, what is most evident is that this doctrine, never without challenge and never perfectly implemented, categorically prioritises church autonomy rights without a proportionality assessment of the competing equality rights of ministerial employees. But more than that, and as will be discussed, this doctrine has recently been extended in a way that now immunises US faith-based employers from non-discrimination claims brought by non-ministerial workers, such as lay personnel and staff.

The "ad hoc balancing" approach

Before looking at church employment disputes at the CoE level, it should be noted that the protection of church employees was initially characterised by extreme shallowness. Early ECommHR case law deemed that the freedom of "dissident" individuals to exit a religious community was a sufficient protection

8 The literature adopting this formula is vast. See generally Lourdes Peroni, 'U.S. Supreme Court and ECtHR: Conflicts between Religious Autonomy and Other Fundamental Rights' (Strasbourg Observers, 2 February 2012) <https://strasbourgobservers.com/2012/02/02/u-s-supreme-court-and-ecthr-conflicts-between-religious-autonomy-and-other-fundamental-rights/> accessed 2 December 2020; Ian Leigh, 'Balancing Religious Autonomy and Other Human Rights under the European Convention' (2012) 1(1) Oxford Journal of Law and Religion 109, 121. Stijn Smet and Eva Brems (eds), *When Human Rights Clash at the European Court of Human Rights. Conflict or Harmony?* (Oxford University Press 2017).

9 This formula can be traced back to Russel Sandberg, 'The Future of Religious Freedom' in Stijn Smet and Eva Brems (n 8)136.

10 Importantly, however, rather than a religious exemption as such, the religious freedom of groups is conceptualised by the ECtHR in terms of "religious autonomy" or "church autonomy". In this sense, see Pamela Slotte and Helge Årsheim (n 3) 180.

of their rights.[11] At any rate, because this "exit/surrender approach"[12] tipped the balance too far in favour of employer autonomy, it left room for debate.

Linked to this, Ian Leigh explained that this doctrine not only risked inflicting costs in terms of social ambitions and expectations of those who were forced to quit but was also flawed from a technical perspective.[13] In this sense, another critic, Ioana Cismas, pointed to the fact that "church autonomy covers solely a *forum externum* that in turn is not absolute",[14] thereby suggesting that autonomy of religious governance should be protected only when it is proportionate to do so. In light of this, instead of requiring an employee to *waive* his or her rights by quitting the workplace, a better approach would be to *weigh* their rights with competing church autonomy claims in a case-to-case balancing analysis. This is the gist of the "ad hoc balancing" exercise that the ECtHR progressively developed in its church employment case law. In effect, and as will be shown, the ECtHR distanced itself from the previous "exit/surrender approach" by requiring proportionality in the employment choices of churches and subjecting them to the limitations under Article 9(2) of the ECHR.

In any case, one should not rush to conclude that the human rights of the others should always take priority; rather, limitations to church autonomy must be construed strictly. Article 9(2) of the ECHR states that restrictions to outward manifestations of religion should be prescribed by law and pursue one of the legitimate aims of protecting public safety and order, health, or morals or protecting the rights and freedoms of the others. Furthermore, they must be "necessary in

11 See *X v Denmark*, App no 7374/76 (ECommHR, 8 March 1976) 5 DR 157, 158; *Karlsson v Sweden*, App no 12356/86 (ECommHR, 8 September 1988). The ECommHR acknowledged an employee's freedom to resign from work as a sufficient standard also in disputes against secular employers. See *Kontinnen v Finland*, App no 24949/94 (ECtHR, 3 December 1996); *Stedman v United Kingdom*, App no 29107/95 (ECtHR, 9 April 1997). For a discussion of this "freedom to resign" doctrine, see Lucy Vickers, *Religious Freedom, Religious Discrimination and the Workplace* (Hart Publishing, 2008) 45–46.

12 In this sense, see Ian Leigh (n 8) 116.

13 ibid 116.

14 Ioana Cismas, *Religious Actors and International Law* (Oxford University Press 2014) 126. This argument drew extensively on Merilin Kiviorg's analysis of collective spheres of religious autonomy. Following examination of which ecclesiastical areas should be protected from state interference, Kiviorg concluded that there are zones in which only religious institutions enjoy "broad, but not absolute autonomy". Merilin Kiviorg, 'Collective Religious Autonomy under the European Convention on Human Rights: The UK Jewish Free School Case in International Perspective' (2010) Max Weber Programme 2010/40, 7 <https://cadmus.eui.eu/bitstream/handle/1814/15236/MWP_2010_40.pdf> accessed 19 November 2020. As an alternative view, Cole Durham rebutted that church autonomy, more than being a simple expression of a *forum externum*, flows directly from the untouchable *forum internum* of church adherents. W. Cole Durham, Jr., 'Facilitating Freedom of Religion or Belief Through Religious Associations Law' in Oslo Conference of Religious Freedom and others (eds), *Facilitating Freedom of Religion or Belief: A Deskbook* (Martinus Nijhoff Publishers 2004) 360. However, the author discusses church autonomy only in terms of "strong protection" and does not conclude anything definitive about the absoluteness of this corporate right. W. Cole Durham, Jr (n 1).

a democratic society";[15] meaning that evidence of a rational connection between FoRB restrictions and one of the legitimate aims mentioned above is required. Additionally, this criterion of "necessity" includes a measure of proportionality to judicially appraise whether or not a restriction constitutes the less intrusive means available to achieve a legitimate aim. It is within this balancing exercise that the breadth of a state's discretion to invoke the "democratic necessity" of a restriction is generally scrutinised (i.e., the "margin of appreciation doctrine").[16]

Based on this analysis, what follows turns to consider how the ECtHR developed in practice this "ad hoc balancing approach". As the Court had the opportunity to demonstrate how it did so in a string of church employment cases between 2009 and 2011, it is with this case law that his section begins.

Lombardi Vallauri v Italy

The profound significance of the ECtHR's departure from an "exit/surrender approach" in church employment disputes was reflected, for the first time ever, in its 2009 decision in *Lombardi Vallauri v Italy*.[17]

In this case, the applicant, Mr. Vallauri, appealed the decision by the Faculty Board of the Catholic University of the Sacred Heart in Milan to not renew his employment contract as a professor in legal philosophy, after holding this position for more than 20 years. The university acknowledged that the applicant failed to meet a necessary condition for faith-based employment: the approval (*gradimento*) by the Congregation of Catholic Education. More exactly, the latter is a department of the Roman Curia, which, in turn, constitutes the central government of the Roman Catholic Church. Overall, while the Congregation issued a letter declaring Mr. Vallauri's views "in clear opposition to Catholic doctrine"[18] on the basis of unspecified concerns, the university did not give any clear explanation about its refusal to examine Mr. Vallauri's application for contract renewal. As a result, Mr. Vallauri had no objective elements to rebut the

15 See European Convention on Human Rights and Fundamental Freedoms, 4 November 1950 (entered into force 3 September 1953) 213 UNTS 221 (ECHR)art 9(2).

16 This doctrine has already been discussed in Chapter I, 45. For a discussion on the ECtHR's requirements of legality, legitimacy, and necessity see Thiago Alves Pinto, 'An Empirical Investigation of the Use of Limitations to Freedom of Religion or Belief at the European Court of Human Rights' (2020) 15(1) Religion and Human Rights 96, 109–120. For a detailed discussion on the structure of the ECtHR' proportionality analysis see: Robert Alexy, *A Theory of Constitutional Rights* (Oxford University Press 2002).

17 *Lombardi Vallauri v Italy*, App no 39128/05 (ECtHR, 20 October 2009). This case has not been published in English. References to the case are drawn from the official translation by the Italian Ministry of Justice available at <https://hudoc.echr.coe.int/eng#{%22fulltext%22:[%22lombardi%20vallauri%22],%22languageisocode%22:[%22ITA%22],%22appno%22:[%2239128/05%22],%22documentcollectionid2%22:[%22GRANDCHAMBER%22,%22CHAMBER%22],%22itemid%22:[%22001-149211%22]}> accessed 21 November 2020.

18 ibid para 8.

charges and defend himself. Thus, having received no explanation either from the Congregation or from the university, as well as having been denied appeal by domestic courts, Mr. Vallauri challenged the dismissal before the ECtHR. He filed an application under Articles 9, 10 (freedom of expression), and 6(1) of the ECHR (right to a fair trial).

On the whole, the ECtHR held that it had no power whatsoever to assess the compatibility of the applicant's position with Catholic doctrine. Relying on an alleged lack of jurisdiction, it then recalled that it is not for civil tribunals to make determinations on matters of orthodoxy and religious teaching.[19] While this may be, the fact remains that, in taking up this case, the Court also proved the non-absoluteness of church autonomy, thus, introducing a procedural limitation to this right. To do that, the Court first considered that the decision by the Faculty Board to not assess Mr. Vallauri's job application interfered with the applicant's right to freedom of expression. Thus, and given the domestic courts' refusal to ascertain why the Board did not do so, it held that the refusal by domestic tribunals to hear Mr. Vallauri's case inhibited his procedural guarantees.[20] In brief summary, and in taking "something of an administrative turn",[21] this is how the ECtHR found a violation of Article 10 of the ECHR on procedural grounds, arguing that the interference with Mr. Vallauri's freedom of expression was not "necessary" in a democratic society.[22]

Beyond that, the Court went on to consider that the Catholic university should have done better to obtain information from the Congregation about the reason for its disapproval. Such information should then have been communicated to the applicant so that he could effectively speak in his own defence, thus the Court held.[23]

In light of the foregoing, the ECtHR found a breach also of the applicant's right to fair trial under Article 6(1) of the ECHR; while with regard to Article 9 of the ECHR, it held that no examination was needed because no further questions added up to those already discussed under Article 10 of the ECHR. In sum, with this decision, the ECtHR set an important precedent recognising that standards of procedural fairness can be effective carve-outs to protect employees in their disputes in religious workplaces.

19 ibid para 50.

20 In this sense, see Ian Leigh (n 8) 120 (arguing that "[T]he Court's use of Article 10 to imply a procedural guarantee based on a supposed principle of adversarial debate is striking and curious, especially when the same conclusion could more naturally be reached under Article 6").

21 Carolyn Evans and Anna Hood, 'Religious Autonomy and Labour Law: A Comparison of the Jurisprudence of the United States and the European Court of Human Rights' (2012) 1(1) Oxford Journal of Law and Religion 81, 99.

22 ibid paras 55–56.

23 *Lombardi Vallauri* (n 17) para 53.

Obst, Schüth, and Siebenhaar v Germany

If in *Vallauri* the ECtHR focused on procedural limitations to church autonomy in employment, in three further cases, it found that substantial limitation grounded in fundamental human rights standards also apply. More exactly, in *Obst*[24] and *Schüth*[25] (2010), the ECtHR addressed conflicts between church autonomy and the right to respect for the private and family life of church employees (Article 8 ECHR). Instead, in *Siebenhaar*[26] (2011), the conflict was between church autonomy vis-à-vis an employee's Article 9 ECHR claim.[27]

Overall, what all these cases have in common is the special attention that the ECtHR paid to the balancing exercise struck by domestic courts in weighing the competing interests at stake. Other things being equal, substantial restrictions to church autonomy apply only and exclusively when it is demonstrated that national courts failed to count the counterposed rights of church employees in their proportionality assessment. In the eyes of the Court, this also implied evaluating the potential repercussions on the employees' personal lives stemming from dismissals justified on the basis of an incomplete assessment at the domestic level.

As will be detailed below, it was precisely in light of this "ad hoc balancing approach" that the three cases generated different outcomes. Briefly summarised, the ECtHR ruled in favour of church employers in *Obst* and *Siebenhaar*, whilst in *Schüth*, it was the applicant-employee who succeeded.

In the first case, Michael Heinz Obst, the Director for Europe in the Department of Public Relations of the Church of Jesus Christ of Latter-Day Saints (the Mormon Church), was terminated after revealing to his superior that he had been involved in an extramarital relationship. Upon an unsuccessful application before domestic courts, Mr. Obst alleged a violation of his right to respect

24 *Obst v Germany*, App no 425/03 (ECtHR, 23 September 2010). This case has not been published in English. References are drawn from an unofficial translation of the case published by the Strasbourg Consortium available at: <https://www.strasbourgconsortium.org/common/document.view.php?DocumentID=5084> accessed 2 December 2020.

25 *Schüth v Germany*, App no 1620/03 (ECtHR, 23 September 2010). This case has not been published in English. References are drawn from an unofficial translation of the case published by the Strasbourg Consortium available at: <https://www.strasbourgconsortium.org/common/document.view.php?DocumentID=5083> accessed 2 December 2020.

26 *Siebenhaar v Germany*, App no 18136/02 (ECtHR, 3 February 2011). This case has not been published in English. References are drawn from an unofficial translation of the case published by the Strasbourg Consortium available at: <https://www.strasbourgconsortium.org/common/document.view.php?docId=5201> accessed 2 December 2020.

27 In 2011 the ECtHR considered three other cases on church autonomy in employment: *Müller v Germany*, App no 12986/04 (ECtHR, 6 December 2011); *Baudler v Germany*, App no 38254/04 (ECtHR, 6 December 2011); and *Reuter v Germany*, App no 39775/04 (ECtHR, 6 December 2011). All cases were declared inadmissible and, therefore, fall outside the scope of this analysis. However, for an extensive comment on these decisions, see Gerhard Robbers, 'Church Autonomy in the European Court of Human Rights — Recent Developments in Germany' (2010) 26(1) The Journal of Law and Religion 281.

for private and family life (Article 8 ECHR) before the ECtHR which, in its judgement of 23 September 2010, upheld the church's decision to dismiss him.

The second case, handed down by the ECtHR on the same day, concerned a conflict between Mr. Schüth, an organist, and his employer, the Catholic Church in Germany. Like in *Obst*, when the church employer discovered that Mr. Schüth was committing adultery, they dismissed him for breach of his duty of loyalty to the church's mission as required by the employment contract. However, unlike in *Obst*, the ECtHR ruled that Mr Schüth's dismissal amounted to a violation of his Article 8 ECHR rights, thus, finding against the church employer.

Before moving to consider *Siebenhaar*, it would be helpful to clarify why the ECtHR reached opposite conclusions in *Obst* and *Schüth*, despite their similar factual backgrounds. Taken together, in both decisions, the ECtHR found it crucial to consider whether the German courts did full justice to all the competing rights at stake. In light of this, the ECtHR acknowledged that Mr. Obst had no cause of complaint. This was because, in its view, the domestic courts had struck a fair balancing exercise between Mr. Obst's Article 8 ECHR rights and his employer's church autonomy.[28] In support of this contention, the ECtHR highlighted that several factors relating to Mr. Obst's background and role had been exhaustively assessed by the national tribunals to justify his dismissal. First, the courts considered that Mr. Obst should have been aware of the absolute importance of marital fidelity within Mormon theology, not only because he grew up Mormon but also because he retained an important position within the church for a long time.[29] Second, and relatedly, it was noted that Mr. Obst had a lifelong knowledge of his faith's requirements. Third, based on this account, the courts observed that Mr. Obst would have no problem finding alternative employment given his professional experience (he held several position within the church) and relatively young age.[30] It was on these grounds that the German courts, thus, found that Mr. Obst's dismissal was legitimate and "necessary to preserve the credibility of the Mormon Church".[31] Drawing on these conclusions, the ECtHR then made it clear that the applicant's dismissal was not justified so much by the adultery itself as by the fact that Mr. Obst was a church senior officer. By virtue of this prominent role, the Court, thus, reasoned that the applicant had a special duty of loyalty to the church's faith and mission; a duty which, so it was felt by the Court, did not raise any issue under the Convention.[32] Thus, the dismissal by the Mormon Church could not be faulted.

By contrast, in *Schüth*, the ECtHR found that the domestic courts had failed to sufficiently evaluate the negative impact that the applicant's dismissal would have on his private and family life as well as in light of his limited prospects of

28 *Obst* (24) para 52.
29 ibid 48–50.
30 ibid 48.
31 ibid.
32 ibid 49.

finding alternative employment.[33] This notwithstanding, the Court noted that, in principle, the plaintiff should have been aware of his duty of loyalty to the church and its mission, having signed an employment contract. For this reason, it considered it necessary to carefully examine the nature of Mr. Schüth's position, and in the end, it found that he was not an ordained minister. This, therefore, led the Court to conclude that, unlike Mr. Obst's employer, Schüth's employer could not demand "excessive" loyalty (one that goes well beyond the professional sphere) from the applicant.[34] This consideration, added to the fact that the domestic courts completely disregarded the applicant's employment status, hinted at a lack of proportionality in the balancing exercise struck at the national level. In consequence, the ECtHR held that Mr. Schüth's termination amounted to a violation of his Article 8 ECHR rights. Having come this far, it only remains to be seen which position the ECtHR took in *Siebenhaar*.

In this case, Astrid Siebenhaar, a teacher of secular subjects in a kindergarten run by a Protestant congregation, was dismissed after church authorities learned of her membership in the Universal Church of Humanism. If that were not enough, they also discovered that Ms. Siebenhaar was teaching introductory courses to the humanist groups of that church that were contrary to the dictates of the Protestant Congregation, her first employer. Before the ECtHR, the applicant complained of a violation of her Article 9 ECHR rights and that the domestic courts did not appropriately count her interests in the balancing exercise. Following the same reasoning as in *Obst*, the ECtHR did not find a violation of the applicant's freedom of religion. Rather, it noted that the domestic courts had taken into account all the relevant factors to justify her dismissal, such as the applicant's relatively young age and her relatively short employment period. That aside, for the Court, it was, however, not inconceivable that the applicant no longer offered "the guarantee that the ideals of her employer would be respected".[35] On the contrary, the ECtHR noted that Ms. Siebenhaar's affiliation with a humanist group could have adversely affected the quality of her work at the congregation, just as the domestic court had previously maintained. In light of this, the ECtHR concluded that Ms. Siebenhaar's termination did not amount to a violation of her Article 9 ECHR rights, finding that her dismissal was necessarily linked to the congregation's need to protect its reputation before the public. Following the analysis of this string of decisions, some final considerations are in order.

To begin, warranting attention is that, in all the cases discussed, all employees were contractually required to properly commit to the ethos of their respective churches as stipulated in their employment arrangements. This could be read to

33 *Schüth* (n 25) para 67.

34 ibid 71.

35 In this sense, see Saïla Ouald Chaib, 'Freedom of Religion in Conflict: Siebenhaar v. Germany' (Strasbourg Observers, 4 March 2011) <https://strasbourgobservers.com/2011/03/04/freedom-of-religion-in-conflict-siebenhaar-v-germany/> accessed 3 December 2020.

mean that the autonomy rights of church employers were "bolstered by contract law and private law notions of consent".[36] Be that as it may, through a "balancing approach" the ECtHR also revealed that the principle of good faith in contractual relations was not enough to protect the interests of churches vis-à-vis their "dissident" employees.

Actually, the ECtHR expected national authorities to consider all the interests at stake and balance them on proportionality grounds. Phrased differently, the ECtHR took the opportunity presented by these church employment disputes to enforce its so-called "doctrine of positive obligations".[37] This is enshrined under Article 1 of the ECHR and provides that: "The High Contracting Parties shall secure to everyone within their jurisdiction the rights and freedoms defined in (…) this Convention". Basically, this formula makes it clear that all member states must commit themselves to protecting the rights set out in the Convention against any potential infringement, whether by a state or by a non-state actor (such as the church employers in the cases at hand). In this sense, this provision offers an important recognition of the so-called horizontal effects of international human rights law (also known under the German term of *Drittwirkung*) at the ECtHR level.[38]

Briefly put, *Drittwirkung* is a complex theoretical concept entailing the possibility for individuals to enforce their human rights in their (horizontal) private law relations with other private persons (including juridical persons, such as churches).[39] This notwithstanding, the fact remains that, under Article 34 of the ECHR, it is only against states that individuals can file a complaint under the Convention.[40] Then, as a matter of logic, individual actors (such as the applicants in *Vallauri*, *Obst*, *Schüth*, and *Siebenhaar*) are, in principle, incapable *rationae personae* to bring a case against another private actor (such as church employers) before the ECtHR.[41] Yet, as Merilin Kiviorg explains, "an individual can bring up an alleged violation of her convention rights by another individual (or religious community) indirectly; for example, when a State can be held responsible for the violation in one way or another".[42]

36 Carolyn Evans and Anna Hood (n 21) 98.
37 In this sense, see Johan D. Van der Vyver 'State Interference in the Internal Affairs of Religious Institutions' (2012) 26(1) Emory International Law Review 1, 6.
38 In this sense, see Ian Leigh (n 8) 122.
39 This theory is masterfully explained in Robert Alexy (n 16) 351–4. See also Pieter van Dijk and others, *Theory and Practice of the European Convention on Human Rights* (Intersentia, 2006) 29.
40 See European Convention on Human Rights (n 15) art 34. ("The Court may receive applications from any person, non-governmental organisation or group of individuals claiming to be the victim of a violation by one of the High Contracting Parties of the rights set forth in the Convention or the Protocols thereto".)
41 In this sense, see Merilin Kiviorg, 'Collective Religious Autonomy versus Individual Rights: A Challenge for the ECtHR?'(2014) 39(1) 315, 323.
42 Ibid 323.

Seen in this way, the four cases examined are an illustrative example of how ECHR norms make states *indirectly* accountable for the potential violations committed by non-state actors under the Convention.[43] In other words, the revolutionary recognition of procedural and substantial limitations on church autonomy by the ECtHR made an important contribution to the issue of the indirect effect of fundamental human rights in the fields covered by the Convention, at least as far as labour relationships in church employment are concerned.

The "one-sided balancing" approach

Having described a first stand of ECtHR's case law on church employment between 2009 and 2011, the following is an analysis of subsequent jurisprudence on the same topic with a view to understanding how the ECtHR's "ad hoc balancing" approach gradually morphed into a "one-sided approach". The latter formula exemplifies the ECtHR's progressive shift toward a judicial reasoning that prioritises church autonomy rights by giving them special weight when balanced against other competing interests.

Sindicatul 'Păstorul cel Bun' v Romania

A good starting point to appraise the ECtHR's change in approach is the case of *Sindicatul 'Păstorul cel Bun' v Romania* and the differences between the Court's reasoning in its Chamber (2012)[44] and Grand Chamber (2013)[45] judgements. The dispute stemmed from a group of priests and lay employees of the Romanian Orthodox Church attempting to register a trade union (*Păstorul cel Bun*) that ecclesiastical authorities opposed because of the lack of permission by the Archbishop.

Overall, the Romanian first-instance court allowed the union's application for legal personality. It relied also on international law (Article 22 ICCPR, Articles 22 and 11 ECHR) to find that the applicant group had a right to form a trade union to protect their non-religious interests (i.e., economic, social, and cultural rights) in their dealings with their church employer.[46] Noting further that the applicants were all contractual employees with salaries funded by state budget, the court held that their trade union rights fell within the scope of civil labour laws. Therefore, the unionisation of church employees could not be made dependent merely on an ecclesiastical rule (i.e., the Archbishop's prior consent). In this connection, the court held that the employees' duty of loyalty to the church's mission did not constitute sufficient ground for restricting rights under labour legislation. By reviewing the union's statutes, it then concluded that restrictions

43 For a discussion on the direct and indirect third-party effects of religious freedom (*unmittelbare* and *mittelbare Drittwirkung*, respectively) in labour law relationships, see Vincenzo Pacillo, *Contributo Allo Studio Del Diritto di Libertà Religiosa Nel Rapporto di Lavoro Subordinato* (Giuffrè, 2003) 43–60.

44 App no 2330/09 (Third Section, 31 January 2012).

45 App no 2330/09 (Grand Chamber, 9 July 2013).

46 *Sindicatul* (n 44) para 11–12.

upon trade union activities were not "necessary in a democratic society" because the applicants allegedly had no intention of challenging the church's tenets and organisational structure. Instead, their official goal was simply to encourage a more positive employee–employer dialogue concerning the negotiation of labour contracts.[47]On appeal by the Orthodox Church, however, the *Doji* County Court quashed the first-instance judgement, holding that the prohibition of setting up a trade union was consistent with the church's statute. It, thus, affirmed the right of religious institutions to autonomously manage their internal affairs.[48]

Following this decision, the applicant group sought redress before the ECtHR, invoking a violation of its Article 11 ECHR rights (freedom of assembly and association). Overall, in disagreeing with the domestic appeal court, the ECtHR's Third Section (a smaller panel of ECtHR judges) ruled in favour of the applicants, finding a breach of their Article 11 rights. In so doing, the Court stuck to its conventional "ad hoc balancing approach". It noted, in fact, that, by allowing a church not to register a trade union for purely religious reasons, the domestic appeal court overlooked several factors relating to the secular rights and interests of church employees. These included the distinction between ministerial and non-ministerial status and their personal backgrounds as well as the compatibility of ecclesiastical rules with national and international labour law standards of protection. Seen in this way, the ECtHR held that the domestic appeal court failed to strike a proportionate balance of rights.[49] Relying on *Schüth*, the ECtHR, thus, found that "a relationship based on an employment contract cannot be "clericalised" to the point of being exempted from all rules of civil law".[50] Following this, it then concluded that the refusal to register the applicant union was not "necessary in a democratic society", despite this denial being grounded on domestic law and pursuing a legitimate aim (i.e., the protection of the defendant church's autonomy rights).[51] In fact, in its view, the domestic appeal court did not establish evidence that recognising the trade union would have jeopardised the Romanian Orthodox Church's traditional hierarchical structure. In conclusion, the interference at hand was not proportionate to the legitimate aim pursued. It, thus, violated the applicants' Article 11 ECHR rights.[52]

On the whole, this decision spurred lively debates not just among legal scholars and practitioners[53] but also (and even more interestingly) among some

47 ibid 13–15.
48 ibid 17–20.
49 ibid para 77–80.
50 ibid para 65.
51 ibid para 67.
52 ibid para 84–86.
53 For instance, Judges Ziemele and Tsotsoria criticised the Third Section's ruling in their dissenting opinion. They noted that the issue of applying Article 11 ECHR rights to church employees is slippery. And this is because the stated purposes of the trade union would easily bleed into religious issues within the church hierarchy. See ibid (joint dissenting opinion of judges Ziemele and Tsotsoria) para 4.

transnational non-governmental organisations (NGOs) with religiously conservative agendas.[54] For instance, the European Centre For Law and Justice (ECLJ) was a third-party intervener in ***Sindicatul*** that made a case for stronger church autonomy before the Third Section.[55] The ECLJ is the European branch of the American Center of Law and Justice (ACLJ), a Christian legal advocacy group engaging in FoRB protection at all levels of the US judiciary and before international tribunals around the globe.[56] Thus, thanks to its European-based branch, the ACLJ is particularly active at the ECtHR in Strasbourg, as well as at the European Parliament in Brussels and the OSCE in Vienna.[57] In light of this, a possible factor for changing course from its Third Section's decision (as it will be detailed below) is that the ECtHR might have felt the influence of American religious activism in Europe favouring stronger church autonomy rights.[58] In effect, Eric Rassbach and Diana Verm, members of the Becket Fund for Religious Liberty (another Christian legal advocacy group based in Washington, DC) urged Romania to request referral of the *Sindicatul* case to the ECtHR's Grand Chamber (the highest panel within the Court). The goal was to convince "Strasbourg" to review and reject its Third Chamber's decision.[59] Toward that aim, they published an article in a Romanian law journal (*Revista de Drept*

54 This is what Clifford Bob dubbed "transnational activism" to describe three main phenomena: "1) non-state actors based in one country forming transnational advocacy networks (TANs) with similar entities in other countries; 2) these networks then seeking to influence ideas and policy in other societies; and 3) the networks seeking to affect international organisations and their member state as they develop global policy". Clifford Bob, 'The Global Right Wing and Theories of Transnational Advocacy' (2013) The International Spectator: Italian Journal of International Affairs 48(4) 71,72.

55 *Sindicatul* (n 44) 54–56.

56 See the ACLJ's webpage at: <https://aclj.org/our-mission/about-aclj> accessed 8 December 2020.

57 See the ECLJ's webpage at <https://eclj.org/about-us> accessed 8 December 2020. See also Katherine Stewards, *The Power Worshippers. Inside the Dangerous Rise of American Nationalism* (Bloomsbury Publishing 2020) 266–273 (exploring some networking activities between US and European Christian conservative advocacy groups).

58 Pamela Slotte and Helge Årsheim (n 3) 198. See also generally Marie Ashe, 'Hosanna Tabor, the Ministerial Exception, and Loss of Equality: Constitutional Law and Religious Privilege in the United States' (2015) Oxford Journal of Law and Religion 4(2) 199–223. For a discussion on direct or indirect lobbying in the ECtHR jurisprudence on FoRB by legal and political groups operating at the national and international level (i.e., "grasstop" mobilisations), see Effie Fokas, 'Directions in Religious Pluralism in Europe: Mobilizations in the Shadow of European Court of Human Rights Religious Freedom Jurisprudence' (2015) 4(1) Oxford Journal of Law and Religion 54. Christopher McCrudden has referred to this phenomenon as "culture wars" in which religiously affiliated NGOs participate in national and transnational FoRB litigation "to attempt to embed particular models of religious rights". See Cristopher McCrudden, 'Transnational Culture Wars' (2015) 13(2) International Journal of Constitutional Law 434, 439.

59 See the Becket Fund for Religious Liberty, 'Eric Rassbach Talks Religious Freedom at the Council of Europe' (21 June 2012) <https://www.becketlaw.org/media/eric-rassbach-talks-religious-freedom-council-europe/> accessed 9 December 2020.

Social),[60] faulting the Third Section's judgement for ignoring the FoRB rights of the respondent church.[61] As per above, perhaps most notable is that the authors also suggested that the ECtHR should align with the practice of exempting the employment relationships of religious ministers from state regulation under US jurisprudence.[62] In their opinion, the ECtHR's Grand Chamber could have benefited from USSC's case law expanding the scope of church autonomy rights to guarantee basic standards of international FoRB protection within democratic governments.[63] Further, and beyond just criticising the ECtHR's handling of religious issues, Eric Rassbach also presented remarks on *Sindicatul* at a conference held at the CoE in June 2012. He clarified on that occasion how the so-called "ministerial exception" doctrine (recently affirmed by the USSC in the high-profile dispute *Hosanna-Tabor v. Equal Employment Opportunity Commission* (2012)) could have offered important insights for strengthening church autonomy protection in the case at hand.[64]

Against this background, a month later, the ECtHR's Grand Chamber re-opened the *Sindicatul* case and permitted the Becket Fund to file an *amici curiae* brief.[65] Eventually, a Grand Chamber hearing took place on 7 November 2012 in which both NGOs reiterated that the ECtHR should apply US-like ministerial exceptions from labour law legislation to church employees, whether members of the clergy or the laity. Putting it starkly, and as remarked by the ECLJ in its second *amici* brief, "where, as in the present case, the facts in dispute were of a religious nature, the interference in issue could not be reviewed by means of a proportionality test".[66]

In 2013, the Grand Chamber overturned the Third Section's judgement.

Importantly, however, the ECtHR did not agree with the third-party interveners that the applicants should waive their Article 11 ECHR rights altogether.[67]

60 Eric Rassbach and Diana Verm, 'Analiza hotărârii Sindicatul "Păstorul cel Bun" împotriva României' (2012) 4(1) *Revista de Drept Social* 1 <https://revistadreptsocial.ro/afisare_detalii.php?id=1701> accessed 9 December 2020.

61 For the English version, see Eric Rassbach and Diana Verm, 'Analysis of Sindicatul "Păstorul cel Bun" v. Romania' (Strasbourg Consortium, 12 March 2012) <https://www.strasbourgconsortium.org/common/document.view.php?docId=5847> accessed 9 December 2020.

62 ibid 7–9.

63 ibid 1.

64 The Becket Fund (n 59).

65 See the Becket Fund for Religious Liberty, 'Sindicatul "Pastorul cel bun" v. Romania' (9 July 2013) <https://www.becketlaw.org/case/sindicatul-pastorul-cel-bun-v-romania/> accessed 9 December 2020. The *amici curiae* was submitted along with the International Center for Law and Religious Studies based at Brigham Young University (BYU) (a conservative Christian university located in Provo, Utah. See 'Case of Sindicatul "Păstorul cel Bun" v Romania *(Application no 2330/09)*. Written Comments of Third-Party Interveners. The Becket Fund for Religious Liberty and the International Center for Law and Religion Studies' <http://s3.amazonaws.com/becketpdf/Sindicatul-v-Romania-brief1-FINAL.pdf> accessed 10 December 2020.

66 *Sindicatul* (n 45) para 126.

67 ibid para 140.

In sum, it did not share the view that religious ministers should be categorically excluded from labour law protection in a US-like "absolutist" fashion.[68] The ECtHR reiterated, in fact, that the applicants were de facto under an employment relationship with the church, also in accordance with several standards of the International Labour Organisations (ILO).[69] Thus, they should be assimilated to public servants or contractual employees. For this reason, the Court found not only that Article 11 of the ECHR was applicable to the unions' members but also that an interference with their free-trade rights occurred.

Despite the foregoing, there was a catch.

In overturning its Third Section's judgement, the ECtHR' s conclusions have, in fact, shown a certain inclination to follow US arguments, thereby stacking the odds in church employers' favour.

To begin with, the ECtHR agreed with the domestic court that the refusal to register the applicant union was proportionate to the legitimate aim of protecting the Romanian Orthodox Church's FoRB rights. In this connection, the Court found that national authorities clearly demonstrated how the existence of a trade union within the Church could have seriously imperilled its traditional hierarchical structure.[70] Yet, the domestic court's analysis was superficial, as it did not properly count the applicant employees' secular rights and interests in the balancing exercise. As such, it focused only on their failure to follow the correct registration procedure because they did not request (and obtain) any prior consent from the Archbishop.[71]

All things considered, an analysis of this situation might lead to assumptions that the issue at hand was not the forming of a trade union per se. As such, and as reiterated by the ECtHR, the defendant church did not absolutely prohibit the right to unionise, as there were several unions in existence that the applicants could join.[72] Rather, what was problematic for both the domestic courts and the ECtHR was the disrespect of ecclesiastical rules requiring the Archbishop's prior consent. However, and despite this one-sided analysis, the ECtHR assumed that the domestic courts sufficiently considered all relevant factors at stake. It then acknowledged their wide margin of discretion in dismissing the applicants' Article 11 ECHR's rights.[73] On this account, the ECtHR's reasoning suggests that it only *formally* stuck to its conventional balancing approach (grounded in the requirements of legality, legitimacy, and necessity/proportionality of an

68 In this sense, see Marie Ashe (n 58) 199–223 (using the adjective "absolute" to describe the special favour that the USSC gives to church employers in the organisation of their workplaces).

69 In this respect, the ECtHR noted that, under the ILO Regulation No. 198, determining the existence of an employment relationship should by guided by the facts relating to (1) the performance of work and (2) the remuneration of that work. See *Sindicatul* (45) para 142.

70 ibid para 162.

71 ibid 168.

72 ibid 170.

73 ibid 172.

interference). While in actually, it did *substantially* recognise a US-like ministerial exception, having justified the refusal to register *Păstorul cel Bun* mostly on the basis of an ecclesiastical rule.[74]

It was, however, in a subsequent case that the ECtHR explicitly broke away from its tried and tested balancing approach. The key moment was its Third Section's decision in *Fernández Martínez v Spain* (2012)[75] in which the Court placed church autonomy beyond the reach of a proportionality analysis altogether. It, thereby, converged its approach to US conservative standards of corporate religious freedom in employment. This is analysed below.

Fernández Martínez v Spain

As to the facts at issue, Mr. Martínez, a married (and "secularised") priest teaching Catholic religion in a state-run secondary school, appealed the decision of a Spanish Catholic diocese to not renew his employment contract. Under a 1979 agreement between Spain and the Holy See, it was the bishop's yearly responsibility to renew the applicant's employment, thus, binding the Ministry of Education to his decision. Of particular interest is the hybrid-nature of the applicant's position: after having been ordained as a priest in 1961, Mr. Martínez applied to the Vatican for dispensation from the obligation of celibacy in 1984. As Javier Martínez-Torrón explains, by virtue of this legal act, the applicant "ceased to be considered a priest and became a lay Catholic" from an outside perspective.[76] But in practice, and from the Church's perspective, Mr. Martínez retained his clerical status for another 13 years. As such, it was only in 1997 that the Holy See granted the applicant's request for dispensation from celibacy. That said, shortly after his petition for secularisation, he got married under Spanish civil law (at that time, he was still a clergyman under canon law and, thus, could not contract a valid canonical marriage.)[77] Eventually, the applicant was included by the bishop of the diocese in the list of prospective employees that could be selected by state authorities to teach Catholic religion and ethics. He then found employment in 1991, regardless of his canonically irregular situation. In November 1996, a Spanish newspaper reported on a seminar organised by the "Movement

74 Marie Ashe (n 58) 202 (noting that also the Grand Chamber decision in *Sindicatul* might be cited as supportive of the preposition that an American "*Hosanna-Tabor* turn" at the ECtHR is underway).

75 In this sense, see Stijn Smet, 'Fernández Martínez v. Spain: Towards a 'Ministerial Exception for Europe?" (Strasbourg Observers, 24 May 2012) <https://strasbourgobservers.com/2012/05/24/fernandez-martinez-v-spain-towards-a-ministerial-exception-in-europe/> accessed 11 December 2020. This observation was cricticised in Dominic McGoldrick, 'Religion and Legal Spaces — In Gods We Trust; In the Church We Trust, but Need to Verify' (2012) 12(4) Human Rights Law Review 759, 786 (describing the ECtHR's approach "sophisticated, balanced and elegant").

76 Javier Martínez-Torrón, '*Fernández Martínez v. Spain.* An Unclear Intersection of Rights' in Stijn Smet and Eva Brems (n 8)192.

77 ibid 192.

for Optional Celibacy". The article included a photograph of the applicant and his family attending the gatherings of this group of "married priests" of which Mr. Martínez was an active member. Furthermore, the article included statements from a number of "married priests" (including the applicant) urging the church to give up the celibacy requirement and become more "democratic rather than theocratic".[78] Statements also included disagreement with the Church's position on abortion, divorce, sexuality, and contraception. Some months later, in 1997, the Vatican issued the secularisation decree and dispensed Mr. Martínez from celibacy. The document explained that he was barred from teaching Catholic religion in public institutions unless the local bishop decided otherwise and only "according to his own prudent judgement and provided that there [was] no scandal".[79] Consequently, the diocese informed the Ministry of Education of its intention to not approve the renewal of Mr. Martínez's contract. The bishop considered, in fact, that Mr. Martínez's marriage had become a public matter after his press appearance. He, thus, indicated that the applicant failed to carry out his duties with discretion and "without any risk of scandal".[80] The Ministry, in turn, notified Mr. Martínez of the decision, who then instituted domestic proceedings.

Having been unsuccessful, Mr. Martínez claimed a violation of his human right before the Spanish Constitutional Court, which found against him, holding that the duty of neutrality under Article 16(3) of the Spanish Constitution meant that no judicial assessment of the notion of "scandal" used in canon law could be done.[81] At this point, and relying on Article 8, in conjunction with Article 14 of the ECHR (prohibition of discrimination), the applicant lodged a complaint before the ECtHR. The Court, in turn, framed the case in terms of Mr. Martínez's right to respect for private and family life (as well as to not be discriminated against for being a married priest) vis-à-vis the church's corporate religious freedom. Hearing the case, however, the ECtHR confirmed the findings at the national level and upheld the dismissal. Remarkably, in doing so, the Third Section categorically deferred to the autonomy of the church in its hiring and firing policies. A key-passage of the Third Section's judgements is a useful case in point to appreciate this argument.

Paragraph 84 reveals that "In the Court's opinion, the requirements of the principles of religious freedom and neutrality preclude it *from carrying out any further examination of the necessity and proportionality* of the non-renewal decision".[82] This was also because, for the Court, it was reasonable to impose an "heightened duty of loyalty" on religious education teachers by virtue of their "special bond of trust" with the church's mission.[83] Taken together, it appeared that the ECtHR relied on the fact that, in the eyes of the Church, Mr. Martínez

78 *Fernández Martínez v Spain*, App no 56030/07 (Third Section, 15 May 2012) para 11.
79 ibid para 12.
80 ibid para 14.
81 ibid paras 24–31.
82 ibid para 84 (emphasis added).
83 ibid para 85.

was still a clergymen when he began to teach. At that time, he had not yet received a waiver from the Vatican that officially recognised his status of "married priest". For this reason, Mr Martínez was under a stronger duty of loyalty to the church, so it was felt by the Court.

On these grounds, the ECtHR also maintained that the dispute at hand was different from the three 2009–10 German cases, noting that the impugned measures taken in the latter "were taken against laymen, whereas the applicant in the present case is a secularised priest".[84] Yet, this was not entirely true because, in *Obst*, the applicant was a church senior officer, and, as discussed, the Court did not focus only on the applicant's ministerial status, but on several other factors concerning his personal background. It is, therefore, noticeable that the ECtHR's reasoning lacked adequate and analytical considerations of the way Mr. Martínez perceived his own identity: a married priest remunerated by the state and father of five children. In sum, and borrowing from Stijn Smet, this is how the ECtHR explicitly affirmed for the very first time the existence of a "ministerial exception for Europe".[85]

This type of "non-balancing" at the ECtHR level, however, has been only a temporary trend. Stijn Smet himself conceded that the Strasbourg Court appeared to hark back to its earlier "ad hoc balancing approach", such as in *Obst*, *Schüt*, and *Siebenhaar*.[86] This became evident in 2014, when the ECtHR handed down a Grand Chamber judgement on the same *Martínez* case which arrived one year after the Grand Chamber decision in *Sindicatul*. In hearing *Martínez* again, the ECtHR realigned to an assessment grounded on the legality, legitimacy, and necessity/proportionality of the interference on the applicant's right to private and family life.[87] In particular, of note was the lack of an explicit language in favour of absolute church autonomy like in the Third Section judgement.[88] Despite this, in a similar manner to its Grand Chamber decision in *Sindicatul*, the ECtHR appeared to de facto recognise a wide and American-style church exception.[89]

84 ibid 83.

85 Stijn Smet (n 75) accessed 11 December 2020.

86 ibid.

87 *Fernández Martínez v Spain*, App no 56030/07 (Grand Chamber, 12 June 2014) paras 113–131.

88 Stijn Smet 'Fernández Martínez v. Spain: The Grand Chamber Putting the Brakes on the "Ministerial Exception" for Europe?' (Strasbourg Observers, 23 June 2014) <https://strasbourgobservers.com/2014/06/23/fernandez-martinez-v-spain-the-grand-chamber-putting-the-breaks-on-the-ministerial-exception-for-europe/> accessed 13 December 2020.

89 In this sense, see Ronan McCrea, 'Singing from the Same Hymn Sheet? What the Differences between the Strasbourg and Luxembourg Courts Tell Us about Religious Freedom, Non-Discrimination, and the Secular State' (2016) 5(2) Oxford Journal of Law and Religion (commenting the approach of the ECtHR in its Grand Chamber judgement in *Martínez* as one in which the Court "took significant steps towards recognizing an American-style, category-based ministerial exemption rather than the balancing approach seen in previous cases")183, 197.

Particularly interesting in this regard is that the Court's reasoning started by explicitly admitting that the applicant's status within the Church was "unclear".[90] Nevertheless, it ended up edging toward the Church's perspective, accepting that Mr. Martínez was still a clergymen bound by an heightened duty of loyalty.[91] Based on this, the ECtHR joined the domestic courts in affirming that the non-renewal was justified by the Church's "necessity" to employ religious teachers whose ways of life do not cause any "scandal".[92] As to this latter concept, the Court also reiterated that civil jurisdictions are precluded from ruling on its meaning and substance, which are better left to ecclesiastical authorities.[93] By doing so, once again the ECtHR justified the restriction of the applicant's right to private and family life on religious reasons that were inconsistent with Mr. Martínez's feeling of being a former priest.

Taken together, it can be noted that, by and large, the ECtHR distanced itself from US discourses on absolute church autonomy. It is fair to say, however, that the Grand Chamber decisions in both *Sindicatul* and *Martínez* crafted the Court's *own* ministerial exception. To do that, and as discussed, the Court's strategy made use of a balancing act that gave special weight to ecclesiastical rules[94] instead of counting them as *one* among the overall elements to be balanced on an equal footing.[95] Interestingly, additional evidence on an ECtHR-style religious exception can be found in the highly contested "exit/surround principle" that the Court re-evoked in this 2012–14 strand of church autonomy case law. Put simply, the ECtHR clarified that Article 9 of the ECHR "does not enshrine a right of dissent within a religious community".[96] It then went on to say that "in the event of any doctrinal or organisational disagreement between a religious community and one of its members, the individual's freedom of religion is exercised by the option of freely leaving the community".[97] This notwithstanding, and quite contradictorily, it also clarified that the employees in *Sindicatul* and *Martínez* could not be considered to have altogether waived their rights under Article 11 and 8, respectively.[98] Despite this, it is easy to see how the ECtHR had already declared churches to be potential "winners" instead of recognising all competing rights as equal.[99] Or, phrased differently, the Grand Chamber seemed to shift from its

90 *Fernández Martínez* (n 87) para 134.

91 ibid paras 132–136.

92 ibid 150.

93 ibid 148.

94 These are the Archbishop's prior consent to form a trade union in *Sindicatul* and the need to avoid "scandal" in *Martínez*.

95 See Ronan McCrea (n 89) (commenting the approach of the ECtHR in its Grand Chamber judgement in *Martínez* as one in which "religion is in some ways special in the sense of being entitled to wider autonomy than other forms of belief") 192, fn 51.

96 *Martínez* (n 87) para 128; in this sense, see also *Sindicatul* (n 45) para 137.

97 ibid; ibid

98 *Sindicatul* (n 45) para 140; *Martínez* (n 87) para 132.

99 For instance, Stijn Smet used the formula "winner-take-all balancing" to describe an approach that tips the scales in favour of one right instead of finding a compromise between both conflicting interests. Stijn Smet, 'Introduction— Conflicts of Rights in Theoretical and Comparative Perspective' in Stijn Smet and Eva Brems (n 8) 14 and 19.

conventional 2009–11 "ad hoc balancing" to a "one-sided approach"[100] that paid less attention to church employees' rights.

What is more, the ECtHR's reasoning in *Martínez* is also less than clear about what exactly the legal differences are between a clergyman and a lay (or "secularised") employee and, above all, whether there are any.[101] Thus, the question here is not just whether, as a matter of principle, religion should be a legitimate trump card for churches vis-à-vis the interests of their employees but also to *which* employees religious exceptions should apply. In sum, should church exemptions extend also to cover non-ministerial personnel?

Completing unfinished business, in its 2017 decision in *Travaŝ v Croatia*,[102] the Court answered this query in the affirmative. This case concerned the dismissal of a lay professor of theology (remunerated by the state) who, in the eyes of the church employer, was under a duty of heightened loyalty toward its religious mission. More exactly, Mr. Travaŝ's canonical mandate was withdrawn when the church employer discovered that he remarried in a civil ceremony without having his first Catholic marriage annulled by an ecclesiastic tribunal. Following its reasoning in *Martínez*, the ECtHR held that the dismissal was lawful, legitimate, and necessary for the Church to employ teachers who are "outstanding in true doctrine".[103] Furthermore, the ECtHR explained, the dismissal was justified in light of an agreement between Croatia and the Holy See that made the religious requirements for church employment part of the law of the land.[104] Yet, Mr. Travaŝ did not hold a ministerial title that *formally* made him a clergyman: he was a layman teacher and, thus, his status was similar to that of the employee in *Siebenhaar*.

However, a major difference is that, in the latter case, the applicant taught secular subjects. Also, Ms. Siebenhaar's dismissal was not justified on grounds that were of exclusively religious/doctrinal nature. Rather, she was terminated because she publicly promoted the views of a humanist group unbeknownst to her church employer. This, in turn, was quantified as an objective and substantial risk to the quality of her work in the Protestant congregation. Instead, in *Travaŝ*, there was no evidence as to how a layman's civil marriage per se could endanger the credibility of the Church toward the public. Further, no particular consideration was given to the repercussions that the dismissal could have on Mr Travaŝ's personal life.[105]

Based on this analysis, at this stage, it seems that the ECtHR is following an approach that not only gives all the advantage to the side of church autonomy, but it is also sceptical of a distinction between ministerial/non-ministerial employees. As noted, this trend has somehow felt the influence of US conservative discourses

100 This term can be traced back to Russel Sandberg (n 9) 136.
101 In this sense, see also Stijn Smet (n 75).
102 App no 75581/13 (ECtHR, 30 January 2017).
103 ibid 75–113.
104 ibid 79.
105 The ECtHR commented briefly only on the fact that "it was open for the applicant to seek other employment in the education system by teaching courses of ethics and culture" ibid para 105.

and constitutional developments. Thus, for the sake of completeness, this chapter turns now to consider the judicial crafting and expansion of ministerial exceptions under US law.

The United States Supreme Court

From the analysis above, it can be seen that church autonomy in employment, in principle, is not fully beyond judicial scrutiny at the CoE level. On the flip side, however, in *Sindicatul* and *Martínez*, the ECtHR created a hierarchy of rights with the autonomy of churches and their religious "specific situation rules"[106] coming above other equality strands.

By contrast, a prominent example of "non-balancing" of religious autonomy rights in church employment disputes can be found at the US regional level. As already discussed, American religious activists lobbying in the ECtHR extensively cited what Marie Ashe has defined as an "absolutist"[107] approach, whereby the USSC held that church governance in employment categorically bars considerations of the rights and interests of church employees. It was precisely on these grounds that in *Hosanna-Tabor v EEOC*, the USSC recognised, for the first time ever, a "ministerial exception" rooted in the Free Exercise and Establishment Clauses of the First Amendment to the US Constitution.

First Amendment

Before turning to consider the case of *Hosanna-Tabor v EEOC*, it is worth briefly zooming in on the content of the First Amendment which declares, *inter alia*,[108] that: "Congress shall make no law respecting an establishment of religion, or prohibiting the free exercise thereof". The first half of this provision is generally known as the Establishment Clause, whilst the second half is known as the Free Exercise Clause. Needless to say, it is clear that both clauses formally address only the legislative branch of the US federal government: the Congress.

Beginning in the 1940s, some jurisprudential developments, however, took the better part of the decade to extend the reach of the religious clauses further to state and local governments as well as the federal government itself.[109] As Winnifred Fallers Sullivan explained, this was accomplished via a broad judicial

106 This term can be traced back to Russell Sandberg, *Law and Religion* (Cambridge University Press 2011) (describing this rule as a principle, whereby "someone has voluntarily submitted themselves to a system of norms, usually by means of a contract".) 84–85.

107 See Marie Ashe (n 58).

108 In addition to protecting FoRB, the First Amendment protects freedom of expression, freedom of speech or of the press, the right of the people peacefully to assemble, and to petition the government for a redress of grievances. See Amendments to the Constitution of the United States of America, Amendment I.

109 These developments can be traced back in particular to the USSC's decisions in *Cantwell v Connecticut*, 310 U.S. 296 (1940) and *Everson v Board of Education*, 330 U.S. 1 (1947).

interpretation that read them into the Fourteenth Amendment.[110] "No State shall (…) deprive any person of life, liberty, or property, without due process of law" runs in fact its Section I. However, judicial interpretations aside, what lies at the heart of these clauses (and their combined effect) is an American "experiment"[111] in religious freedom that had the political and constitutional commitment to promote equality among all religions at its centre. In order for the project to succeed, in the eyes of the Founding Fathers it was necessary to combine the protection of individuals and groups of any kind in their religious expression (i.e., free exercise) with the removal of church–state alliances privileging major denominations (i.e., non-establishment).[112] In this connection, John Witte explained that the religious clauses, in fact, have their roots in an American cultural synthesis of theological and political views (Puritan, Evangelical, Enlightenment, and Civic Republican movements) sharing a historical aversion to religious establishments. More exactly, the early American settlers left the British homeland to break away from an Anglican establishment that combined ecclesiastical and governmental powers to control religious exercise and compel attendance and support to state-favoured churches.[113] On this reading, one could see why the Establishment Clause was conventionally designed to prohibit governments "from asserting a preference for one religious denomination or sect over others".[114] Yet, constitutional debates over the religious clauses also support somewhat different interpretations.

As will be shown, in carving out a religious exception from the First Amendment in *Hosanna-Tabor*, the USSC signalled what Philip Hamburger described as a reconceptualisation of the Establishment Clause from a ban against establishments to an all-out jurisdictional separation between church and state.[115] In essence, autonomy of church governance in employment came to be seen as an expression of a proper church jurisdiction in which "the state cannot enter not because it would be an invasion of rights, but because it would be an invasion

110 Winnifred Fallers Sullivan, *Church State Corporation: Construing Religion in US Law* (The University of Chicago Press 2020) 2.

111 For a historical and legal introduction to the idea of an American experiment in religious freedom see John Witte, Jr. and Joel A. Nichols, *Religion and the American Constitutional Experiment* (Oxford University Press 2016).

112 Understood this way, the First Amendment has been generally associated with a "religious free market model" that minimises governmental influence to maximise the autonomy of religious choice and overall religious freedom. See Rex Ahdar and Ian Leigh, *Religious Freedom in the Liberal State* (Oxford University Press 2013) 119–22.

113 John Witte (n 111) 24–39.

114 ibid 161 (quoting *Wallace v. Jaffree*, 472 U.S. 38, 107, 113 (1985) (Rehnquist, J., dissenting).

115 See Philip Hamburger, *Separation of Church and State* (Harvard University Press 2004) 11 (arguing that "Americans took their religious liberty in a new direction when they reconceived their constitutional freedom from an establishment to a separation between church and state"). See also Marc O. De Girolami, 'Constitutional Contraction: Religion and the Roberts Court' (2015) 26(2) Stanford Law & Policy Review 385, 405 (arguing that at its strongest, a broad interpretation of the Establishment Clause reads this principle to demand strict separation of church and state).

of sovereignty".[116] From this vantage point, the USSC seemed to suggest that where civil courts impose an unwanted minister upon a church, they violate both the Free Exercise clause (preventing states from interfering with the FoRB rights of groups) and the Establishment Clause (prohibiting states from appointing ministers).

Against this background, if similar patterns can be inferred from the ECtHR and US jurisprudence (reflected in the wide church exemptions that both courts derived from their respective constitutional texts), their approaches are, however, intrinsically distinct.[117] If the ECtHR framed "church autonomy" in the language of human rights, the USSC, instead, favoured a jurisdictional language that phrased this concept in terms of "freedom of the church",[118] to wit, a way of thinking of corporate religious freedom, according to which, "dealing with a church is not a matter of applying domestic law, but rather as negotiating with an independent entity".[119] Taken at its extreme, independent religious governance is, in fact, framed as an absolute and sovereign power in ecclesiastical matters that states and civil courts lack the authority to assess.[120] In other words, and borrowing from Pasquale Annicchino, church autonomy disputes in the US seem to have morphed from being human rights conflicts to become proper conflicts of church–state jurisdictions.[121] With this in mind, the following turns to discuss the "absolutist" approach that the USSC took in deciding some high-profile cases on church employment.

116 Richard Schragger and Micah Schwartzman, 'Against Religious Institutionalism' (2013) 99(5) Virginia Law Review 917, 922.

117 In this sense, see also Brett G. Scharffs, 'The (Not So) Exceptional Establishment Clause of the United States Constitution' (2018) 33(2) Journal of Law and Religion 137, 154.

118 In this sense, see Steve D. Smith, 'The Jurisdictional Conception of Church Autonomy' in Micah Schwartzman, Chad Flanders, and Zoë Robinson (eds), *The Rise of Corporate Religious Liberty* (Oxford University Press 2016) 19–37, 19.

119 Micah Schwartzman, Chad Flanders, and Zoë Robinson (n 118) xvi.

120 Richard Schragger and Micah Schwartzman (n 115) (distinguishing "freedom of the church" as a jurisdictional claim from "church autonomy" as a human right claim) 919. The literature in support of a jurisdictional sovereignty of churches in the US is vast. Examples include Steve D. Smith (n 118); Richard W. Garnett, 'The Freedom of the Church: (Toward) an Exposition, Translation and Defense' in Micah Schwartzman, Chad Flanders, and Zoë Robinson (n 118) 39. Paul Horwitz, 'Freedom of the Church without Romance' (2013) 21(1) Journal of Contemporary Legal Studies. See also the issues collected in the symposium: 'The Freedom of the Church in the Modern Era' (2013) 21(1) The Journal of Contemporary Legal Issues 1–279. It should be noted, however, that not all US proponents of "church autonomy" necessarily support a jurisdictional interpretation of this concept. See Douglas Laycock, 'Towards a General Theory of the Religious Clauses: The Case of Church Labor Relations and the Right to Church Autonomy' (1981) 81(7) Columbia Law Review 1373.

121 See Pasquale Annicchino, 'Il conflitto tra il principio di autonomia dei gruppi religiosi ed altri diritti fondamentali: recenti pronunce della Corte Suprema degli Stati Uniti e della Corte Europea dei Diritti dell'Uomo' (2013) 1(1) Quaderni di Diritto e Politica Ecclesiastica 55, 56, fn 4. Winnifred Fallers Sullivan (n 110) 10 (describing current US church–state relationships in terms of "churchstateness") 10.

The "absolutist" approach

This section begins by detailing the case of *Hosanna-Tabor v EEOC.*[122] It then explores the contemporary scene, considering how the scope of the ministerial exception has been further stretched during the USSC's October Term 2019–2020.

Hosanna-Tabor Evangelical Lutheran Church & School v. Equal Employment Opportunity Commission

On the facts, this case involves the dismissal of Ms. Cheryl Perich, a member of the Lutheran Church-Missouri Synod congregation and a fourth-grade teacher of secular subjects at the Hosanna-Tabor Evangelical Lutheran School. Ms. Perich was originally hired as a "lay" teacher, but near the end of her first year, the Hosanna-Tabor congregation appointed her as a "called" Lutheran teacher.

The latter term is a designation indicating a class of "commissioned ministers" who serve only in an auxiliary capacity (such as directing music or teaching in schools, such as in the case at hand). Being "called" for the Lutheran congregation requires completion of a course of theological study and the endorsement by the local synod to receive the title of "Minister of Religion, Commissioned". This label is, however, different from proper "ordained ministers", who instead engage in core religious activities, such as preaching the doctrine and administering the sacraments.[123] Having clarified this, it has to be noted that Ms. Perich developed narcolepsy and began the 2004–05 school year on disability leave. When she sought to return to her classroom in January 2005, the school principal answered that the school had already contracted another lay teacher to fill her position. Also, because doubts were raised as to Ms. Perich's readiness to teach again, the principal refused her return.

Subsequently, the Lutheran congregation offered to pay part of Ms. Perich's health insurance in exchange for her resignation as a "called teacher". By declining the offer, Ms. Perich notified her church employer that she would take legal action. In consequence, the congregation voted to rescind Ms. Perich's call, whilst the school sent her a letter of dismissal. As grounds for termination, the letter cited Ms. Perich's "insubordination and disruptive behaviour", as well as the damage she had done to her "working relationship" with the school by "threatening to take legal action".[124]

At this point, Ms. Perich filed a charge of discrimination with the Equal Employment Opportunity Commission (EEOC), claiming that her employment had been terminated in violation of the Americans with Disabilities Act (ADA).[125]

122 132 S. Ct. 694 (2012).
123 The distinction between "called" and "ordained" minister is explained in Winnifred Fallers Sullivan (n 110) 25, fn 8.
124 *Hosanna Tabor* (n 122) ibid 701.
125 1990,42 U.S.C.A. § 12112.

Thus, the EEOC, acting on her behalf, brought a suit against Hosanna-Tabor, alleging that Ms. Perich had been fired in retaliation for threatening to file an ADA lawsuit. The school, however, moved to dismiss the action on the basis that its employment relationship with a minister presented an ecclesiastical issue on which secular courts had no jurisdiction. In doing so, Hosanna-Tabor claimed immunity under a judicially created ministerial exemption that American appellate courts have recognised over the past 40 years to be grounded in the First Amendment of the Constitution.[126] As will be discussed, in *Hosanna-Tabor*, the USSC took no issue with that foundation. Rather, for the first time in American history, the Court confirmed that the religious clauses under the First Amendment immunise churches from the purview of employment anti-discrimination laws.

To begin with, Ms. Perich's claim was brought before the US District Court for the Eastern District of Michigan, which granted summary judgement in Hosanna-Tabor's favour. The court explained that it had no jurisdiction because the ministerial exception blocks lawsuits against religious institutions for discrimination in employment.[127] Thus, in supporting the school's characterisation of Ms. Perich as a minister, it concluded that it could inquire no further into the latter's claim of retaliation.[128] The US Court of Appeals, however, overturned this decision. Although it recognised the existence of a ministerial exception rooted in the First Amendment, it found that Ms. Perich was not a minister under this provision because her work was predominantly secular. The Court then clarified that after Ms. Perich was promoted to "called teacher", her employment duties remained identical to those that she performed as a contract teacher. Ms. Perich continued to teach math, language arts, social studies, science, gym, art, and music, the Court noted, without incorporating religion into these secular subjects. Also, she dedicated very little time to the school's religious education activities (from giving religion classes to leading students in prayer).[129]

By contrast, and reversing the judgement of second instance, the USSC confirmed that Ms. Perich's complaint was barred by the religion clauses of the First Amendment. In reaching this decision, three specific points of criticism were raised. First, the appellate court was questioned for its failure to acknowledge that Ms. Perich was a "commissioned minister". The applicant had a religious duty of loyalty, the USSC noted, regardless of the fact that "commissioned ministers" do not generally engage in core religious activities. Second, the USSC also challenged the appeals tribunals' emphasis on the fact that lay teachers at the school performed the same religious duties as Ms. Perich. Third, the USSC considered that too much weight was assigned to Ms. Perich's primarily secular tasks.[130] In other words, and borrowing from Winnifred Fallers Sullivan, the USSC looked at

126 ibid 701. For a discussion on the constitutionalisation of the ministerial exception in pre-*Hosanna-Tabor* US circuit courts, see Marie Ashe (n 58) 214–16.

127 *EEOC v. Hosanna-Tabor Evangelical Lutheran Church & Sch.*, 582 F. Supp. 2d 881 (2008).

128 ibid 892.

129 *EEOC v. Hosanna-Tabor*, 597 F.3d 796, 780.

130 *Hosanna-Tabor* (122) 708.

Ms. Perich and saw a minister, largely accepting the church's characterisation of her role.[131] Understood it this way, one could easily see how the legal meaning of "religious" that the Court adopted also extended to cover the applicant's secular tasks. Based on this, the USSC implicitly concluded that no ECtHR-style proportionality analysis was needed because, in the words of Chief Justice Roberts, "the First Amendment has struck the balance for us".[132]

At this point, a final remark warrants consideration. It is of note that the USSC never mentioned the formula "church autonomy" in its judgement, nor did it go so far as to accept that the ministerial exception operates a jurisdictional bar.[133] Clearly, this does not seem to lend support to what has been argued so far. Nevertheless, it is fair to say that, with this judgement, the USSC did implicitly acknowledge the de facto jurisdiction of churches in employment matters.[134] The majority opinion of the Court, authored by Chief Justice Roberts, is a case in point. To begin with, and oddly enough, Chief Roberts addressed the issue of the exception, starting with a historical reconstruction of the European struggle between popes and kings over the selection of bishops and church officers in the Middle Ages.[135] Elaborating on this historical issue, he then concluded that "[t]he church must be free to choose those who will guide it on its way".[136] A moment's reflection discerns that Chief Roberts apparently engaged in an all-out exercise of political theology to justify the sovereign authority of churches as the structural logic behind the First Amendment.[137] This approach might be contested on several grounds.

In this regard, some rebutted that neither the word "church" nor the phrase "separation between church and state" appear in the First Amendment (or in the US Constitution in general).[138] Others would go even further and say that the church in the US is just disestablished and not separated.[139] Religious institutions with no constitutional ties with the state (such as in the US) need some sort of contact with governments to obtain legal entity status and produce legal effects into the civil sphere. In other words, the conferral of legal personality is a helpful clue to see how no structural separation between church and state formally exist, for it takes a "state" to enable "the church" under the law.[140]

131 Winnifred Fallers Sullivan (n 110) 28.
132 *Hosanna-Tabor* (122) 710.
133 ibid 709, fn 4.
134 In this sense, see Winnifred Fallers Sullivan (n 110) 28.
135 *Hosanna-Tabor* (122) 702–3.
136 ibid 710.
137 Winnifred Fallers Sullivan (n 110) 34.
138 ibid 29; Brett G. Scharffs (n 117) 143.
139 Winnifred Fallers Sullivan (n 110) 39; see generally Philip Hamburger (n 114).
140 ibid 9 and 21. See also Marco Ventura, 'L'Eccezione Ministeriale in Hosanna-Tabor. Dall'Ingerenza visibile all'Ingerenza Invisibile' in Pasquale Annicchino (eds), *La Corte Roberts E La Tutela Della Liberta` Religiosa in America* (European University Institute 2017) 72–3 (arguing that, when a religious institutions invokes a civil court to protect its autonomy rights, it indirectly accepts state interference).

Our Lady of Guadalupe School v Morrisey-Berru

In a series of decisions over the past few years (and particularly during the USSC's October Term of 2019–20 during President Trump's administration)[141] the "ministerial exception" doctrine has been further strengthened and enlarged under the lead of Chief Justice Roberts.[142] In particular, the Court's recent decision in *Our Lady of Guadalupe School v Morrisey-Berru*[143] of July 2020 (consolidated with *St. James School v Biel*)[144] has been said to be the most "direct outgrowth"[145] of its judgement in *Hosanna-Tabor*. All things considered, what is noteworthy in this case is that the USSC did not seem to have just reconfirmed the "ministerial exception" doctrine elaborated in *Hosanna-Tabor*. Rather, the key takeaway from this decision appeared to be the USSC's willingness to go even further by elaborating a more potent version of this First Amendment protection.[146] It remains to be seen how this happened in practice.

The case at hand arose from the suits brought by two lay teachers at Catholic schools against which they alleged violations of anti-discrimination laws after their employment was terminated. More exactly, Ms. Morrissey-Berru complained that she had been dismissed on the grounds of age, whilst Ms. Biel on the basis of her disability. Interestingly, like in *Hosanna-Tabor*, the Court overlooked the issue of whether a dismissal from church employment could be justified on grounds that are anything but religious. Instead, the bone of contention was whether the two

141 Worthy of attention are four cases decided between June and July 2020: *Espinoza v. Montana Department of Revenue*, 140 S. Ct. 2246 (2020) (not only allowing but also *requiring* government funding of religious private schools); *Our Lady of Guadalupe School v Morrissey Berru*, 140 S. Ct. 2049 (2020) (extending the "ministerial exception" to lay personnel teaching secular subjects in faith-based schools); *Little Sisters of the Poor Saints Peter & Paul Home v. Pennsylvania*, 140 S. Ct. 2367 (2020) (upholding regulations promulgated by the Trump administration that exempted religious employers from contraceptive coverage requirements); *Bostock v. Clayton City.*, 140 S. Ct. 1731 (2020) (guaranteeing LGBTQ rights' protection in employment but also allowing employers to discriminate against them if they could articulate religious motives for it). For a comment on these cases, see Marci A. Hamilton, 'Religious Entities Flex Their Muscles Through the Roberts Court, Playing Both Sides of the Discrimination Coin' (*Justia*, 4 August 2020) <https://verdict.justia.com/2020/08/04/religious-entities-flex-their-muscles-through-the-roberts-court-playing-both-sides-of-the-discrimination-coin> accessed 28 December 2020.

142 For some, this is because the USSC has become increasingly religiously conservative over time. In this sense, see Erwin Chemerinsky, 'Supreme Court—October Term 2009 Foreword: Conservative Judicial Activism' (2011) 44(3) Loyola of Los Angeles Law Review 863.

143 591 U.S. (2020).

144 140 S.Ct. 680 (2019).

145 Ira C. Lupu and Robert W. Tuttle, 'The 2020 Ministerial Exception Cases: A Clarification, Not a Revolution' (*Take Care*, 8 July 2020) <https://takecareblog.com/blog/the-2020-ministerial-exception-cases-a-clarification-not-a-revolution> accessed 28 December 2020.

146 In this sense, see Elizabeth Sepper, 'Ever-Expanding Immunity for Religious Institutions Augurs Trouble for Worker Protections' (Expert Forum, 14 July 2020) <https://www.acslaw.org/expertforum/ever-expanding-immunity-for-religious-institutions-augurs-trouble-for-worker-protections/> accessed 28 December 2020.

teachers counted as "ministers" for the purpose of triggering the ministerial exception. Overall, both applicants taught secular subjects as well as some religious ones. In fact, they educated students in religious ethics from textbooks chosen by their respective school administrations and led them in worship service. Yet, unlike Ms. Perich in *Hosanna-Tabor*, they had neither a liturgical title nor a formal religious training.[147]

As to the domestic proceedings, both applicants won their claims before the Court of Appeals for the Ninth Circuit. which held that none of them were "ministers" for purposes of the ministerial exception. In an unbalanced 7–2 decision, the USSC, however, reversed the decision. It found that, although the applicants were not ordained ministers, there was, however, "abundant record evidence that they both performed vital religious duties".[148] Thus, Justice Alito, writing the majority opinion, concluded that the ministerial exception should also include "any employee (…) who serves as a messenger or teacher of its faith".[149] Two aspects of the case are worthy of note.

First, in determining which positions fall within the ministerial exception, Justice Alito held that "[w]hat matters, at bottom, is what an employee does".[150] This stress on an employee's job function was a notable shift from the USSC's position in *Hosanna-Tabor*, which instead focused on Ms. Perich's title of "commissioned minister".

Following this new track, it would, therefore, have been reasonable to expect the Court to rule in favour of the applicant employees, given their "primarily secular"[151] tasks. Yet, the Court deferred to the ultimate authority of church employers in determining who should count as a "minister".

The emphasis that the Court put on the importance of the "school's definition" and own "explanation" of the role of their employees "in the life of the religion in question" is a helpful hint in this regard.[152] Against this background, this latest decision is authority for the proposition that the new USSC trend "treads perilously close to saying a minister is whomever an employer says she is".[153]

Second, the fact that the liberal Justices Breyer and Kagan signed a conservative majority opinion (thus, leaving Justices Sotomayor and Ginsburg as the only two dissenters) without writing to explain their votes was a puzzle to some commentators.[154] For Nelson Tebbe and Micah Schwartzman, one possibility is that they were acting tactically. In practice, both liberal justices already knew "that

147 *Our Lady of Guadalupe* (143) 2.
148 ibid 3.
149 ibid 16.
150 ibid 18.
151 ibid 2 (dissenting opinion by Justice Sotomayor and Ginsburg).
152 ibid 22.
153 Elizabeth Sepper (n 146).
154 In this sense, see also Noah Feldman, 'Why Supreme Court Liberals Joined Conservatives on Religion' (Bloomberg, 8 July 2020) <https://www.bloomberg.com/opinion/articles/2020-07-08/supreme-court-expands-religious-exemptions-with-liberals-help> 28 December 2020.

Justice Alito had the votes to rule in favor of the schools even without them. So perhaps they joined his decision so they could help to *shape* it".[155] Based on this, they concluded that, after all, "Justice Alito's decision was not as radical as it might have been".[156] In fact, in his opinion, he clarified that the *Our Lady of Guadalupe* ruling "does not mean that religious institutions enjoy a general immunity from secular laws".[157] This was an important outcome that "might have been the product of an agreement"[158] between the liberal and conservatives wings of the USSC. From this analysis of *Our Lady of Guadalupe* and several other FoRB cases decided on a 7–2 margin, Tebbe and Schwartzman suggest that a new pattern in US law and religion is now emerging: one in which some liberal justices dissent, while others join conservative majorities or concur separately. The authors call the approach of the latter "judicial appeasement";[159] that is to say, a "sustained strategy of offering unilateral concessions"[160] to conservative judges for the purpose of adjusting their overly ideologically oriented constitutional interpretations. At any rate, some questions still remain open, such as whether, in the future, an "appeasement" strategy will be capable of placating a broad doctrine of church autonomy that (in the words of Frederick Gedicks) has made religious governance a proper "constitutional right on steroids".[161]

The Court of Justice of the European Union

So far, this chapter has explored the ECtHR case law in the area of religious exemptions, to then contrast it with relevant jurisprudence of the USSC. Although the USSC handled the issue of exceptions in ways that the ECtHR would not (i.e., by categorically excluding a balancing of church employer/employee rights), the goal, nevertheless, was to highlight how there has been a "recognizable convergence"[162] in their approaches since 2012. These developments have then resulted in the judicial crafting of a broad theory of church autonomy at the CoE

155 Nelson Tebbe and Micah Schwartzman, 'Re-upping Appeasement: Religious Freedom and Judicial Politics in the 2019 Term' (2020) Virginia Public Law and Legal Theory Research Paper No. 2020-68, Cornell Legal Studies Research Paper No. 20-40, 2019-2020 ACS Supreme Court Review 115, 16 <https://papers.ssrn.com/sol3/papers.cfm?abstract_id=3694589> accessed 28 December 2020 (emphasis added).
156 ibid; in this sense, see also Ira C. Lupu and Robert W. Tuttle (145).
157 *Our Lady of Guadalupe* (143) 10.
158 Nelson Tebbe and Micah Schwartzman (155).
159 Nelson Tebbe and Micah Schwartzman, 'Establishment Clause Appeasement' (2020) 2019 Supreme Court Review 271, Virginia Public Law and Legal Theory Research Paper No. 2020-17, Cornell Legal Studies Research Paper No. 20-12 <https://ssrn.com/abstract=3541906>
160 ibid 272.
161 Frederick Mark Gedicks, 'Narrative Pluralism and the Doctrine Incoherence in *Hosanna-Tabor*' (2013) 3(64) Mercer Law Review 405, 429.
162 In this sense, see Brett G. Scharffs (n 117) 140.

and US level by virtue of what have been called a "one-sided" and "absolutist" approach to corporate religious freedom, respectively.

From this view, it is worth noting that, in both its 2013 and 2014 judgements in *Martínez*, the ECtHR also made reference to EU religious exemptions in employment (in the form of a directive: Directive 2000/78EC) to strengthen its support to a "heightened duty of loyalty" on church employees.[163] However, and perhaps more interestingly, at the time that the ECtHR decided *Martínez*, there was no CJEU case law yet clarifying the scope of Directive 2000/78 EC vis-à-vis religious exemptions in church employment.[164] It was not until 2018 that the CJEU issued its first major rulings on the matter.

At this point, and given this ECtHR/EU interlacing, it is sensible to conclude this chapter by considering the posture of the EU to questions of corporate religious freedom in employment and the availability of special religious exemptions for churches. From this discussion, it will emerge how, unlike the USSC and the ECtHR, the CJEU found that the religious exception under Directive 2000/78E/EC could not go so far as to categorically prioritise church autonomy over the counterposed rights and interests of church employees. But before dealing with this issue, this section begins with a summary overview of Directive 2000/78/EC, which provided the interpretative framework inspiring the CJEU's action.

Directive 2000/78/EC

In the previous chapter, it was observed that the EU took an ambivalent posture toward FoRB. On the one hand, it gave constitutional protection to the autonomy rights of majority religious/ideological institutions as fundamental expressions of the cultural heritage of the member states that the Union is bound to respect. While on the other, and in parallel with this aforesaid "protectionist" approach, it also established a guarantee of protection for new minority faiths that facilitates their FoRB claims on a basis that values their connection to EU market structures rather than to the cultural traditions of states. This second and "competitive" approach to religion, in turn, resonates with the EU effort to harmonise standards of human rights protection generally, and FoRB in particular, as an instrumental means to ensure the effective functioning of the single market.[165]

At this point, it has to be noted that, in the year 2000, this ambivalent system of FoRB regulation took concrete form in the Framework Directive 2000/78/EC, which forbids employment discrimination on a number of grounds. In keeping with a "competitive" approach to FoRB, the Directive aims at removing all those discriminatory "entry barriers" (also on grounds of religion or belief) that

163 *Martínez* (n 78) para 87; *Martínez* (n 87) para 138.

164 In this sense, see Emma Svensson, 'Religious Ethos, Bond of Loyalty, and Proportionality—Translating the "Ministerial Exception" into "European" (2015) 4(2) 224, 241.

165 For a discussion on this topic see Chapter I, 58–61.

would make it difficult for individuals to access basic market structures (in this case, the labour market).[166] Thus, the Directive has sketched a system of neutral rules that builds on the concepts of direct and indirect discrimination.

Under Article 2(2)(a), direct discrimination is defined as an "in-your-face", less favourable treatment that explicitly targets an employee (or prospective employee) on protected grounds, such as when an employer decides not to hire a Muslim woman because of her religion. Instead, under Paragraph (2)(b), indirect discrimination is meant to cover apparently neutral workplace rules that *prima facie* apply equally to everyone but, in practice, are likely to put some employees at a particular disadvantage compared with others. For instance, a business policy prohibiting visible signs of political, philosophical, or religious beliefs at work will create more difficulties for religious staff wearing conspicuous symbols (e.g., Islamic headscarves or Sikh turbans) than for, say, Marxist employees hiding Che Guevara shirts under their work clothes.[167]

Against this background, it is easy to see how, for the EU, there is an unquestionable relationship between the promotion of FoRB and the economic-oriented goals of the single market.[168] For, if the Union aims at fostering a "highly competitive social market economy",[169] building a religiously inclusive workplace would then appear to be a winning strategy for better economic growth.[170] Benefits provided by workplace religious diversity might include greater employment opportunities, increased morale and productivity of the workforce, larger capital funding by socially responsible investors, or less liability for litigation and reputational damages to cite but a few.[171] At the same time, however, and coherently with a "protectionist" approach to FoRB, a broad exception to the prohibition of indirect discrimination exists when the employers are churches

166 See Ronan McCrea, *Religion and the Public Order of The European Union* (Oxford Scholarship Online 2011) (describing the Directive as the expression of the EU effort to recognise the "market as an arena within which individuals of all religious backgrounds have an equal opportunity to take part") 151.

167 For a critical analysis of the potential shortcomings of the concept of "indirect discrimination" see the collection of essays in: Hugh Collins and Tarunabh Khaitan (eds), *Foundations of Indirect Discrimination Law* (Hart Publishing 2018).

168 In this sense see Emilios Christodoulidis, 'The European Court of Justice and "Total Market" Thinking' (2006) 14(10) German Law Journal 2006, 2015.

169 Consolidated Version of the Treaty on European Union [2012] OJ C 326/13, art 3(3).

170 In this sense see Council Regulation (EC) 2000/78 establishing a general framework for equal treatment in employment and occupation (EC Employment Equality Directive) [2000] L 303/16, preamble (recital 11) (stating that, "[d]iscrimination based on religion or belief (…) may undermine the achievement of the objectives of the EC Treaty, in particular the attainment of a high level of employment and social protection, raising the standard of living and the quality of life, economic and social cohesion and solidarity, and the free movement of persons").

171 For a discussion over the positive correlation between FoRB and economic competitiveness in business see: Brian J Grim, Greg Clark and Robert Edward Snyder, 'Is Religious Freedom Good for Business?: A Conceptual and Empirical Analysis' (2014) 10(4) Interdisciplinary Journal of Research on Religion 2–19.

or "public or private organisations the ethos of which is based on religion or belief".[172] Article 4(2) enables religious or ideologically oriented enterprises to require compliance of specific (and potentially discriminatory) codes of conduct from their employees in the pursuit of goals related to their corporate mission. Its Subsection 3 reads:

> [T]his Directive shall thus not prejudice the *right* of churches ***and other public or private organisations, the ethos of which is based on religion or belief***, acting in conformity with national constitutions and laws, ***to require individuals working for them to act in good faith and with loyalty to the organisation's ethos.***[173]

Several features of this article are worthy of attention.

First, and as noted, this provision does not simply protect church autonomy rights, but it extends to also cover ideologically oriented enterprises, such as hospitals or a schools informed by a religious ethos. Moreover, because there is no legal definition of "ethos" under EU law,[174] Article 4(2) opens up the possibility to broaden this concept to include institutions informed by non-conventionally religious moralities.[175] As will be seen later, these grounds will prove useful in Chapter III when discussing the extension of EU ***church autonomy*** rights to the

172 See Council Regulation (EC) 2000/78 (n 170), art 4(2). See also ibid, preamble (recital 24) (explaining that the scope of the Directive also keeps in line with the recognition of the status under national law of churches and religious associations or communities in the member states under Declaration No. 11 annexed to the Amsterdam Treaty. Instead, direct discrimination, in principle, is never permitted also on religious grounds. A general exception can only be made when it is "necessary for public security, for the maintenance of public order and the prevention of criminal offences, for the protection of health and for the protection of the rights and freedoms of others"). ibid, art 2(5).

173 ibid (emphasis added).

174 Ronan McCrea (n 166) 164.

175 Also, the EU did not even give a definition of "religion". Interestingly, its repeated reference to "religion or other forms of philosophy" in its 1988 decision in *Udo Steymann v Staatssecretaris van Justitie* suggests that, for the Court, "religion is not entitled to any greater consideration or role in public life than other beliefs". In this sense, see Ronan McCrea (n 166) 146–7. See also Case 196/87 *Udo Steymann v Staatssecretaris van Justitie* [1988] ECR 6159. In this respect, the EU gave a very broad definition of the "concept of religion" (and not of *what* is religion in an essentialist perspective) as including the "holding of theistic, non-theistic and atheistic beliefs". See Council Directive 2004/83/EC on minimum standards for the qualification and status of third country nationals or stateless persons as refugees or as persons who otherwise need international protection and the content of the protection granted [2004] 304/12, art 10(1)(b). From this angle, Marco Ventura explains that "[t]he religious diversity of the European Union is thus a true diversity 'of religion and belief' in the sense that it does not limit itself to religions, but extends to every religious or belief-based conviction". Marco Ventura, 'Non-Discrimination and Protection of Diversity and Minorities' in Giuliano Amato and others (eds), *The History of the European Union. Constructing Utopia* (Hart, 2019) 254.

business autonomy of another type of mission-driven entity: the secular for-profit corporation.

Second, if religious/ideological enterprises have the right to demand "loyalty" and adherence from their staff to a certain corporate culture and lifestyle, an employer's discriminatory practice, to that end, must, nevertheless, comply with the occupational requirements under Subsection 2 of Article 4(2). This section states that an employee's differential treatment shall not be viewed as discriminatory only whereby reason of (i) *the nature* of employment activities or of (ii) *the context* in which they are carried out, a person's (iii) *religion* or (iv) *belief* constitute a genuine, legitimate, and justified occupational requirement, having regard to the organisation's ethos. This means that exceptions that apply to religious/ideological enterprises do not cover discrimination on any other non-religious grounds (i.e., sexual orientation, disability, and age).[176] Reasonably, this is because the latter grounds have no *prima facie* connection with an employee's "duty of loyalty" to the organisation's ethos. On further inspection, however, because Article 4(2) de facto allows religious employers to import into the law religious rules (relating, for example, to appropriate sexual behaviour), it might somehow touch upon other protected grounds (such as sexual orientation and respect to private life). Article 4(2), therefore, has the potential to give rise to a significant amount of litigation.

Third, what is, perhaps, most striking is its textual lack of any requirement of proportionality to limit the scope and breadth of such religious exemptions. Based on this, it goes without saying, then, that this provision contains the greatest statutory leeway for religious institutions that one could find in the European discourse as a whole. The argument has been made, in fact, that Article 4(2) presents features of a typical US "ministerial exception".[177]

The "competitive" approach

In its two major rulings on church employment in Germany, *Egenberger* and *IR v JQ* (2018), the CJEU clarified that religious exceptions under Article 4(2) need to be balanced against the secular interest of church employees. The result of this was that such exceptions were substantially narrowed down, in marked contrast to the US and the ECtHR. As will be discussed, this was certainly the outcome of a combined application of Directive 2000/78/EC with the constitutionalisation of human rights law through the Nice Charter. At any rate, to think that this judicial balancing was only dictated by the logic of human rights protection might, perhaps, be somehow unsatisfying. In fact, a second analysis of this case law might lead to assume that, drawing on a "competitive" approach to FoRB,

176 In this sense, see Lucy Vickers (n 11) 208.

177 See generally Emma Svensson (n 164) (describing art 4(2) as the translation of the US "ministerial exception" into "European").

the CJEU deemed that the religious exceptions in exam hindered too much the economic goals of the market.

In other words, it is possible to think that, for the Court, over-broad immunities for churches from employment anti-discrimination laws could significantly reduce an employee's prospect to participate in the processes of wealth production and income distribution via the labour market. Therefore, limitations shall apply when special religious exceptions risk frustrating the EU goal of achieving a competitive social market economy.[178] This would be even more the case for Christian churches in Germany that are now said to be among the largest private employers in the country. It should be borne in mind, however, that direct reference to this reasoning was missing from both *Egenberger* and *IR v JQ*. Against this background, the following is a brief overview of these cases to see how limitations to church autonomy rights took place in practice.

In *Egenberger*, a job applicant to a position offered by the *Evangelisches Werk für Diakonie und Entwicklung* (a welfare organisation affiliated with the Protestant Church in Germany) challenged the refusal to hire her for her lack of affiliation to any of the German Protestant Churches belonging to the Working Group of Christian Churches in Germany. Ms. Egenberger was of no denomination. Also, she applied to a non-ministerial position for which the church had advertised concerning the preparation of a report on Germany's compliance with the United Nations International Convention on the Elimination of All Forms of Racial Discrimination.[179] As to the second case, *IR v JQ* arose out of the dispute between a physician (JQ) and his employer (IR), a private hospital formed under German law and subject to the supervision of the Archbishop of Cologne. When IR discovered that JQ remarried in civil ceremony without having his first Catholic marriage declared null by an ecclesiastic tribunal, it dismissed him for breach of the duty of loyalty to its Catholic mission, as required by the employment contract.[180] Taken together, both cases have in common an interpretative issue around the scope of Paragraphs 9(1) and 9(2) of the General Law on Equal

178 In support of this contention, see Ronan McCrea (n 166) (arguing that, although the EU respects mainstream churches as fundamental expressions of the cultural heritage of the member states, their protection, however, is "limited by the need to respect the overarching structures of the market (…) which are also part of the EU's public order" (193). Linked to this, the author argues that Article 4(2) contains "anachronistic and anomalous exceptions" (resulting from intense lobbying by churches) to an EU balancing approach that also counts the need to respect basic market structures). ibid 195. See also Sionaidh Douglas-Scott, 'The Problem of Justice in the European Union Values, Pluralism, and Critical Legal Justice' in Julie Dickson and Pavlos Eleftheriadis (eds), *Philosophical Foundations of European Union Law* (Oxford University Press, 2012) 416 (arguing that "the benefits of EU law and Court of Justice case law (…) have been market-driven, by the need to secure a level playing field in an area of free movement, rather than by a freestanding concern for equality").

179 Case C-414/16, *Vera Egenberger v Evangelisches Werk für Diakonie und Entwicklung e.V.* [2018] EU:C:2018:257.

180 Case C-68/17, *IR v JQ* [2018] EU:C:2018:696.

Treatment, which implements Article 4(2) of the above-mentioned Directive 2000/78EC. In fact, pursuant to these provisions, church employers are allowed a wide scope to authoritatively determine religious occupational requirements.[181] This broad interpretation of church autonomy raised questions concerning the compatibility with Article 4(2) of the Directive. In both cases, the German Federal Labour Court asked the CJEU to clarify the matter through a preliminary ruling.

In response, the CJEU considered that, in principle, churches and ideologically oriented organisations can lay down occupational requirements connected to their ethos. However, the Court rejected the excessively "church-friendly" perspective offered by German law. It noted that an employee's duty to comply with a certain religious mission must be read in light of the general purpose of the Directive; to wit, the prohibition of discrimination and the right to a fair trial and effective remedy that find protection under Article 21 and 47 of the Charter, respectively.[182] Based on this, for a religious exception to justify a differential treatment, the Court argued that it must fulfil the objective criteria set under Article 4(2). This, in turn, should be taken to mean that it must be a "genuine, legitimate and justified occupational requirement".[183] In such way, the CJEU established that the review of compliance with the criteria under Article 4(2) cannot be entrusted to the "self-perception" of the religious body concerned.[184] In contrast, the decisions of religious organisations must be amenable to substantial judicial review by civil courts.[185]

Remarkably, as a consequence of this constitutionally oriented interpretation of Directive 2000/78EC, the CJEU read a proportionality requirement into Article 4(2) that, as noted, does not explicitly appear in the text of this provision.[186] What is more, the CJEU did not simply clarify that the objective of Article 4(2) is to ensure a fair balance between church autonomy rights and the competing employees' rights,[187] but it also gave guidance as to how such balance should be carried out. Consequently, the Court developed a test, according to which religious bodies must show an "objectively verifiable existence of a direct link between the occupational requirement imposed by the employer and the activity concerned".[188] In practice, in order to appraise whether a religious occupational requirement is "genuine, legitimate and justified", it must be shown that such requirement has a casual connection with the need to protect churches in their

181 *Vera Egenberger* (n 179) para 16; *IR v JQ* (n 180) para 17.
182 ibid 47–9; ibid 72.
183 ibid para 61; ibid 43.
184 In this sense, see Luísa Lourenço, 'Religion, Discrimination and the EU General Principles' Gospel: Egenberger' (2019) 56(1) Common Market Law Review 193, 198.
185 *Vera Egenberger* (n 179) para 55, *IR v JQ* (n 180) para 43.
186 In this sense, Ronan McCrea, 'Salvation Outside the Church? The ECJ Rules on Religious Discrimination in Employment' (EU Law Analysis, 18 April 2018) <http://eulawanalysis.blogspot. com/2018/04/salvation-outside-church-ecj-rules-on.html> accessed 15 February 2021.
187 This is explicitly acknowledged in *Vera Egenberger* (n 179) para 51.
188 ibid 63; *IR v JQ* (n 180) para 50.

autonomy rights (i.e., genuine and justified). Further, it must not go beyond what is necessary to attain a religiously oriented objective (i.e., legitimate).[189]

In conclusion, through these findings, the CJEU reiterated and consolidated well-known case law principles on the horizontal effects of fundamental rights in EU law (*Drittwirkung*) in labour disputes between private parties.[190] But more than this, these decisions finally offered authority to the proposition that, from now on, the direct effect of EU law should also extend to cover the prohibition of discrimination on grounds of religion and the right of an effective remedy (Articles 21 and 47 CFREU).

Conclusion

In this chapter, the approaches of the CoE and the EU to the issue of religious exemptions in employment have been analysed. The conclusions reached regarding the above show that the current trend of ECtHR case law is toward an increased entitlement of religious exemptions to church employers.

It has been explained that this ECtHR approach has been mapped based on the so-called "ministerial exception" doctrine that has developed over 40 years of American case law but only gained constitutional status in 2012 with the USSC decision in *Hosanna-Tabor v EEOC*. In a word, this doctrine is conceived as a judicially created immunity that puts church autonomy beyond the reach of proportionality balancing. As discussed, while this doctrine may have inclined the ECtHR toward following an US "absolutist" and "non-balancing approach" for some time, it has, nevertheless, been noted that the Court has returned to its tried and tested balancing formula. This notwithstanding, the way in which the ECtHR applies proportionality in its balancing exercise is still being questioned, as it seems to give special favour to church autonomy instead of counting it as one among the elements to be balanced on an equal footing. This is what has been defined a "one-sided" approach to corporate religious freedom in employment.

In marked contrast to this position, the CJEU substantially narrowed down exceptions for religious employers in its two 2018 decisions on church employment. It has been assumed that one reason the CJEU did so was the need to balance corporate religion with one of the basic pillars of the single market: employment equality. Fundamentally, because the latter is seen as crucial for the achievement of an "highly competitive economy", this might explain why the CJEU stuck to a "competitive" approach to FoRB that values and protects religion only insomuch as it meets the goals of the EU single market.

189 ibid paras 63–68; ibid paras 50–54.

190 In this sense, see Aurelia Colombi Ciacchi, 'The Direct Horizontal Effects of EU Fundamental Rights' (2019) 15(2) European Constitutional Law Review 294, 305.

Reference list

Ahdar R. and Leigh I., *Religious Freedom in the Liberal State* (Oxford University Press, 2013) (DOI: 10.1093/acprof:oso/9780199253623.001.0001).

Alexy R., *A Theory of Constitutional Rights* (Oxford University Press, 2002).

Amato G. and others (eds), *The History of the European Union. Constructing Utopia* (Hart, 2019) (DOI: 10.5040/9781509917440).

Annicchino P., 'Il conflitto tra il principio di autonomia dei gruppi religiosi ed altri diritti fondamentali: recenti pronunce della Corte Suprema degli Stati Uniti e della Corte Europea dei Diritti dell'Uomo' (2013) 1(1) Quaderni di Diritto e Politica Ecclesiastica, 55–70.

Ashe M., 'Hosanna Tabor, the Ministerial Exception, and Loss of Equality: Constitutional Law and Religious Privilege in the United States' (2015) Oxford Journal of Law and Religion, 199–203 (DOI: 10.1093/ojlr/rwv007).

Chaib S. O. and Valeska D., 'European Court of Justice Keeps the Door to Religious Discrimination in the Private Workplace Opened. The European Court of Human Rights could Close it' (*Strasbourg Observer*, 27 March 2017).

Chemerinsky E., 'Supreme Court—October Term 2009 Foreword: Conservative Judicial Activism' (2011) 44(3) Loyola of Los Angeles Law Review, 863–888.

Christodoulidis E., 'The European Court of Justice and 'Total Market' Thinking' (2006) 14(10) German Law Journal, 2006–2020.

Cismas I., *Religious Actors and International Law* (Oxford University Press, 2014) (DOI: 10.1093/acprof:oso/9780198712824.001.0001).

Clifford B., 'The Global Right Wing and Theories of Transnational Advocacy' (2013) 48(4) The International Spectator: Italian Journal of International Affairs, 71–85 (DOI: 10.1080/03932729.2013.847685).

Collins H. and Khaitan T. (eds), *Foundations of Indirect Discrimination Law* (Hart, 2018) (DOI: 10.5040/9781509912551.ch-011).

Colombi Ciacchi A., 'The Direct Horizontal Effects of EU Fundamental Rights' (2019) 15(2) European Constitutional Law Review, 294–305 (DOI: 10.1017/S1574019619000154).

De Girolami Marc O., 'Constitutional Contraction: Religion and the Roberts Court' (2015) 26(2) Stanford Law & Policy Review, 385–410.

Dickson J. and Eleftheriadis P. (eds), *Philosophical Foundations of European Union Law* (Oxford University Press, 2012) (DOI: 10.1093/acprof:oso/9780199588770.001.0001).

Douglas-Scott S., 'The Problem of Justice in the European Union Values, Pluralism, and Critical Legal Justice' in Julie Dickson and Pavlos Eleftheriadis (eds), *Philosophical Foundations of European Union Law* (Oxford University Press, 2012), 412–447 (DOI: 10.1093/acprof:oso/9780199588770.003.0016).

Durham Jr. W. C., Facilitating Freedom of Religion or Belief Through Religious Associations Law' in Oslo Conference of Religious Freedom and others (eds), *Facilitating Freedom of Religion or Belief: A Deskbook* (Martinus Nijhoff Publishers, 2004), 321–406.

———, The Right to Autonomy in Religious Affairs: A Comparative View' in Robbers Gerhard (ed), *Church Autonomy: A Comparative Survey* (Peter Lang, 2001).

Esau A. J., ''Islands of Exclusivity': Religious Organizations and Employment Discrimination' (2000) 33(3) British Columbia Law Review, 390–434.

Evans C. and Anna H., 'Religious Autonomy and Labour Law: A Comparison of the Jurisprudence of the United States and the European Court of Human Rights' (2012) 1(1) Oxford Journal of Law and Religion, 81–107 (DOI: 10.1093/ojlr/rwr030).

Feldman N., 'Why Supreme Court Liberals Joined Conservatives on Religion' (*Bloomberg*, 8 July 2020).

Fokas E., 'Directions in Religious Pluralism in Europe: Mobilizations in the Shadow of European Court of Human Rights Religious Freedom Jurisprudence' (2015) 4(1) Oxford Journal of Law and Religion, 51–74 (DOI: 10.1093/ojlr/rwu065).

Garnett R. W., 'The Freedom of the Church: (Toward) An Exposition, Translation and Defense' in Micah Schwartzman, Chad Flanders and Zoë Robinson (eds), *The Rise of Corporate Religious Liberty* (Oxford University Press, 2016), 39–62.

Gedicks F. M., 'Narrative Pluralism and the Doctrine Incoherence in *Hosanna-Tabor*' (2013) 3(64) Mercer Law Review, 405–435.

Grim B. J., Clark G. and Snyder R. E., 'Is Religious Freedom Good for Business?: A Conceptual and Empirical Analysis' (2014) 10(4) Interdisciplinary Journal of Research on Religion, 1–19.

Hamburger P., *Separation of Church and State* (Harvard University Press, 2004).

Hamilton M. A., 'Religious Entities Flex Their Muscles Through the Roberts Court, Playing Both Sides of the Discrimination Coin' (*Justia*, 4 August 2020).

Horwitz P., 'Freedom of the Church Without Romance' (2013) 21(1) Journal of Contemporary Legal Studies, 60–126.

Kiviorg M., 'Collective Religious Autonomy Under the European Convention on Human Rights: The UK Jewish Free School Case in International Perspective' (2010) Max Weber Programme 2010/40, 1–14.

———, 'Collective Religious Autonomy versus Individual Rights: A Challenge for the ECtHR?' (2014) 39(1) Review of Central and East European Law, 315–341.

Laycock D., 'Towards a General Theory of the Religious Clauses: The Case of Church Labor Relations and the Right to Church Autonomy' (1981) 81(7) Columbia Law Review, 1373–1417.

Leigh I., 'Balancing Religious Autonomy and Other Human Rights Under the European Convention' (2012) 1(1) Oxford Journal of Law and Religion, 109–129 (DOI: 10.1093/ojlr/rwr015).

Lourenço L., 'Religion, Discrimination and the EU General Principles' Gospel: Egenberger' (2019) 56(1) Common Market Law Review, 193–208.

Lupu I. C. and Tuttle R. W., 'The 2020 Ministerial Exception Cases: A Clarification, Not a Revolution' (*Take Care*, 8 July 2020).

Martínez-Torrón J., '*Fernández Martínez v. Spain*. An Unclear Intersection of Rights' in Stijn Smet and Eva Brems (eds), *When Human Rights Clash at the European Court of Human Rights. Conflict or Harmony?* (Oxford University Press, 2017), 192–217 (DOI:10.1093/oso/9780198795957.001.0001).

McCrea R., *Religion and the Public Order of the European Union* (Oxford Scholarship Online, 2011) (DOI: 10.1093/acprof:oso/9780199595358.001.0001).

———, 'Salvation Outside the Church? The ECJ Rules on Religious Discrimination in Employment' (*EU Law Analysis*, 18 April 2018).

———, 'Singing from the Same Hymn Sheet? What the Differences Between the Strasbourg and Luxembourg Courts Tell Us About Religious Freedom, Non-Discrimination, and the Secular State' (2016) 5(2) Oxford Journal of Law and Religion, 183–210 (DOI: 10.1093/ojlr/rwv067).

McCrudden C., 'Transnational Culture Wars' (2015) 13(2) International Journal of Constitutional Law, 434–462 (DOI: 10.1093/icon/mov018).
McGoldrick D., 'Religion and Legal Spaces — In Gods We Trust; in the Church We Trust, But Need to Verify' (2012) 12(4) Human Rights Law Review, 759–786 (DOI: 10.1093/hrlr/ngs026).
Pacillo V., *Contributo Allo Studio Del Diritto di Libertà Religiosa Nel Rapporto di Lavoro Subordinato* (Giuffrè, 2003).
Peroni L., 'U.S. Supreme Court and ECtHR: Conflicts Between Religious Autonomy and Other Fundamental Rights' (*Strasbourg Observers*, 2 February 2012).
Pinto T. A., 'An Empirical Investigation of the Use of Limitations to Freedom of Religion or Belief at the European Court of Human Rights' (2020) 15(1) Religion and Human Rights, 134–152.
Rassbach E. and Verm D., 'Analysis of Sindicatul 'Păstorul cel Bun' v. Romania' (*Strasbourg Consortium*, 12 March 2012) <https://www.strasbourgconsortium.org/common/document.view.php?docId=5847>.
Robbers G. (ed), *Church Autonomy: A Comparative Survey* (Peter Lang, 2001).
———, Church Autonomy in the European Court of Human Rights — Recent Developments in Germany' (2010) 26(1) The Journal of Law and Religion, 281–320 (DOI: 10.1017/S0748081400000989).
Sandberg R., *Law and Religion* (Cambridge University Press, 2011) (DOI: 10.1017/CBO9780511976865).
———, 'The Future of Religious Freedom' in Stijn Smet and Eva Brems (eds), *When Human Rights Clash at the European Court of Human Rights. Conflict or Harmony?* (Oxford University Press, 2017), 130–147 (DOI: 10.1093/oso/9780198795957.003.0008).
Scharffs B. G., 'The (Not So) Exceptional Establishment Clause of the United States Constitution' (2018) 33(2) Journal of Law and Religion, 137–154.
Schragger R. and Schwartzman M., 'Against Religious Institutionalism' (2013) 99(5) Virginia Law Review, 917–985.
Schwartzman M., Flanders C. and Robinson Z. (eds), *The Rise of Corporate Religious Liberty* (Oxford University Press, 2016) (DOI: 10.1093/acprof:oso/9780190262525.001.0001).
Sepper E., 'Ever-Expanding Immunity for Religious Institutions Augurs Trouble for Worker Protections' (*Expert Forum*, 14 July 2020).
Slotte P. and Årsheim H., 'The Ministerial Exception — Comparative Perspectives' (2015) 4(2) Oxford Journal of Law and Religion, 171–198 (DOI: 10.1093/ojlr/rwv008).
Smet S., 'Fernández Martínez v. Spain: The Grand Chamber Putting the Brakes on the "Ministerial Exception" for Europe?' (*Strasbourg Observers*, 23 June 2014).
———, 'Fernández Martínez v. Spain: Towards a "Ministerial Exception" for Europe?' (*Strasbourg Observers*, 24 May 2012).
———, 'Introduction— Conflicts of Rights in Theoretical and Comparative Perspective' in Stijn Smet and Eva Brems (eds), *When Human Rights Clash at the European Court of Human Rights. Conflict or Harmony?* (Oxford University Press, 2017) (DOI: 10.1093/oso/9780198795957.003.0001).
———, and Brems E. (eds), *When Human Rights Clash at the European Court of Human Rights. Conflict or Harmony?* (Oxford University Press, 2017) (DOI: 10.1093/oso/9780198795957.001.0001).

Smith B. C., *Baptizing Business. Evangelical Executives & the Sacred Pursuit of Profits* (Oxford University Press, 2020).

Smith S. D., 'The Jurisdictional Conception of Church Autonomy' in Micah Schwartzman, Chad Flanders and Zoë Robinson (eds), *The Rise of Corporate Religious Liberty* (Oxford University Press, 2016).

Stewards K., *The Power Worshippers. Inside the Dangerous Rise of American Nationalism* (Bloomsbury Publishing, 2020).

Sullivan W. F., *Church State Corporation: Construing Religion in US Law* (The University of Chicago Press, 2020).

Svensson E., 'Religious Ethos, Bond of Loyalty, and Proportionality—Translating the "Ministerial Exception" into "European"' (2015) 4(2) Oxford Journal of Law and Religion, 224–243 (DOI: 10.1093/ojlr/rwv006).

Tebbe N. and Schwartzman M., 'Establishment Clause Appeasement' (2020) 2019 Supreme Court Review 271, Virginia Public Law and Legal Theory Research Paper No. 2020-17, Cornell Legal Studies Research Paper No. 20-12, 271–311.

———, 'Re-upping Appeasement: Religious Freedom and Judicial Politics in the 2019 Term' (2020) Virginia Public Law and Legal Theory, Research Paper No. 2020-68, Cornell Legal Studies Research Paper No. 20-40, 2019–2020 ACS Supreme Court Review, 115–141.

The Becket Fund for Religious Liberty, 'Eric Rassbach Talks Religious Freedom at the Council of Europe' (21 June 2012) <https://www.becketlaw.org/media/eric-rassbach-talks-religious-freedom-council-europe/>.

———, 'Sindicatul "Pastorul cel bun" v. Romania' (9 July 2013) <https://www.becketlaw.org/case/sindicatul-pastorul-cel-bun-v-romania/>.

Van der Vyver J. D., 'State Interference in the Internal Affairs of Religious Institutions' (2012) 26(1) Emory International Law Review, 1–9.

Van Dijk P. and Van Hoof F., *Theory and Practice of the European Convention on Human Rights* (Kluwer Law International, 1998).

Ventura M., 'L'Eccezione Ministeriale in Hosanna-Tabor. Dall'Ingerenza visibile all'Ingerenza Invisibile' in Pasquale Annicchino (ed), *La Corte Roberts E La Tutela Della Liberta` Religiosa in America* (European University Institute, 2017), 66–73.

———, 'Non-Discrimination and Protection of Diversity and Minorities' Giuliano Amato and others (eds), *The History of the European Union. Constructing Utopia* (Hart, 2019), 239–256.

Vickers L., *Religious Freedom, Religious Discrimination and the Workplace* (Hart Publishing, 2008) (DOI: 10.5040/9781474203395).

Witte J. and Green M. C. (eds) *Religion and Human Rights: An Introduction* (Oxford University Press, 2011) (DOI: 10.1093/acprof:osobl/9780199733453.001.0001).

Part II

Business autonomy

3 Neutrality-based companies

Matteo Corsalini

The previous chapter documented how, in a series of cases prioritising religious autonomy in employment, the ECtHR tilted the balance of rights in favour of churches in a way that underplayed the importance of preventing church employees from being discriminated against on religious grounds. In marked contrast, it was noted that the CJEU, instead, took a narrow view on the matter and required proportionality in the employment choices of religious institutions. When a religious exception is likely to upset the conditions for free access to the labour market, the CJEU reasoned that it will trigger the horizontal effects of the equality rights of employees (or prospective ones), implementing the non-discrimination objectives of Directive 2000/78/EC. Taken together, this line of reasoning has been welcomed as a considerable step forward by those scholars who believe that the decision to carve out religious exceptions from a rule of general applicability should always follow a careful weighing of the competing rights at stake. However, that is only part of the story.

The fuller picture of the issue of religious exemptions at the EU level has recently been complicated by some twists and turns that merit further attention because, at the very least, they seem to have undermined the EU goal of equality and social justice. As will be shown, this has much to do with an emerging trend of CJEU decisions that extended religious exemptions under Article 4(2) of Directive 2000/78/EC to protect what this book will dub "neutrality-based companies" with an entire focus on profit-maximisation objectives. However, before moving forward, it is important to set the parameters of this discussion through a working definition of what, precisely, a "neutrality-based company" is. Later in this chapter, a more subtle account of the intellectual backdrop that informs this idea will be discussed.

For now, suffice it to say that a "neutrality-based company" can be thought of as an "economic institution"[1] that exists solely to increase productivity and is established on a purely commercial (and secular) business model. However, this is not saying much. It can be added that, with its pure focus on profits, a

1 See Oliver E. Williamson, *The Economic Institutions of Capitalism. Firms, Market, Relational Contracting* (The Free Press, 1985).

DOI: 10.4324/9781003340829-6

"neutrality-based company" is one that keeps a detached and "neutral" stance on several public issues (from human rights to the environment) to dodge unwanted political exposure and potential loss of income for actively addressing them.[2] The idea of "neutrality-based companies" is not unusual in this sense. In fact, and despite a recent increase in demands that companies serve a social purpose,[3] profit at all costs still seems to be an appealing idea for too many businesses to not take a stand on sustainability matters or, worse, justify their bad track records of caring about human rights.[4] In light of this, the hereby proposed definition of "neutrality-based company" is anything but a purely theoretical exercise. Rather, it aims at capturing the concrete and topical problem of scarce human rights due

2 Conventional economics literature has gone a long way to explain that individuals incorporate business entities for purely economic reasons, namely to maximise the efficiency of their commercial transactions while reducing the costs of production (including social ones). See Ronald Coase, 'The Nature of the Firm' (1937) 4(16) Economica 386–405. See also Ronald Coase, 'The Problem of Social Cost' (1960) 3(1) The Journal of Law and Economics 1–44. From this transaction–costs perspective, one author suggests that "in competitive environments, a neutrality principle economizes on the social costs of production". See Vincent S.J. Buccola, 'Corporate Rights and Organizational Neutrality' (2016) 101(2) Iowa Law Review 499, 512. Another argument in favour of "neutrality" is that it just makes no sense to impute social and moral responsibilities to for-profit corporations insofar as they are "artificial" and not "real" persons. This is discussed and criticised in Kennet E. Goodpaster and John B. Matthews, Jr., 'Can a Corporation Have a Conscience?' (Harvard Business Law Review, January 1982) <https://hbr.org/1982/01/can-a-corporation-have-a-conscience#> accessed 9 April 2021.

3 In the US, the American Business Roundtable officially announced in 2019 that the new purpose of the corporation would put ethical conduct and stakeholders first. Alan Murray, 'America's CEOs Seek a New Purpose for the Corporation' (Fortune, 19 August 2019) <https://fortune.com/longform/business-roundtable-ceos-corporations-purpose/> accessed 8 April 2021. Also, since 2018 to date, Larry Fink, founder and chief executive of the asset manager company BlackRock, addressed four letters to his investors urging them to deliver not only financial but also social performance. His latest annual letter is available at: <https://www.blackrock.com/corporate/investor-relations/larry-fink-ceo-letter> accessed 4 July 2022. Discourses on "sustainable corporate governance" have recently reached Europe and are particularly perceivable at the EU policymaking level; see European Commission, 'Study on Director's Duties and Sustainable Corporate Governance' COMM (2020). See also the 2021 'Call for Reflection on Sustainable Corporate Governance' issued by the European Corporate Governance Institute (ECGI) available at <https://ecgi.global/content/call-reflection-sustainable-corporate-governance> accessed 20 April 2021. At the European regional level, see OECD, *OECD Guidelines for Multinational Enterprises* (OECD Publishing, 2011) available at <https://www.oecd-ilibrary.org/governance/oecd-guidelines-for-multinational-enterprises_9789264115415-en> (accessed 8 April 2021).

4 The latest 2020 report by the Corporate Human Rights Benchmark has shown that, on average, 230 companies across five sectors (agricultural, apparel, extractives, ICT manufacturing, and automotive manufacturing) have scored poorly in terms of social performance. A detailed briefing of the results is available at: <https://assets.worldbenchmarkingalliance.org/app/uploads/2020/11/WBA-2020-CHRB-Key-Findings-Report.pdf> (accessed 8 April 2021).

diligence in business that, today, is among the major impediments to a smooth transition to a "mission-oriented economy"[5] working for societal goals.

Also, as explained through this definition, it becomes clear that "neutrality" in the globalised marketplace is far from denoting objective impartiality. On the contrary, by approaching social and human rights issues with utilitarian calculus, "neutrality" unavoidably boils down to an ideological justification for business plans that prioritise *private* profits over *public* interests.[6] It goes without saying, then, that "neutrality-based companies" are not value-neutral but inherently value-laden.[7] It is from this perspective that "neutrality" obtains a pejorative connotation insofar as it becomes a proper *function* of economic interest, or, in the worst case, a sleight of hand enabling employers to shirk the responsibilities incurred by their business.

Equally troubling is that a for-profit entity might choose to behave "neutrally" not only toward communities but also toward the individuals holding its offices. For instance, and interestingly enough, from a law and religion perspective, "neutral" employers might want to avoid any social and welfare changes in their company's governance system that are expected to frustrate financial returns such as, say, religiously friendly workplace adjustments.[8]

Following from this, these entrepreneurs can argue that religious diversity at work is at odds with the secular business image that they wish to present to customers and investors as part of her/his core strategy for maximising profitability. Concerned that the market will wrongly associate any display of religious affiliation by employees with its core secular values, a "neutral" company ultimately has the "power"[9] to impose occupational requirements on its workforce, such as a ban from wearing visible religious symbols at work.

5 This term can be traced back to Mariana Mazzucato, *Mission Economy. A Moonshot Guide to Changing Capitalism* (Allen Lane, 2021).

6 This cost-benefit logic is akin to what Richard Posner and Michael W. McConnell call "an economic definition of 'neutrality'". In applying economic analysis to state–religion relationships, they argue that "governmental neutrality" is justified only when the resulting benefits outweigh those of accommodating religion. For example, if Mormon religious courses in public schools produced superior societal benefits (i.e., more educated and productive citizens) then their teaching would be permitted. Richard A. Posner and Michael W. McConnell, 'An Economic Approach to Issues of Religious Freedom' (1989) 56(1) University of Chicago Law Review 1, 1 and 9.

7 In this sense, see Azza Karam, 'Religion at the United Nations. Challenges or Opportunities?' in Sherrie M. Steiner and James T. Christie (eds), *Religious Soft Diplomacy and the United Nations. Religious Engagement as Loyal Opposition* (Lexington Books, 2021) (arguing that "secular organisations are erroneously considered "neutral", when they are themselves guided by values and ideologies which, incidentally, may not always be transparent") 24.

8 See Lucy Vickers, *Religious Freedom, Religious Discrimination and the Workplace* (Hart Publishing, 2008) (discussing the major legal issues about religious expressions in UK workplaces and placing this analysis in a comparative context).

9 See Dennis Robertson, *The Control of Industry* (James Nisbet and Co, 1923) 85 (describing for-profit corporations as "islands of conscious powers" that regulate their internal relationships via governance mechanisms that are tailored for their specific business needs).

Understood this way, at the heart of this "obligation of neutrality"[10] is the compelling need to test an employee's commitment to the "belief-based system"[11] underpinning a profit-maximising behaviour through proper command-and-control managerial tools.

By way of analogy, this is very much like the "duty of loyalty" that enables religious institutions to exclude "dissidents" from membership under Article 4(2) of Directive 2000/78/EC.

This parallel can be taken a step further with the argument that in the same way that churches can claim corporate freedom of religion to protect their *church autonomy*, "neutrality-based companies" can similarly invoke corporate freedom from religion to protect their *business autonomy*. And no matter how divergent churches and secular businesses may be in their purposes, they, thus, represent two variations on the same phenomenon of corporate religious freedom, be it in its positive (corporate freedom *of* religion) or negative modality (corporate freedom *from* religion).[12]

Having come this far, the trajectory of the legal relationship between business and religion can finally be mapped out. As documented in Part I of this book, this moved initially from an existing pattern of corporate rights to maximise the autonomy of religious institutions in the organisation of their internal affairs (*business*) to then evolve into something new in the CJEU case law. A closer look at this shift makes it possible to glimpse a "corporate/business turn" in law and religion in which, this time, it is *business* entities as such that benefit from "church-like" exemptions to maximise profits in secular commerce under Article 4(2) of Directive 2000/78/EC. As counterintuitive as this contention may be, there are at least three good reasons for taking it seriously.

10 Recently, the CJEU made multiple references to the formula "neutral obligations" (in French, *obligation en apparence neutre*) to describe a ban from wearing religious attire in the secular and for-profit workplace. See Case C-157/15, *Samira Achbita and Centrum voor Gelijkheid van Kansen en voor Racismebestrijding v G4S Secure Solutions NV* [2017] EU:C:2017:203, paras 34; 44 and 45 (this case will be discussed at length in what follows).

11 Organisation theorists argue that the differences between religious and non-religious institutions in their organisational structures depend on the different belief-systems underpinning them. Thus, it is precisely the primacy of belief within these entities (whether theological or otherwise) to be the central (and common) feature of their institutional environments. For an introduction to this topic, see C.R Hinings and Mia Raynard, 'Organizational Form, Structure and Religious Organizations' in Paul Tracey, Nelson Phillips and Michael Lounsbury (eds), *Religion and Organization Theory* (Emerald, 2014) (suggesting that future research should consider the question of whether statements of faith in religious organisations are equal to secular mission statements in non-religious entities (such as businesses)) 179. For a similar discussion from a law and economics perspective, see Richard A. Epstein, 'The Nature of the Religious Firm' (2018) 21(1) Journal of Markets & Morality 141–66.

12 In this sense, see Jeroen Temperman, *Corporate Religious Freedom and the Rights of Others* (Eleven 2019) 46. See also Natan Lerner, *Religion, Belief and Secular Human Rights. 25 Years After the 1981 Declaration* (Martinus Nijhoff Publishers, 2006) (arguing that: "[f]reedom of religion in a strict sense includes freedom of belief and freedom from religion") 8.

One is that the subjects covered by Article 4(2) span from churches to "other public or private organisations the ethos of which is based on religion or belief". This is how a wide array of belief diversities and ideological bents were tucked into the same single provision. Another is that, relatedly, neither EU law generally, nor the Directive in particular, have clarified what is actually meant by "ethos" or "religion".[13] Or, even better, because, for the EU, the latter includes the "holding of theistic, non-theistic and atheistic beliefs",[14] this could be taken to mean that "religion (...) is not entitled to any greater consideration or role in public life than other beliefs".[15] Ultimately, it is expected that the pressures of economic competition could lead the CJEU, a court mostly focused on free-trade issues, to apply proportionality in a way that categorically benefits "neutral" companies, placing the interests of capital owners beyond judicial scrutiny.[16]

Having gathered the basic elements of an argument, it only remains to assemble them into a cohesive whole. For this purpose, the first part of this chapter begins by discussing the high-profile case of *Achbita v G4S Secure Solutions*,[17] to then illustrate how the defendant corporation involved is an example of "neutrality-based company" that benefitted from an exceptional treatment in a "church-like" fashion. An analysis of profit-maximisation as a corporate ethos that can fall within the scope of EU religious exemptions is included in this discussion. The second part then turns to consider some CJEU developments that post-dated *Achbita* and which seem to confirm how this "corporate/business turn" in law and religion is a rising trend under EU law.

The Court of Justice of the European Union

The business model of the Belgian branch of G4S Secure Solutions, a for-profit corporation which provides security services globally, exemplifies the vision of "neutrality-based companies". At a board meeting, G4S adopted a policy of

13 This point was already discussed in Chapter II, 101.

14 See Council Directive 2004/83/EC on minimum standards for the qualification and status of third country nationals or stateless persons as refugees or as persons who otherwise need international protection and the content of the protection granted [2004] 304/12, art 10(1)(b).

15 Ronan McCrea, *Religion and the Public Order of the European Union* (Oxford Scholarship Online 2011) 147.

16 This approach resonates with the EU "competitive" approach to FoRB (and human rights generally) described in Chapter I, 58–61. See also Joseph H.H. Weiler, 'The Transformation of Europe' (1991) 100 (8) The Yale Law Journal (describing the EU single market not just as a mere technocratic project but as "a highly politicized choice of ethos, ideology, and political culture" aimed at removing all barriers that hinder the maximisation of utility") 2403, 2477. In this sense, one author describes the CJEU as a powerful instrument for implementing the EU "free-market ideology" also at the expenses of social harmony. See Alan Supiot, *The Spirit of Philadelphia. Social Justice vs the Total Market* (Verso, 2012) 50–55.

17 *Samira Achbita* (n 10).

workplace neutrality according to its mission to provide excellent customer service and maximise profits to increase its shareholders' dividend pay-outs.[18] The consequence of this policy was that a Muslim employee wearing a headscarf was dismissed, as the company wanted to maintain a certain neutral image. In brief summary, the CJEU took this case in its Grand Chamber and found that G4S's policy did not directly discriminate against the applicant. Several scholars have criticised this decision for the reckless manner in which the Court handled the proportionality analysis.[19] But technicalities aside, it is fair to say that the *Achbita* case has now become the symbol of something larger.

In fact, this case has epitomised a marked judicial effort to rework the "old" and narrow paradigm of state neutrality (one prohibiting the religious expressions of those charged with performing *public* duties) into a "new" and widened duty of neutrality for individuals operating in *private* employment contexts.[20] In essence, the *Achbita* case has become the symbol for a pervasive and secular "employment ethos"[21] that some members of the private business community deem necessary to remain economically productive in the long term. It is hoped that this section will demonstrate how, in deciding *Achbita*, the CJEU indirectly suggested that even a "for-profit and secular ethos" falls within Article 4(2) of Directive 2000/78/EC, with its specific regulation of religious or ideological organisations. As will be explained, there is much to suggest that the "duty of loyalty" to an organisation's ethos under Article 4(2) was translated into an all-out duty of neutrality in the dress-code for a Muslim employee.

To make this argument as convincing as possible, this section discusses the interpretation of *Achbita* as given by most scholars to offer an alternative construction of it as a case of corporate religious freedom in its negative modality (corporate freedom *from* religion). The relationship with the judgement in

18 More information about G4S's corporate mission can be found at <https://www.g4s.com/who-we-are> accessed 19 April 2021.

19 See, for instance, Joseph H.H. Weiler, 'Je Suis Achbita!' (2017) 15(4) International Journal of Constitutional Law 879–906; Erica Howard, 'Islamic Headscarves and the CJEU: Achbita and Bougnaoui' (2017) 24(3) Maastricht Journal of European and Comparative Law 348–66; Lucy Vickers, '*Achbita* and *Bougnaoui*: One Step Forward and Two Steps Back for Religious Diversity in the Workplace' (2017) 8(3) European Labour Law Journal 232–57.

20 For a discussion on the extension of state secularism to the private sphere in the French context, see Eoin Daly, 'Laïcite in the Private Sphere? French Religious Liberty after the Baby-Loup Affair' (2016) 5(2) Oxford Journal of Law and Religion 211–9. See also Marco Ventura, *Nelle Mani di Dio. La Super-Religione del Mondo che Verrà* (Il Mulino, 2021) (using the dichotomy "old/new secularism" to describe the regression of conventional state neutrality into a check upon public expressions of religiosity in the private sector) 215, fn 23.

21 In this sense, see Emmanuelle Bribosia and Isabelle Rorive, 'ECJ Headscarf Series (4): The Dark Side of Neutrality' (*Strasbourg Observers*, 14 September 2016) <https://strasbourgobservers.com/2016/09/ 14/ecj-headscarf-series-4-the-dark-side-of-neutrality/> accessed 19 April 2021 (arguing that "[w]hile there are a few examples of corporate enterprises expressly being based on an atheistic, agnostic or humanist ethos, quite a few companies are by default secular because they do not have a religious mission statement"). Jeroen Temperman (n 12) 37.

Bougnaoui v. Micropole[22] that the CJEU decided on the same day of *Achbita* is also noted and incorporated into the argument to highlight the inconsistent levels of protection against employment discrimination between the two cases. As will be shown, such inconsistencies occur because, for the Court, there is an obvious difference between companies that explicitly include "neutral" rules in their governance system (as in the case of G4S) and those that do not (as in the case of Micropole). This discussion on corporate freedom *from* religion at the EU level is established by first introducing the contextual background to the cases to then analysing the decisions taken by the CJEU, including the respective opinions of the Advocates General when relevant to this discussion.[23]

The Achbita and Bougnaoui cases

In the first case, Ms. Achbita worked as a receptionist for the Belgian branch of G4S for three years and complied until then with an unwritten corporate policy of neutrality prohibiting any visible signs of political, philosophical, or religious beliefs in the workplace.[24] When, in April 2006, she informed G4S of her intention to keep wearing an Islamic headscarf a work, she was dismissed. More exactly, following the employee's refusal to take off her headscarf at work, G4S adopted a change to workplace regulations, thereby making its corporate policy of neutrality a written rule. The policy change at G4S, which officially made it "neutral", determined the termination of Ms. Achbita. Ultimately, both the Labour Court and the Higher Labour Courts in Antwerp rejected Ms. Achbita's claim of discrimination on religious grounds contrary to Directive 2000/78/EC. In the second case, Ms. Bougnaoui was a design engineer who was hired by Micropole in February 2008. Initially, she wore a bandana and then a headscarf. Following complaints from customers and their requests that there be "no veil next time" in their relations with Micropole, Ms. Bougnaoui was dismissed in June 2009 after she refused to comply with her employer's request to take off the headscarf. Like Ms. Achbita, her claim that the termination constituted discrimination on religious grounds under Directive 2000/78/EC was also unsuccessful, as the Labour Tribunal of Paris rejected her complaint.

Although the common factual background in both cases was the wearing of an Islamic headscarf at work, the preliminary questions referred by the Belgian and French Courts of Cassation to the CJEU were different. In *Achbita*, the Belgian

22 Case C-188/15, *Asma Bougnaoui, Association de Defense des Droits de l'Homme (ADDH) v Micropole Univers SA*, [2017] EU:C:2017:204.

23 The institution of the Advocate General was introduced by the 1957 Treaty of Rome "to make, in open court, reasoned submissions on cases brought before the Court of Justice, in order to assist the Court in the performance of the task assigned to it". Treaty establishing the European Economic Community, 25 March 957 (unreported) art 166.

24 What follows contains reformulated excepts from the author's prior published work in Matteo Corsalini, 'Religious Freedom Inc: Business, Religion and the Law in the Secular Economy' (2020) 9(1) Oxford Journal of Law and Religion 28, 34–40.

Supreme Court asked the CJEU to determine whether a ban from wearing the headscarf at work constituted direct discrimination within the meaning of Article 2(2)(a) of Directive 2000/78EC.[25] Instead, in *Bougnaoui*, the French Court asked the CJEU to consider whether the wish of a customer not to have services supplied by an employee wearing an Islamic headscarf amounts to a genuine and determining occupational requirement under Article 4(1) of the Directive.[26]

The analysis of the cases should begin with some explanatory remarks. First, because the CJEU is the tribunal that implements the EU market-oriented goals,[27] it will generally abstain from reviewing or overturning managerial decisions that an employer believes to be in the best interest of economic efficiency (such as a policy of neutrality in *Achbita*). The lawfulness of these discretional policies is usually within the competence of national courts.[28] Second, and relatedly, judges are, in principle, neither businessman nor business experts. Thus, it follows that even domestic courts would refrain from reviewing corporate decisions (unless those decisions may constitute fraud, illegality, or self-dealing) in accordance with the corporate law's pivotal doctrine of the "business judgment rule".[29] This doctrine entails that directors, executives, and managers are better suited to make corporate decisions and, thus, left to their discretionary business judgement, as they are the involved in the day-to-day running of the corporation. Importantly, the fact that judges are not business experts complicates judicial intervention against employers who illegally discriminate.[30] Taken together, the bottom line here is that it is a company's specific corporate governance framework (i.e., a set of rules conventionally directed to maximise either profits or

25 The Belgian court referred the following question: "[s]hould Article 2(2)(a) of Directive 2000/78 be interpreted as meaning that the prohibition on wearing, as a female Muslim, a headscarf at the workplace does not constitute direct discrimination where the employer's rule prohibits all employees from wearing outward signs of political, philosophical and religious beliefs at the workplace?" See *Samira Achbita* (n 10) para 21.

26 The French court referred the following question: "should [...] Article 4(1) of Directive 2000/78 be interpreted as meaning that the wish of a customer of an information technology consulting company no longer to have the information technology services of that company provided by an employee, a design engineer, wearing an Islamic headscarf, is a genuine and determining occupational requirement, by reason of the nature of the particular occupational activities concerned or of the context in which they are carried out?" See *Asma Bougnaoui* (n 22) para 19.

27 In this sense, see Alan Supiot (n 16)50.

28 In *Achbita*, the CJEU stated that it was up to the national court to decide whether a policy of neutrality constituted direct or indirect discrimination, as the Court was only required to settle interpretative issues under the Directive. See *Samira Achbita* (n 10) para 36.

29 For an introduction to this doctrine, see Stephen M. Bainbridge, *Corporate Law* (Foundation Press 2002) 115–50.

30 Elaine Luthens, 'Racial Discrimination or Valid Business Judgments: Employment Discrimination and the Business Judgment Rule' (2017) 20(1) The Journal of Gender, Race & Justice 381, 399 (discussing how eliminating the business judgement rule in US employment discrimination suits might guarantee employees a better chance for a fair trial).

other stakeholder interests and human rights)[31] that shapes the judicial outcomes of corporate business rulings. Apparently, the *Achbita* and *Bougnaoui* cases confirmed this general rule.

As noted, in *Achbita*, the presence of an explicit policy of neutrality to maximise commercial performance led the CJEU to develop what Alan Supiot called a "total market"[32] approach that underestimated the possibility of a malign intent to directly discriminate under the guise of a "neutral" internal rule. But despite this risk, in the eyes of the Court, religion must categorically yield to the freedom to conduct business whenever a policy of neutrality is clear and well-established. By contrast, in *Bougnaoui*, it was the absence of an explicit ban on religious garments that offered an opportunity for the CJEU to incorporate the ECtHR's human rights-based approach on religious accommodation at work in its analysis.[33] Lucy Vickers described this approach as a substantial step forward in promoting equality at work for Europe's religious minorities.[34] With these preliminary remarks, the following turns to detail these CJEU diverging approaches in *Bougnaoui* and *Achbita*.

Bougnaoui v Micropole

In reaching a decision in *Bougnaoui*, the CJEU heavily relied on the opinion by Advocate General (AG) Sharpston who clarified that the "business interest in generating maximum profit should (…) give way to the right of the individual employee to manifest his religious convictions".[35]

It was precisely this premise that informed her interpretation of the "occupational requirements" under Article 4(1) of Directive 2000/78/EC.

In any case, before going further, it has to be noted that this latter provision is almost identical to Article 4(2), with the only difference that it does not contain

31 Alex Edmans, *Grow the Pie. How Great Companies Deliver Both Purpose and Profit* (Cambridge University Press, 2020) (describing this either/or attitude in corporate governance as a "pie-splitting mentality", meaning that business leaders conventionally believe that the maximisation of one slice of the pie (i.e., profits) necessarily involves the minimisation of another (i.e., stakeholders' interests) and vice-versa. The author criticises this approach as a zero-sum game that fails to fairly distribute costs and benefits to both shareholders and stakeholders).

32 Alan Supiot (n 16) (using the formula "total market" to describe a mode of organising production in business that considers human rights only insofar as they can facilitate the ability to trade and perform economic activities) 44.

33 See the seminal ECtHR decision in *Eweida and Others v UK* Apps Nos 48420/10, 59842/10, 51671/10 and 36516/10 (ECtHR, 15 January 2013) (clarifying that an employer's wish to communicate a corporate image is a legitimate aim for dismissal on grounds of religion, on condition that that there is evidence that religious manifestations at work constitute a substantial encroachment on the commercial undertaking or the interests of others).

34 Lucy Vickers (n 19)

35 Case C-188/15, *Asma Bougnaoui, Association de Defense des Droits de l'Homme (ADDH) v Micropole Univers SA*, [2017] EU:C:2017:204, Opinion of AG Sharpston, para 133.

the specific "ethos requirement" for churches or ideological organisations.[36] Article 4(1) exempts employers from the applicability of EU anti-discrimination legislation when an employee's differential treatment is motivated by:

> [T[he *nature* of the particular occupational activities concerned or of the *context* in which they are carried out, such a characteristic constitutes a genuine and determining occupational requirement, provided that the objective is legitimate and the requirement is proportionate.[37]

Overall, it was against this background that AG Sharpston framed her analysis. To begin with, she considered that, for a differential treatment to be justified, any occupational requirement (dictated by the *nature* of the job and the *context* in which it is carried out) must be "genuine" and "determining".[38] Furthermore, the objective must be legitimate, and the requirement proportionate. In other words, any restriction concerning religious garments must be *objectively* dictated by the nature and context of the job, AG Sharpston instructed, which is why Article 4(1) does not cover *subjective* considerations. Following from this, AG Sharpston considered that Micropole's termination letter expressly praised the claimant's professional competence, acknowledging that the dismissal lacked any objective basis other than the customer's request to avoid the *hijab* in the future.[39] And because the commercial interest of Micropole to accommodate customer's prejudices against religious minorities cannot be a basis for employment restrictions,[40] it became unnecessary to analyse the proportionality of the measures adopted. On these grounds, AG Sharpston concluded that Ms. Bougnaoui's dismissal was directly discriminatory under Article 2(2)(a) of Directive 2000/78/EC, as she was treated less favourably than any other would have been treated in a comparable situation for religious reasons.[41]

Eventually, in endorsing this finding, the CJEU confirmed that the applicant's termination was excessively biased in favour of a customer's prejudice and was not the result of an internal managerial rule. In consequence, Ms. Bougnaoui's differential treatment amounted to direct discrimination.[42] However, the Court went further to clarify that had the dismissal been supported by an explicit internal rule (such as a corporate policy of religious, political, and philosophical neutrality, such as in *Achbita*), the differential treatment would have not amounted to an indirect discrimination. Under these circumstances, the employer's busi-

36 The content and scope of Article 4(2) has already been discussed in Chapter II, 101–102.
37 Council Regulation (EC) 2000/78 establishing a general framework for equal treatment in employment and occupation (EC Employment Equality Directive) [2000] L 303/16, art 4(1) (emphasis added).
38 Opinion of AG Sharpston (n 35) para 96.
39 ibid para 102.
40 ibid para 95.
41 ibid para 108.
42 *Asma Bougnaoui* (n 22) para 34.

ness judgement would have counted as a legitimate aim to justify restrictions, provided that the means are proportionate and necessary.[43]

This is how the CJEU anticipated that the presence of an internal policy of neutrality would add a layer of evidentiary presumption in favour of the employer. In the wake of this decision, it is clear that, in future cases, employees might run the risk of being affected by an extra burden requiring them to prove that an apparently neutral rule conceals an intent to directly discriminate.[44] In this regard, deep concerns relate to the fact that the CJEU could dangerously set different standards of protection depending on the presence or absence of a corporate policy of neutrality. Because this actually happened in *Achbita*, the next subsection turns to its analysis.

Achbita v G4S Solutions

In *Achbita*, both AG Kokott and the CJEU agreed that an internal dress code applicable to political, philosophical, and religious signs was not directly discriminatory under Article 2(2)(a).[45] Basically, they both answered the question made by the Belgian Court of Cassation in the negative, for they did not spot any direct discriminatory intent masqueraded as a blanket ban.[46] However, because it was "not inconceivable"[47] that Ms. Achbita's treatment could be indirectly discriminatory under Article 2(2)(b) of the Directive, the CJEU went further to give guidance on this matter. In doing so, the Court applied a "fairly loose justification test"[48] that was incongruent with its previous judgement in *Bougnaoui*, as it cancelled out the claimant's right to manifest her religion from the balancing exercise.[49]

To demonstrate this, it has to be noted how the Court initially followed the lead of the ECtHR in *Eweida and Others v UK*, by acknowledging that an

43 ibid para 33.

44 This was subject to debate by academic opinion. Lucy Vickers writes that "discrimination based on a generally applicable dress code is not direct discrimination". See Lucy Vickers, 'Direct Discrimination and Indirect Discrimination: Headscarves and the CJEU' (Oxford Human Rights Hub, 15 March 2017) <http://ohrh.law.ox.ac.uk/direct-discrimination-and-indirect-discrimination-headscarves-and-the-cjeu/> accessed 22 October 2021. Instead, Schona Jolly QC says that "a rule expressed neutrally on workplace attire or apparel is more likely to constitute indirect discrimination, unless there is evidence of particular stereotyping, prejudice or intent behind the rule which could lead it to be direct discrimination". See Schona Jolly QC, 'Islamic Headscarves and the Workplace Reach the CJEU: The Battle for Substantive Equality' (2016) 6(1) European Human Rights Law Review 672, 675.

45 *Samira Achbita* (n 10) para 30; Case C-157/15, *Samira Achbita and Centrum voor Gelijkheid van Kansen en voor Racismebestrijding v G4S Secure Solutions NV* [2017] EU:C:2017:203. Opinion of AG Kokott para 49.

46 Ibid para 32; ibid para 49.

47 *Samira Achbita* (n 10) para 34.

48 In this sense, see Erica Howard (n 19) 359.

49 Joseph H.H. Weiler (n 19) 989, 997.

employer's wish to project a certain business image to the public is a *prima facie* legitimate aim.[50] But from there, it moved to categorically prioritise G4S's aim of religious neutrality vis-á-vis its customers as a freestanding principle derived from the freedom to conduct a business under Article 16 of the Charter of Fundamental Rights of the European Union (CFREU).[51] This reasoning cannot be justified under the ECtHR, as restrictions based on claims of neutrality concern, mainly, public service[52] and must be applied narrowly to private employees.[53] At this point, it is no wonder that it was precisely this broad reading of neutrality as a means to regulate public expressions of religiosity also in the private employment sphere that tipped the balancing scales in favour of G4S. However, for a better understanding of how this happened in practice, one should look more closely at the AG Kokott's opinion on which the CJEU heavily relied before issuing its judgement.

To begin with, and upon recognition that neutrality was a legitimate aim that *prima facie* justified indirect discrimination, AG Kokott turned to assess the appropriateness and necessity for the means to achieve such an aim. As to the first element (the appropriateness of FoRB restrictions), AG Kokott clarified that the desire to preserve corporate neutrality is acceptable only insomuch as an internal rule to that effect is unambiguously understandable and known to employees.[54] After that, she turned to discuss the issue of necessity in relation to Article 4(1) of the Directive, which included examining whether the legitimate aim could have been achieved by less restrictive means than a ban on religious/ideological attire.[55] In making this evaluation, she noted that, although providing female employees with an optional headscarf as part of their uniforms would be a less intrusive solution, this would be "much less satisfactory, not to say entirely inappropriate, for the purposes of achieving the objective of religious and ideological neutrality".[56] Alternatively, she suggested that employees could be moved to back-office positions with no duties to interact with customers.[57]

In reflecting AG Kokott's arguments, the CJEU stopped short of demanding proportionality from "neutrally religious" business entities. The Court first considered that a neutrality policy was appropriate to the extent that it was

50 *Samira Achbita* (n 10) paras 38–9.
51 ibid, para 37–8.
52 In this sense, see *Dahlab v Switzerland*, App no 42393/98 (ECtHR, 15 February 2001); *SAS v France*, App no 43835/11 (ECtHR, 1 July 2014); *Ebrahimian v France*, App no 64846/11 (ECtHR, 26 November 2015).
53 The ECtHR always requires that business autonomy rights be balanced on grounds of proportionality and reasonability. Thus, when it comes to religious accommodation, the balancing exercise must be narrow and give careful consideration of the "possibility of changing job" and "the seriousness of losing one's job" on religious grounds. *Eweida* (n 33) para 83 and 109.
54 *Opinion of AG Kokott* (n 45) para 101–2.
55 ibid 104.
56 ibid para 107.
57 ibid para 108.

"genuinely pursued in a consistent and systematic manner".[58] Second, and while analysing the necessity of the rule, it stated that the prohibition must be "limited to what is strictly necessary" and cover "only G4S workers who interact with customers".[59] Following from this, the CJEU concluded that indirect discrimination might occur only if it is established that religious employees will bear most of the disadvantageous effects of this policy, and the means of achieving neutrality are unnecessary and inappropriate.[60] Be that as it may, in finding that employers might, in principle, ban religious manifestations at work, the CJEU omitted any consideration of Ms. Achbita's right to freedom of religion, failing to provide national courts with guidance concerning the proportionality analysis. In conclusion, not only the CJEU's argumentative discourse is inconsistent with settled ECHR case law on FoRB in employment but it also lacks coherence with *Bougnaoui*. For it is hard to conceive how, if customer preferences can never justify direct discrimination, they can, however, do so when they are included in a corporate policy of neutrality.[61]

The Achbita case: an alternative reading

In the previous section it was shown how the presence of a market-oriented rule of corporate "neutrality" in *Achbita* was key to understanding why, unlike in *Bougnaoui*, the CJEU categorically privileged the defendant company's economic interests over equality (and FoRB) rights. Taken together, this outcome is hardly surprising when analysed in light of an EU "competitive approach" to human rights that accommodates FoRB claims only insofar as they could adapt "to the profit motive and the need for efficiency in the market".[62]

Instead, what is surprising is that the CJEU took for granted that secular employers could impose a "duty of neutrality" onto their employees to remove

58 *Samira Achbita* (n 10) para 40.

59 ibid para 42.

60 ibid para 45.

61 In this sense, see Saïla Ouald-Chaib and Valeska David, 'European Court of Justice Keeps the Door to Religious Discrimination in the Private Workplace Opened. The European Court of Human Rights Could Close it' (Strasbourg Observer, 27 March 2017) <https://strasbourgobservers.com/2017/03/27/euro pean-court-of-justice-keeps-the-door-to-religious-discrimination-in-the-private-workplace-opened-theeuropean- court-of-human-rights-could-close-it/> accessed 25 April 2021. See also Steve Peers, 'Headscarf Bans at Work: Explaining the ECJ Rulings' (EU Law Analysis, 14 March 2017) <http://eulawanalysis.blogspot.com/2017/03/headscarf-bans-at-work-explaining-ecj.html#> accessed 25 April 2021.

62 Ronan McCrea (n 15)154. As far as human rights in employment are concerned, the TFEU is emblematic of this state of affairs. It states that the EU's goal is to facilitate "a coordinated strategy for promoting a skilled, trained and adaptable workforce ***responsive to economic change***". Consolidated Version of the Treaty on the Functioning of the European Union [2012] [2008] OJ C 326/47, art 145 (emphasis added).

any form of "deviance" from the authority of their profit-maximising business model without a proper balancing exercise.

Understood this way, the organisational autonomy of "neutrality-based companies" then looks no different from the autonomy of church employers to terminate employees disloyal to the religious mission of their institution, as analysed in Chapter II.[63] In light of this, one must ask whether this analogy justifies a reading of *Achbita* as a case on negative corporate religious freedom (i.e., corporate freedom *from* religion). This will be further examined below.

Old rules, new "religious" players in the EU single market

To defend the claim that, in *Achbita*, there has been a de facto extension of the EU "ministerial exception" under Article 4(2) of Directive 2000/78/EC to a secular for-profit corporation, a word of caution first needs to be made.

As noted, the case came to the CJEU by way of preliminary reference only with respect to the issue of whether a corporate policy of neutrality constitutes direct discrimination under Article 2(2)(a) of the Directive. Thus, no mention whatsoever to Article 4(1), let alone to the religious exemption under Article 4(2), appears in the CJEU's judgement.[64] But picking up on the lines of argument taken by AG Kokott, it is possible to see how her opinion lends itself to a reading of *Achbita* as a case of corporate religious freedom under Article 4(2). To fully appreciate this "business turn" in EU law and religion, this section, therefore, now briefly returns to Kokott's reasoning, in which the recognition of the right of a for-profit company to have and maintain its right to freedom *from* religion is most fully set out.

To begin with, and unlike the CJEU's decision in the case, AG Kokott *did* consider the potential discriminatory nature of G4S's policy of neutrality from the point of view of the occupational requirements under Article 4(1) of the Directive.[65] As to the first requirement (the *nature* of the job), the AG noted that Ms. Achbita's receptionist work in itself did not require a ban on religious attire. In any case, she accepted that the removal of the headscarf could be necessary because of the *context* of the job (the second occupational requirement).[66] "[O]ne of the conditions of carrying out that work may nonetheless be compliance with the dress code laid down by the employer", she held.[67] This conclusion was, however, contradictory. First, the AG admitted that the work of a receptionist could be performed both with and without a headscarf. However, she then concluded that a less intrusive means than a headscarf ban, such as a uniform

63 The author already suggested this argument in Matteo Corsalini (n 24) 40.

64 The author wishes to thank Daniele Ferrari, law and religion scholar at the University of Siena's law department for suggesting that this point be made clear from the start.

65 *Opinion of AG Kokott* (n 45) para 64.

66 ibid para 75.

67 ibid.

including an optional headscarf, would have been "entirely inappropriate, for the purposes of achieving the objective of religious and ideological neutrality *which G4S has laid down as an occupational requirement*".[68] The last sentence in italics is noteworthy because the AG framed G4S's neutrality not so much as a mere governance rule but as a proper "occupational requirement" that has the character of an "obligation"[69] for its employees. On closer inspection, this looks no different from the "ethos requirement" that ideologically oriented entities could impose onto their staff under Article 4(2). In other words, it is the argument of this book that, through her opinion, AG Kokott indirectly (and perhaps unwittingly) conflated Article 4(1) with the mechanisms for exemptions for churches under Article 4(2). As a result of this, she seemed to have crafted a "church-like" exemption for commercial (and "neutral") companies that tilted the proportionality analysis in favour of their business autonomy. As noted elsewhere, it follows from this analysis that whenever for-profit entities enjoy "church-like" special benefits to fulfil their profit-oriented mission, by logical extension, they themselves become "religious"(legally speaking, at least).[70]

At any rate, this contention should not be taken to mean that for-profit entities share the absolute, infinite, and complete characters of conventional religions. Rather, here, the argument is only that, very much like religious institutions, business entities (including "neutrality-based" ones) are legally construed, for strategic purposes, as derivatively embracing the value-laden conceptions of the good life shared by their individual members. From this vantage point, even a for-profit corporation might well be said to have a "conscience" in the sense that it "serves as a venue and vehicle for the sharing of conscience-driven claims among its constituents".[71] And to the extent that such corporate "conscience claims" are by default "non-neutral" (that in fact might clash and stand against other counterposed values), it is not unreasonable to think of secular corporations, be they for-profit or non-profit, as all-out "ideologically oriented"[72] entities.

As further evidence of this, one only needs to look to the French *Baby-Loup* affair[73] to see how this assumption is not beyond the bounds of possibility. The *Baby-Loup* case concerned the dismissal of a Muslim nanny who was not allowed

68 ibid para 107.
69 ibid para 75 and 77.
70 See Matteo Corsalini (n 24) 44–5.
71 Robert K. Vischer, *Conscience and the Common Good. Reclaiming the Space Between Person and State* (Cambridge University Press, 2010) 179.
72 Azza Karam (n 7) 24. One commentator has labelled neutral for-profit corporations as "entreprises postséculières" and their desire to maximise commercial performance as "le nouvel esprit du management". See Louis-Leon Christians, 'Le bien-être Spirituel en Management. Approches Juridiques' in Sophie Izoard-Allaux, Louis-Léon Christians, and Walter Lesch (eds), *Le Nouvel Esprit du Management Interrogations Interdisciplinaires sur la Spiritualite' en Entreprise* (Presses Universitaires de Louvain 2018) 36. See also Louis-Leon Christians, 'Ideologically Oriented Enterprises Faced with the Reconfiguration of Ethics and Spiritual Management' (2014) 1(3) Brigham Young University Law Review 565–84.
73 Cass Ass Plén 25 June 2014 (2014) Recueil Dalloz, 1386.

to wear a *hijab* because her employer, a private kindergarten, had an internal regulation prohibiting religious garments to protect constitutional *laïcitè*. This saga involved five separate judgements, of which only the most relevant ones will be examined.[74] In 2013, the Social Chamber of the Court of Cassation held that the extension of *laïcitè* to private employees, beyond reasons of occupational necessity, was discriminatory. This judgement was then remitted to the Paris Court of Appeal in 2014. Interestingly, this latter court described *Baby-Loup* precisely as an ideologically oriented organisation (*entreprise de conviction*) promoting a "neutrally religious" ethos under Article 4(2) of Directive 2000/78 EC. All things considered, there might be a temptation to suggest that this depiction of *Baby-Loup* was a convenient expedient to justify the extension of the constitutional neutrality principle to a purely private law employment context. But strategic reasoning aside, the Court de facto acknowledged that *Baby-Loup*'s moral conviction of religious neutrality was a means of "transcending multiculturalism" which justified discrimination against private employees.[75] Ultimately, and drawing on this Lower Court's decision, the French Court of Cassation, sitting in its Plenary Chamber, then reviewed its earlier judgement and ruled in favour of the defendant kindergarten. Despite this, it rejected the interpretation of *Baby-Loup* as an *entreprise de conviction* because, in its eyes, neutrality in that context only amounted to a mere managerial rule rather than a conviction per se.

With this in mind, it is now possible to link the findings in *Baby-Loup* with those in *Achbita* and see how the French Court of Cassation's conclusion clashed head-on with AG Kokott's reasoning, as the latter accepted neutrality well-beyond matters of managerial organisation. Despite their differences, both cases shared the same outcome: an extensive interpretation of "neutrality" as a fully fledged "ethos" requirement under Article 4(2) of Directive 2000/78/EC that holds sway over behaviours and practices in a given working environment. At this stage, because it is generally expected that only religious and comprehensive moral/philosophical foundations fall under this EU "ministerial exception",[76] this chapter now lays out the case for profit-maximisation as a corporate ethos which might benefit from this special concession. The following sub-section aims at tracing the contours of this perspective.

The moral obligation of profit-maximisation

On the face of it, the belief that business should focus on nothing but profit-maximisation as a proper moral duty is a highly contentious idea. In any case, one

74 For a description of this complex legal battle, see Eoin Daly (n 20) 211; Myriam Hunter-Henin, 'Living Together in an Age of Religious Diversity: Lessons from Baby Loup and SAS' (2015) (4)1 Oxford Journal of Law and Religion 94, 101–106.

75 In this sense, see Eoin Daly (n 20) 219.

76 See Commission Staff Working Document Annexes to the Joint Report on the application on the Racial Equality Directive (2000/43/EC) and the Employment Equality Directive (2000/78/EC) SWD(2014) 5 final, Brussels 17 January 2014.

can only understand the moral connotation of this single-minded objective by contextualising it within some ideological and intellectual trends that have been inspiring the efficiency-oriented commitments of "neutrality-based companies" since the middle part of the twentieth century.

To start, conventional economics literature has gone a long way to explain that, quite intuitively, individuals use for-profit corporations as legal devices to structure their business activities (i.e., firms) for purely economic reasons. In this specific view, for-profit corporations are legal entities that exclusively aim at maximising the efficiency of commercial transactions, while minimising their costs of production (including the social costs of paying attention to their obligations toward the public).[77] Understood this way, this line of economic thinking offered a normative basis against which businessmen were encouraged to prioritise their "neutral" *financial performance* over their *social performance.*

An interesting variation of this efficiency-oriented argument is that it simply makes no sense to impute social responsibilities to for-profit corporations insofar as they are not flesh and blood persons but only "artificial" ones.[78] However, even tough corporations are fictitious entities under the law, in the eyes of one leading economist and Nobel prize winner, Milton Friedman, businesses *do* have social responsibilities nonetheless. Writing in the *New York Times Magazine* in 1970, he famously (or infamously) argued that: "There is one and only one social responsibility of business—to (…) make as much money as possible".[79] As will be shown, it was with these words that Friedman created an open door for fostering a vision of the profit motive as some sort of categorical and moral imperative.

Echoing the intellectual legacy of Adam Smith, the doyen of the modern political economy and interdisciplinary studies that cut across the borders of economics, philosophy, and even theology,[80] Milton Friedman was the most eloquent spokesman of Smith's "invisible hand" of the market.[81] According to this theory, it is only by leaving markets free from governmental regulation that the (invisible) force of private competition, demand, supply, and self-interested behaviour will naturally generate economic and social utility for communities.[82]

77 See also Ronald Coase (n 2) 1- 44. For an introduction to the notion of "firms" and "corporations" as well as their differences see Robé Jean-Philippe, 'The Legal Structure of The Firm' (2011) 1(1) Accounting, Economics and Law: A Convivium 1–86.

78 This is discussed and criticised in: Kennet E. Goodpaster and John B. Matthews, Jr. (n 2).

79 Milton Friedman, 'The Social Responsibility of Business is to Increase its Profits' (*The New York Times*, 13 September 1970) <https://www.nytimes.com/1970/09/13/archives/a-friedman-doctrine-the-social-responsibility-of-business-is-to.html> accessed 2 May 2021.

80 For a theological reading of Adam Smith see Paul Oslington (eds), *Adam Smith as Theologian* (Routledge, 2011); see also Harvey Cox, *The Market as God* (Harvard University Press, 2016) 156–175.

81 In this sense see Kennet E. Goodpaster and John B. Matthews, Jr. (n 2).

82 Smith's "invisible hand" argument appears three times in his writings: first in his essay *History of Astronomy* (unpublished) then in the *Theory of Moral Sentiments* (1759) and ultimately in *The Wealth of Nations* (1776). In this sense see John D. Bishop, 'Adam Smith's Invisible Hand Argument' (1995) 14(3) Journal of Business Ethics, 165, 166.

Other things being equal, the higher the freedom to maximise *private* profits, the greater the incentives to produce and offer valuable services to the *public* community as a whole.[83] At any rate, it should be borne in mind that Smith's theory was only intended to be a purely scientific observation, according to which "in certain situations (a free market), certain types of actions (everything pursuing their own interests), will cause a certain result (promoting of the public good)".[84] In practice, Smith did not mean to draw a moral conclusion from his argument. Nor, as a consequence, did he claim that, because the common good is best served when everyone pursues its own self-interest, then individuals have a *moral duty* to do so.[85] Yet, two centuries later, some free-marketers did cling to the "invisible hand" argument to draw this kind of moral conclusion.

Beginning in the 1980s, and thanks to Friedman's growing popularity, the "invisible doctrine" argument began to enter mainstream politics on both sides of the Atlantic. At that time, *laissez-faire* economics, with its prescriptions for deregulation and minimal government, was best embodied by Margaret Thatcher's administration in the UK and Ronald Reagan's government in the US, respectively. Most remarkable here is that both Thatcher and Reagan's agendas assimilated ideological themes to defend the moral appropriateness of advancing competitive free markets.

Somewhat more specifically, Thatcher had Christian religious beliefs that very much influenced her programme and provided a foundation for the idea that "self-reliance is the first step towards helping others".[86] In this way, she spoke from an ideological paradigm that anchored free-market principles to her reading of Christian charity.[87] Instead, Reagan's enthusiasm for free markets should be generally framed within the broader theme of his staunch anti-communist policies exalting the pursuit of maximal individual freedoms.[88]

More than this, and because it is the freedom of private enterprises in particular that is essential for guaranteeing freely functioning markets, in the same period, scholars from the US "law and economics" movement began to take on

83 In this sense, see for instance Michael C. Jensen, 'Value Maximization, Stakeholder Theory, and the Corporate Objective Function' (2001) 14(3) Journal of Applied Corporate Finance 7, 9 (arguing that a for-profit corporation increases social welfare whenever it "produces an output (…) that is valued by its customers at more than the value of the inputs it consumes").

84 John D. Bishop (n 82) 167.

85 ibid.

86 See Margaret Thatcher, 'Speech to Conservative Women's Conference' (Margaret Thatcher Foundation, 22 May 1988) <https://www.margaretthatcher.org/document/107248> accessed 4 May 2021.

87 For a discussion on Thatcher and religion, see Florence Sutcliffe-Braithwaite, 'Neo-Liberalism and Morality in the Making of Thatcherite Social Policy' (2012) 55(2) The Historical Journal 497–520.

88 Reagan's anti-communist line is now dubbed 'Reagan Doctrine'. For a discussion on this topic, see Robert H. Johnson, 'Misguided Morality: Ethics and the Reagan Doctrine' (1988) 103(3) Political Science Quarterly 509–30.

questions about the governance of for-profit corporations.[89] In doing so, they offered some suggestions on how to take the "moral version" of the "invisible hand" argument further. In this regard, for-profit businesses have been somehow rendered morally justified by a powerful theory of the corporation as a "nexus of contracts"; that is, a bundle of "contractual" relationships between its board of directors and all the inputs of production, including its creditors and investors (i.e., shareholders).[90] One author in particular, Theo Vermaelen, drew from this "contractarian" theory the moral corollary that corporate directors have the "ethical imperative"[91] to maximise profits and, thereby, ensure an healthy return for their investors in the form of a higher share price. As he explains it, this is because whenever a company explicitly mentions the pursuit of shareholder value in its statements of purpose, it makes a contractual and "implicit promise"[92] to serve the interests of those who originally committed financial contributions to the corporation.[93] Thus, should the "promise" of maximising shareholder value remain unfulfilled, this might prove a serious inconvenience to the expectations of shareholders, who also provided the business capital which is at risk and over which they have no contractual rights of return.[94] In light of this, the interests of

89 See generally Richard A. Posner, *Economic Analysis of Law* (Wolters Kluwer, 1986). In the interests of simplicity, the formulas "law and economics" and "economic analysis of law" are used interchangeably here. Distinctions, however, exist and should be briefly mentioned. Guido Calabresi explains that "while in Economic Analysis of Law economics dominates and law is its subject of analysis and criticism, in Law and Economics the relationship is bilateral". Meaning that "economic theory examines law, but not infrequently this examination leads to changes in economic theory rather that changes in law". See Guido Calabresi, *The Future of Law and Economics* (Yale University Press, 2016) 6.

90 For a discussion of this theory, Michael C. Jensen, William H. Meckling, 'Theory of the Firm: Managerial Behaviour, Agency Costs and Ownership Structure' (1976) 3 Journal of Finance and Economics 305–57. See also Eugene F. Fama, 'Agency Problems and the Theory of the Firm' (1980) 88(2) Journal of Political Economy 288, 290.

91 Theo Vermaelen, 'Maximising Shareholder Value: An Ethical Responsibility?' in N. Craig Smith and Gilbert Lenssen (eds), *Mainstreaming Corporate Responsibility* (Wiley 2009) 206.

92 ibid 210–211. See also Christopher McMahon, 'Morality and the Invisible Hand' (1981) 10(3) Philosophy & Public Affairs 247, 255 (discussing the "implicit morality of the market"). For a more recent discussion on the "moral status of markets" as a normative foundation for contract law, see Nathan B. Oman, *The Dignity of Commerce. Markets and the Moral Foundations of Contract Law* (The University of Chicago Press, 2016).

93 In this sense, see also Stephen M Bainbridge, 'Director Primacy: The Means and Ends of Corporate Governance' (2002) 97(2) Northwestern University Law Review 547 (arguing that "the board of directors has a contractual obligation to maximize the value of the shareholders" residual claim".) 551.

94 This is because, upon incorporation, shareholders convert their property rights on the assets that they conferred in the first place into the ownership of shares. Meaning that, from that moment on, it is the new corporate entity that holds title to all the assets, whilst it would be difficult (if not impossible) for shareholders to claim back their original contributions. In this sense, see Lynn A. Stout, 'The Corporation as a Time Machine: Intergenerational Equity, Intergenerational Efficiency, and the Corporate Form' (2015) 38(2) Seattle University Law Review 685, 692; see also Robé Jean-Philippe (n 77) 23.

stakeholders (e.g., employees, trade associations, and local communities) might be attended only when these do not compromise shareholder wealth.

Based on this analysis, it is now easy to see how the "moral" argument for maximising profits resonates with the business model of G4S, the defendant company in *Achbita*. G4S's statement of purpose reads that: "Our mission is to create material, sustainable value for our customers and *shareholders* by being the supply partner of choice in all our markets".[95] This is how its board of directors established a strategy of corporate governance that evaluates its decisions only on the basis of its implicit contractual promises to customers and shareholders, while paying little attention to stakeholders (such as *hijab*-wearing employees). At any rate, things would have turned out differently if G4S had, since the beginning, established a declared purpose of giving, for example, 50% of profits to charity in its mission statement. Theo Vermaelen conceded that a business entity could not be accused of destroying shareholder wealth when its corporate purpose, announced from the outset, would include the social interests of many other stakeholders and not simply those of shareholders.[96]

Linked to this, a significant number of scholars have analysed the importance of maximising stakeholder value as opposed to shareholder value.[97] Discussions on stakeholder theory aside, it is enough to note that it was precisely through a critique of businesses that give overly broad consideration to the social interests of third parties that leading economist Michael Jensen offered another foothold for moral reasoning. In his own terms, he admonished that a business entity cannot "serve many masters".[98] In his view, expenditures on progressive values, such as corporate social responsibility (CSR) to benefit communities, not only amount to an unethical behaviour toward investors but also risk diverting resources away from the ultimate goal of making money. As a result of this, societies themselves will bear the costs of inefficient businesses incapable of creating superior quality products for human use.[99] Further, and building on this argument, Jensen proposed an "enlightened value maximisation" approach as an alternative organi-

95 See <https://www.g4s.com/who-we-are> accessed 5 May 2021 (emphasis added).

96 Theo Vermaelen (n 91) 211. See also Jill E. Fisch and Steven Davidoff Solomon, 'The "Value" of a Public Benefit Corporation' (2020) Institute for Law and Economics Research Paper no 20-54 <https://papers.ssrn.com/sol3/papers.cfm?abstract_id=3712532> accessed 5 May 2021 (analysing corporate legal devices allowing directors to include non-shareholder interests (e.g., stakeholders, statutes, and benefit corporations) and discussing their structural limitations).

97 An often-cited source of stakeholder theory is R. Edward Freeman, *Strategic Management. A Stakeholder Approach* (Boston Pitman 1984).

98 See Michael C. Jensen (n 83) 9.

99 Clearly, this argument does not entirely justify why the business world should not take seriously its duties to the public. On the flip side, however, there is much evidence to indicate that CSR can be reduced to mere tokenism that does not fully serve society and sustainable development goals. To take just one example, the fact that a tobacco company gives, say, 50% of revenues to cancer treatment centres will not stop it from producing addictive and harmful goods to earn a profit. For an interesting critique on CSR, see Alex Edmans (n 31).

sational strategy to meet stakeholders claims without sacrificing profitability, revenue growth, and other indicators of financial performance. He argued that "in order to maximise value, corporate managers must not only satisfy, but enlist the support of, all corporate stakeholders".[100] In short, by infusing the corporation with a "strategic corporate vision",[101] he assumed that a strong sense of corporate affiliation would follow. This, in turn, entails that the more stakeholders identify with the corporation, the greater their alignment to the profit motive and the fewer their negative reactions to organisational changes (such as downsizing and layoffs).[102]

Treading this path, Jesper Kunde, management strategist and CEO of the Scandinavian advertising agency Kunde & Co., took Jensen's argument even further. In an era in which consumers demand not simply products but brands, he argued that the most lucrative businesses are those build around a strong idea, a shared vision, that shapes their marketing concept. In sum, the more a company's *internal* management is bound together in a common "belief"[103] (what Kunde dubs "corporate religion"),[104] the stronger its ability to define and communicate an inspiring corporate brand to the public, thereby strengthening its *external* market positioning.[105]

In the author's opinion, the meaning of "religion" that Kunde is adopting (which extends to commercial businesses that are not tied to religion in the strict sense) constitutes a fairly radical deconstruction of the religious/secular divide. In sum, Kunde's theory, combined with the insights discussed above, not only entertains the idea that commercial companies might be *prima facie* conscience-exemption claimants under EU law, but it also makes the whole argument more sound and easily defendable.

100 Michael C. Jensen (n 83) 9.
101 ibid 7.
102 This, however, largely depends on the subjective attitudes of each corporate constituent.
103 See Jesper Kunde, *Corporate Religion* (Pearson Education, 2000) 2.
104 ibid. Kunde & Co.'s mission statement speaks eloquently for itself, as its opening banners announce, "200 employees, 1 religion". See <https://www.kunde.dk/about/> accessed 6 May 2021.
105 One author applies sociological analysis to religion to describe it as a "power of communication". Phrased differently, religion is seen as a device allowing not only the construction of belief systems via the sharing of values and doctrines but also their interaction (communication) with other social systems, be they religious or otherwise. See Enzo Pace, *Religion as Communication. God's Talk* (Routledge, 2011). In a similar vein, see Pierre Bordieu, 'Genesis and Structure of the Religious Field' in Craig Calhoun (eds) *Comparative Social Research. A Research Annual. Religious Institutions* (Jai Press, 1991) (arguing that "religious" might be considered as "a language, that is both an instrument of communication and an instrument of knowledge, or more precisely, (…) a *symbolic medium*".) 2.

Sequel: in the aftermath of *Achbita v. G4S Secure Solutions*

So far, it has been the hope of this chapter to demonstrate how churches and "neutrality-based companies" can be seen as instances of the same legal phenomenon—that is, a growing recognition of the rights of corporate entities to have and manifest a corporate image, be it religious or secular (read: "neutral"). For this purpose, it has been shown how the CJEU decision in *Achbita* has de facto extended religious exemptions for churches to a commercial business's wish to present a secular image to customers and investors as part of its strategy for maximising profitability. Understood this way, it has been introduced and defended the claim that *Achbita* is about corporate freedom of religion (in its negative modality: corporate freedom *from* religion). To appreciate this argument fully, a crucial segment of a discussion in business theory justifying the moral obligation of pursuing maximum profit was also considered. This also gave the key to this chapter's purpose to introduce the idea of profit-maximisation as a corporate "ethos", falling within the scope of the EU "ministerial exception" under Article 4(2) of Directive 2000/78/EC; however, all this is with a caveat.

The author arrived at this final consideration despite his awareness that there are good reasons to be cautious about making an argument for exceptional treatment of for-profit companies on conscience grounds. One such reason is that, for orthodox believers, on no account it is permissible to mention religious institutions and for-profit corporations in the same breath. This study does not mean to be offensive; nevertheless, the reader is invited to consider how economic theory, today, is increasingly interested in drawing this kind of analogy.[106] Also, the EU itself has put religious institutions and other non-confessional organisations on the same footing, as emerges from Article 17 TFUE and Article 4 of Directive 2000/78/EC. Another reason for criticising the idea of for-profit entities as conscience-exemption claimants is that this could open a grim Pandora's box of new corporate claims of special pleading, ignoring the checks and balances of the human rights system. On the flip side, however, denying the plausibility of this new "business turn" in law and religion merely out of fear and rejection is not viable and even less justifiable.

106 As early as 1776, Adam Smith discussed churches as firms producing and selling religious goods and services to consumers. This is explained in Book V of Adam Smith, *An Inquiry into the Nature and Causes of the Wealth of Nations* (University of Chicago Press 1976). The analysis of churches as "firms" offering spiritual commodities in the market is now at the centre of the "economics of religion" approach. For one of the first scholarly articles on this topic see Laurence R. Iannaccone, 'Introduction to the Economics of Religions' (1998) 36(3) Journal of Economic Literature 1465–1495. See also Robert B. Ekelund, Jr. and others, *Sacred Trust: The Medieval Church as an Economic Firm* (Oxford University Press, 1996). For a recent literature review of the "economics of religion" see Sriya Iyer, 'The New Economic of Religion' (2016) 54(2) Journal of Economic Literature 395–441. For one of the most recent publications in the field, see Rachel M. McCleary and Robert J. Barro, *The Wealth of Religions. The Political Economy of Believing and Belonging* (Princeton University Press, 2019).

Assuming that there is always a good basis for respecting conscience in human rights law (be it individual, collective, or corporate), then the decision to carve out a corporate exemption from general applicable rules should not be discarded *a priori* but, rather, genuinely appraised on a proportional and case-by-case basis. It is, therefore, in light of impartial and analytic criticism that the goal here was only to signal an important extensive interpretation of the "ministerial exception" doctrine at the EU level so as to also include non-conventional religious actors.[107] For that reason, this chapter should be seen as only part of a broader effort to reconstruct developments over the scope and breadth of religious exceptions across different jurisdictions. Having clarified this, it remains only to conclude by considering some judicial developments on FoRB in the private workplace that post-dated *Achbita*.

Belgian level

This section analyses the case follow-up on the Belgian level that brought the *Achbita* saga to a close. A discussion on the impact of *Achbita* on new religious non-discrimination claims recently decided by the CJEU is included in the next section.

Achbita's journey: to the Belgian Supreme Court and back (for re-examination)

Readers will recall that, in deciding *Achbita*, the CJEU found that a corporate policy of neutrality did not amount to direct discrimination against a *hijab*-wearing employee. Following this decision, the Belgian Court of Cassation also dismissed Ms. Achbita's appeal on points of law.[108] This notwithstanding, the Court of Cassation accepted that Ms. Achbita's termination amounted to an "abuse

107 This, in turn, resonates with the EU's broad definition of the "concept of religion" (and not of *what* is religion in an essentialist perspective) as including the "holding of theistic, non-theistic and atheistic beliefs". See Council Directive 2004/83/EC (n 14). For a comment on this "very broad definition", see Marco Ventura, 'The Formula "Freedom of Religion or Belief" in the Laboratory of the European Union' (2020) 23(1) Studia z Prawa Wyznaniowego 7, 36–7.

108 The judgement is only available in Dutch. See *S A & Centrum voor Gelijkheid van Kansen en voor Racismebestrijding t G4S Secure Solutions nv* (2017) *Hof van Cassatie van België* Nr S.12.0062.N. For a full analysis of the case, see Fabienne Kéfer, 'Religion at Work. The Belgian Experience' (2019) 41(1) Hungarian Labour Law E-Journal 41; Frank Cranmer, 'Achbita: The (interim) Domestic Outcome' (Law & Religion UK, 4 December 2017) <https://www.lawandreligionuk.com/2017/12/04/achbita-the-in terim-domestic-outcome/> accessed 8 May 2021; Emmanuelle Bribosia, 'Ruling of the Belgian Court of Cassation (Cour de cassation) in the Achbita Case' (European Network of Legal Experts in Gender Equality and Non-discrimination, 23 October 2017) <https://www.equalitylaw.eu/downloads/ 4465-belgium-ruling-of-the-belgian-court-of-cassation-cour-de-cassation-in-the-achbita-case-pdf-158-kb> accessed 8 May 2021.

of the right to dismiss"[109] and, therefore, to unjustified indirect discrimination "even in the absence of fault and even if the employer's wrongful conduct had been committed unknowingly".[110]

Hence, although the Court upheld the CJEU's decision on the issue of direct discrimination, it annulled the remainder and sent the case back to a different labour court of appeal (the Ghent labour court) for a ruling on the issue of indirect discrimination.

At the appeal stage, the goal was then to formulate a qualification of indirect discrimination that would have been "decisive in determining whether Ms. Achbita was subject to unfair dismissal".[111] On 12 October 2020, the appeal court ruled on the issue.[112] In brief summary, because G4S's policy of neutrality applies to everyone, the court began by considering that such an internal rule could not *prima facie* amount to indirect discrimination on grounds of religion. Further, even if the policy had been shown to concretely disadvantage a category of staff (e.g., all *hijab*-wearing employees), the Court reasoned that indirect discrimination would have been objectively justified by G4S's legitimate aim to present itself neutrally to its customers and investors. Following in the footsteps of the CJEU's decision in *Achbita*, the Court, thus, confirmed that a policy that is systematically adopted to prohibit religious/ideological expressions at work "due to anticipation to customer reactions"[113] categorically trumps a Muslim employee's FoRB rights. Tellingly, if with this decision, the Ghent labour court had a chance to bring insights from equality law to the protection of FoRB at work, it clearly missed it, thus, retaining the same lack of proportionality as the CJEU.

Achbita's alternative journey: new references for preliminary rulings to the CJEU

Before the Ghent labour court's judgement came out, the author had advanced elsewhere some insights into an alternative direction that the Court could have followed in re-examining *Achbita* and which is briefly re-proposed here.[114] In doing so, it is hoped to present a viable option for addressing future cases concerning "neutrality-based companies" vis-à-vis their religious employees. Below is how the arguments break down.

Overall, it might have been preferable if the Ghent labour court had considered a new reference for a preliminary ruling to the CJEU before rendering

109 Bribosia (n 108).
110 ibid.
111 Kéfer (n 108) 53.
112 For an analysis of the case, see Inger Verhelst and Lauren Daniels, 'Can Employers in Belgium Ban the Wearing of a Headscarf?' (Monday, 6 May 2021) <https://www.mondaq.com/employee-rights-labour-relations/1065386/can-employers-in-belgium-ban-the-wearing-of-a-headscarf> accessed 10 May 2021.
113 Steve Peers (n 61).
114 See Matteo Corsalini (n 24) 49–55.

a judgement in the main proceedings.[115] From this angle, the referring court could have begun by noting that the CJEU did not examine the claimant's religious freedom. Consequently, it might have asked the CJEU to clarify whether this was because Directive 2000/78 allows a secular for-profit corporation to determine authoritatively that a philosophy of neutrality is a genuine, legitimate, and justified occupational requirement in view of its secular self-perception and proclaimed mission.

Phrased differently, this new reference for preliminary ruling would have opened the door to fully deliberate the question of whether G4S might be considered an ideologically oriented organisation benefitting from the EU "ministerial exception" under Article 4(2) of Directive 2000/78.[116] Following from this, a second question might have been whether such conscience exemption effectively inhibits the judicial protection of employees or, instead, whether there is a possibility to balance G4S's right to organisational autonomy (freedom *from* religion) against Ms. Achbita's freedom of religion. Having come this far, it might also be worth speculating about what answers the CJEU could have given in this hypothetical scenario.

As to the first question, the CJEU could have begun by examining the scope *ratione personae* of Article 4(2), namely "churches and other public or private organisations". In this analysis, the fact that the defendant is a private limited company cannot affect the applicability of that provision.[117] At the same time, however, Article 4(2) applies exclusively to corporate entities "the ethos of which is based on religion or belief", meaning that the CJEU would have been challenged with the task of describing G4S as an ideologically oriented corporation on objective grounds. Other things being equal, the Court's analysis should have been carried out without making value judgements on the truth or falsity of G4S's subjective and secular beliefs.

In order for the CJEU to do so, a possible solution could have been to appraise the "objectively verifiable existence of a direct link between the occupational

115 The authority of a preliminary ruling does not prevent the national court concerned from making a new reference before giving judgement in the main proceedings (e.g., when the referring court encounters difficulties in understanding or applying the earlier preliminary ruling). See Case C-466/00 *Kaba* [2003] ECR-I2219, para 39. See generally Morten Broberg and Niels Fenger, *Preliminary References to the European Court of Justice* (Oxford University Press 2014) 187–9.

116 In this respect, one author argued that the *Achbita* case does not "exclude the view that freedom of enterprise allows a private company to make neutrality a philosophy in the service of its other workers, who have the right not to have a religion at all". Because the question has not been before the Court, "[f]or more certainty in this regard, the Court must be asked a specific question on this point". See Kéfer (108) 55.

117 In this sense see Case C-68/17, *IR v JQ* [2018] EU:C:2018:696 (stating that "considerations as to the nature and legal form of the entity concerned cannot affect the applicability" of Article 4(2)).

requirement imposed by the employer and the activity concerned".[118] Then, by relying on this "objective link" requirement, the CJEU could have, thus, acknowledged that G4S's "ethos of neutrality" is genuinely linked to the profit-maximisation objectives in question. This would especially be the case given that neutrality, although developed from a simple and unwritten rule, was later adopted as a bylaw to govern G4S's internal affairs. Also, this policy change might be read as meaning that G4S did not want to assert a moral claim against *hijab*-wearing employees per se. Rather, it only aimed at hindering any undue interference with G4S's right to put a "neutral" mark on its commercial activities. It is on these grounds that the CJEU could have ultimately conceded that the requirement of neutrality is legitimately connected to G4S's secular purpose and, therefore, justified according to the company's business autonomy. In other words, if the CJEU were to pursue the judicial path described above, it could have found that G4S *prima facie* qualifies for protection under the EU "ministerial exception".

Be that as it may, it takes no great stretch of the imagination to envisage that, in replying to the question as to whether G4S can authoritatively determine its neutral occupational requirements, the CJEU would have answered in the negative. All things considered, this is because the Court already clarified in *Egenberger* and *IR v JQ* that Article 4(2) requires a certain ethos to be objectively dictated; meaning that it must necessarily comply with the rights derived from EU primary law (i.e., the Treaties and the CRFEU). In sum, through its findings in *Egenberger* and *IR v JQ*, the CJEU could have reiterated how the principle of non-discrimination (Article 21 CFREU) is the ratio of Directive 2000/78. In consequence, G4S's board of directors cannot authoritatively make neutrality an occupational requirement insomuch as it undermines proportionality as established under EU law principles. This is an outcome that, turning now to the second question over the need for a proportionality assessment, would have required the Ghent labour court to include the horizontal effects of Ms. Achbita's right to not be discriminated against on religious grounds in its proportionality assessment.

CJEU level

At the time of writing, the question as to whether the conscience exemption under Article 4(2) of Directive 2000/78/EC also extends to cover secular corporations has not been formally referred to the CJEU yet. Nevertheless, in his 2021 joint opinion on a preliminary ruling request in the new German cases *IX*

118 It will be recalled that the CJEU developed this test in is 2018 church-employment decisions in Case C-414/16, *Vera Egenberger v Evangelisches Werk für Diakonie und Entwicklung e.V.* [2018] EU:C:2018:257 paras 63, 65, 66, 67. See *IR v JQ* (n 117) para 50. These cases have already been discussed in Chapter II, 102–105.

v. WABE e.V and *MH Müller Handels GmbH v. MJ*[119] on the wearing of Islamic headscarves at work, AG Rantos implicitly hinted at this possibility.

As will be shown, the AG initially reaffirmed the controversial idea of an "obligation of neutrality" in private business relationships that had already emerged in *Achbita* and which, as noted, functions in the same way as the "ethos" requirement in church-employment relationships. But perhaps more striking is the fact that, moving from this assumption, the AG took the "neutrality" argument further. When the freedom to conduct business is at stake for a "neutrality-based company", he reasoned, any interference with the counterposed FoRB rights of its employees could not be reviewed by means of a proportionality test. Granted, this line of reasoning is resoundingly reminiscent of the US "ministerial exception" doctrine that, as discussed in Chapter II, categorically bars civil courts from interfering with the internal-governance rights of religious institutions. From this perspective, and as far-fetched as it might sound, the above analogy can lead to the realisation that the AG indirectly "translated"[120] the *religious autonomy* rights under Article 4(2) of Directive 2000/78/EC into a broader EU law principle of secular *business autonomy*. It remains to be seen how this happened in practice.

However, before moving on, the reader is invited to take note that the CJEU finally reached a decision in *WABE* and *Müller* on 15 July 2021, one month after the drafting of this section. For this reason, the paragraphs that follow are largely centred on the opinion of AG Rantos. At any rate, for the sake of completeness, a brief analysis of the new CJEU judgements has been integrated into the text. The latter has been added immediately after a discussion on the AG opinion on which, *inter alia*, the Court heavily relied to implement the rulings that it gave.

The WABE and Müller cases

In *IX v. WABE e.V*, the claimant is a *hijab*-wearing Muslim employee who worked as a special-needs carer at WABE, a non-denominational charitable association running a number of nurseries. From October 2016 to May 2018, Ms. IX was on parental leave and, upon returning to work, was asked to remove her headscarf because it violated the policy of neutrality that WABE had adopted during her absence. Following a series of warnings, Ms. IX was temporarily suspended

119 Joined Cases C-804/18, *IX v WABE e.V* and *C-341/19 MH Müller Handels GmbH v MJ*, [2021] EU:C:2021:144 Opinion of AG Rantos.

120 One author discusses the possibility of "translating" the old idea of the "freedom of the church" into new secular terms to justify the legal protection of "church autonomy" on non-theological grounds. See Richard W. Garnett, 'The Freedom of the Church: (Toward) an Exposition, Translation and Defense' in Micah Schwartzman, Chad Flanders, and Zoë Robinson (eds), *The Rise of Corporate Religious Liberty* (Oxford University Press 2016) 39–63. From this perspective, it is not unreasonable to think that "church autonomy" is not so different from "business autonomy" in that both corporate liberties stem "from the right of association and self-determination of organised institutions *qua* institutions and, thus, regardless of a theological foundation". See Matteo Corsalini (n 24) 40.

because of her insistence to not comply with WABE's internal regulations. The policy at hand integrated specific guidelines (i.e., *Instructions on observing the requirement of neutrality*) prohibiting customer-contact employees from wearing any signs of political, religious, and ideological nature including, among others, Christian crosses, Muslim headscarves, and Jewish skullcaps. The AG opinion recorded that a Christian employee was also required to remove a cross necklace at exactly the that WABE asked Ms. IX to take off her veil.[121]

All that said, the applicant challenged her suspension from work before the *Arbeitsgericht Hamburg* (Hamburg labour court), which, in turn, referred two preliminary questions to the CJEU.

These questions asked, respectively, whether WABE's policy of neutrality constituted direct or indirect discrimination within the meaning of Directive 2000/78/EC. It is noteworthy that, in its second question, the referring court also mentioned indirect discrimination on grounds of gender.

Additionally, this latter question was split in two parts. Part A asked whether indirect discrimination on the grounds of religion and/or gender can be justified by the employer's subjective desire to pursue a policy of neutrality to anticipate the wishes of its potential customers.

Part B of the question asked whether, in light of Article 8 of the Directive, the freedom to conduct a business (Article 16 CFREU) inhibits the applicability of domestic laws that offer greater protection to FoRB in employment than the Directive and, according to which, FoRB restrictions shall be justified:

> [N]ot simply on the basis of an abstract capacity to endanger the neutrality of the employer, but only on the basis of a sufficiently specific risk, in particular of a specifically threatened economic disadvantage for the employer or an affected third party.

All that said, if WABE might be compared with the non-profit kindergarten in *Baby-Loup*, the second case, *H Müller Handels GmbH v. MJ*, draws, instead, a close parallel with the "neutrality-based" for-profit company in *Achbita*.

This latter case concerns a conflict between the German branch of *Müller*, a chain of retail stores, and Ms. MJ, a practicing Muslim who was employed as a sales assistant and cashier since 2002. Upon returning to work after maternity leave in 2014, the applicant started wearing the *hijab* despite her employer's admonition not to wear the headscarf at work. Eventually, in 2016, Ms. MJ was informed that, from that year onward, all *Müller* stores would follow an internal policy forbidding the wearing of conspicuous religious, political, and ideological signs at work. Because the rule aimed to preserve neutrality, as well as avoiding conflicts between employees, she was eventually sent home for non-compliance. In the end, Ms. MJ challenged the applicability of Müller's policy suspension before the *Bundesarbeitsgericht* (the German federal labour court), taking the

121 See Joined Cases *WABE* and *MH* (n 119) para 24.

view that she could rely on her FoRB right as protected under German constitutional law. The German court, in turn, submitted three questions for preliminary ruling to the CJEU.

The first asked whether indirect discrimination resulting from a policy of neutrality can be justified only if that rule forbids the wearing of *all* visible signs of religious, ideological, or political expression and, thus, not only of conspicuous and large-scale symbols. In the case of a negative answer, the Court posed a second question. That is, whether in determining the justifiability of the neutrality policy at hand, FoRB rights as guaranteed under (a) Article 10 of the CFREU and Article 9 of the ECHR as well as (b) more favourable constitutional provisions at the domestic level should be counted in the balancing exercise. In case this question was also answered in the negative, the Court ultimately asked whether national rules of constitutional status on FoRB can "be set aside because of primary EU law, even if primary EU law, such as, for example, Article 16 of the Charter of Fundamental Rights, recognises national laws and practices".[122]

The opinion of AG Rantos and the decision of the CJEU

On 25 February 2021, the newly appointed AG Rantos delivered a joint opinion on the above cases that has been described by critics as "ever more unpalatable than the *Achbita* judgment itself".[123]

In *WABE*, the answer to the first question as to whether a corporate policy of neutrality directly discriminated the applicants was answered in the negative. Following the decision in *Achbita*, the AG confirmed that an internal rule indistinctly covering any ideological expression at work, whether religious or not, does not amount to direct discrimination within the meaning of Article 2(2)(a) of Directive 2000/78/EC.[124] Instead, as regards Part A of the second question (about whether the introduction a policy of neutrality justifies a differential treatment indirectly based on religion or gender), the AG made the preliminary determination that "gender" does not fit into the scope of the Directive. In saying so, he narrowed down the focus of his analysis to indirect discrimination on grounds of religion or belief only.[125] Having clarified this, the AG then decided that, in principle, the prohibition of religious symbols at work is justified as long as it stems from a neutrality policy that is applied in a general and coherent manner to customer-contact employees only.[126] Further, he accepted that an employer's wish to project an image of neutrality constitutes a legitimate

122 ibid para 40(3).

123 Martijn Van Den Brink, 'Preserving Prejudice in the Name of Profit. AG Rantos "Opinion in IX v WABE and MH Müller Handels GmbH"' (*Verfassungblog*, 1 March 2021) <https://verfassungsblog.de/preserving-prejudice-in-the-name-of-profit/> accessed 14 May 2021.

124 Joined Cases *WABE* and *MH* (n 119) paras 50.

125 ibid 59.

126 ibid paras 64–8.

aim which is covered by his/her freedom to conduct a business under Article 16 of the CFREU.[127] In this way, he entirely subscribed to the CJEU's logic in *Achbita* that, while customers' wishes for "no veil next time" do not amount to a legitimate occupational requirement, nevertheless, they do become legitimate whenever they are incorporated into a policy of neutrality or, alternatively, into a rule book for employees (recall WABE's *Instructions on observing the requirement of neutrality*).

At this stage, the AG turned to address the first question in *Müller* and replied that only a "partial" policy of neutrality (that is, one prohibiting only conspicuous signs at work) can be justified. In other words, the AG conceded that an employer can *prima facie* allow employees to wear symbols of religious, political, or ideological affiliation only insomuch as they are "small in scale" and "not noticeable at first glance;"[128] however, no matter how discreet these symbols might be, the AG went further to note that they sometimes "may reveal to an attentive and interested observer the political, philosophical or religious beliefs of a worker".[129] Thus, the AG reasoned, a proportionality analysis balancing an employee's right to manifest religion against his/her employer's freedom to conduct a business in compliance with workplace neutrality rules should always and necessarily be undertaken.[130]

This notwithstanding, the way in which the AG effectively weighed the competing rights at issue was not without its fair share of critics, with some even going so far as to say that the AG took a "schizophrenic" approach to the matter, to say the least.[131] More exactly, major doubts over the coherence and consistency of the AG reasoning related to the fact that he justified the imposition of corporate neutrality on private employees on the grounds of human rights law (Article 16 CFREU) while simultaneously denying the applicability of this same standard to a company's workforce.[132] To expand further on that point, it will be necessary to consider the AG's answers to Part B of the second questions in *WABE* and *Müller*. Both questions concerned whether national constitutional laws offering more favourable protection to FoRB than Directive 2000/78/EC could be taken into account when examining the justifiability of an indirectly discriminatory treatment. Both questions were examined jointly and answered in the negative.

National constitutional laws, the AG explained, "can be applied by the Member States, but in a different context from that of Directive 2000/78",[133] as this piece of EU law should be read only in light of the prohibition against discrimination

127 ibid para 36.
128 ibid para 74.
129 ibid.
130 ibid para 75.
131 In this sense see Martijn van den Brink (n 123).
132 In this sense see ibid.
133 Joined Cases *WABE* and *MH* (n 119) para 88.

under Article 21 CFREU.[134] By the same token, and in reply to Part A of the second question in *Müller*, the AG also denied that FoRB standards of protection under Article 10 of the CFREU and 9 of the ECHR can be brought into a balancing exercise when considering the appropriateness of requiring "neutrality" to employees.[135] In other words, because Directive 2000/78/EC is solely and exclusively about non-discrimination and, unlike Article 10 of the CFREU, does not cover FoRB rights,[136] the argument goes that "there is no need to balance"[137] the employees' religious freedom rights vis-à-vis the freedom to conduct business. Eventually, and in reply to the third question in *Müller*, the AG did not exclude that somehow there might be scope for the applicability of more favourable national provisions on FoRB at the domestic level, provided, however, that the non-discrimination rationale of the Directive is respected.[138]

Although, with his last answer, the AG left room for domestic constitutional laws to complement the non-discrimination objectives of the Directive, this conclusion was, nonetheless, contradictory. When it comes to examining the scope of corporate neutrality, it is, in fact, unclear why more favourable constitutional FoRB provisions can be taken into account at the domestic level, whilst Article 10 of the CFREU and 9 of the ECHR should be totally excluded from the balancing exercise at the CJEU level.[139] All things considered, the impression here is that, from the start, AG Rantos uncritically accepted the narrative that the CJEU set forth in *Achbita* as well as its cursory application of proportionality vis-à-vis corporate neutrality. More than this, one might venture to add that the AG even expanded the breadth of *Achbita* by allowing "neutrality-based companies" to categorically derogate from EU anti-discrimination laws in employment without requiring proportionality in their business choices. Seen in this way, it is the argument of this chapter that, in doing so, the AG de facto crafted an EU "business exemption" that looks no different from the EU "ministerial exception" under Article 4(2) of Directive 2000/78/EC. Based on this analysis, it takes no great stretch of the imagination to envisage that the "business turn" in EU law and religion discussed in this chapter is, seemingly, on an upward trend in the CJEU case law.

In fact, the CJEU recently provided final confirmation of this hypothesis by rendering a final judgement in the *WABE* and *Müller* cases on 15 July 2021.[140] On its face, this decision first echoed *Achbita* and then AG Rantos' opinion. It reiterated that Directive 2000/78EC totally bans employment policies and

134 ibid para 97.
135 ibid 100.
136 ibid 103.
137 ibid 95.
138 ibid 112.
139 In this sense, see also Martijn van den Brink (n 123).
140 Joined Cases C-804/18, *IX v WABE e.V* and *C-341/19 MH Müller Handels GmbH v MJ*, [2021] ECLI:EU:C:2021:594.

practices that directly discriminate the workforce, while, at the same time, it also carves out “a limited space for indirect discrimination”.[141]

The point being that a policy of corporate neutrality that indirectly puts someone at a particular disadvantage compared with others will pass CJEU muster only insomuch as it is “objectively justified by a legitimate aim and the means of achieving that aim are appropriate and necessary”.[142] Other things being equal, if, for the CJEU, the internal neutrality rules at hand did not directly discriminate the applicants,[143] such rules could, nevertheless, survive judicial scrutiny solely and exclusively if they respected the CJEU requirements of legitimacy and proportionality. In any case, once again, the criteria that the Court applied in its balancing exercise proved to be one-sided, thus, confirming the trend of *Achbita* and, more recently, the opinion of AG Rantos.

To see this, it is enough to note the ease with which the Court accepted that any infringement of employees’ FoRB rights could be justified by a company’s stated purpose to present a neutral image to its customers.[144] Beyond that, in the eyes of Court, neutrality in employment served *inter alia* the purpose of preventing “social conflicts” between the workforce.[145] Needless to say, the result of this was that the CJEU tilted the balancing of rights in the defendant companies’ direction, paying little attention (if any) to the applicants’ religious freedom. In doing so, the Court, thus, seemed to confirm that an employer’s freedom to conduct a business could easily trump FoRB rights without conceding the relevance of the latter in the proportionality assessment.

But on top of that, perhaps the most obvious difference from AG Rantos’ opinion is that the CJEU argued in favour of a “total prohibition”[146] of the wearing of any sign of ideological, political, or religious affiliation. What this means, in practice, is that, contrary to what the AG concluded, for the Court, a policy of neutrality could be justified “only if that prohibition covers *all* visible forms of expression of political, philosophical or religious beliefs”,[147] not just those that are small in scale. On closer inspection, this finding does not necessarily have more negative implications for religious freedom in employment. In fact, and as some observed, if a policy prohibiting only large-scale symbols is certainly less restrictive than an all-out prohibition covering all signs; however, it is also true that the former could more easily legitimise a malign intention to directly

141 In this sense, see Andrea Pin, ‘The EU Needs an RFRA: The Leftovers of Religious Freedom in the Case Law of the Court of Justice’ (*Canopy Forum*, 3 August 2021) <https://canopyforum.org/2021/08/03/the-eu-needs-an-rfra-the-leftovers-of-religious-freedom-in-the-case-law-of-the-court-of-justice/> accessed 5 August 2021.

142 Joined Cases (n 140) para 60 and 74.

143 ibid 55.

144 ibid 76.

145 ibid.

146 In this sense, see Andrea Pin (n 141).

147 Joined Cases (n 140) ibid 77 and 78 (emphasis added).

discriminate in disguise.[148] In any case, it remains that the CJEU's endorsement of a "total" policy of neutrality, combined with an approach that de facto cancelled any consideration of FoRB rights at work, seems to imply (in the words of Andrea Pin) that "neutrality does not seem to require balancing, but rather strict adherence" at the EU level.[149]

More than this, the CJEU eventually recalled that the goal of Directive 2000/78/ is only to establish a general framework for equal treatment in employment and occupation. Following from this, the Court reasoned that this piece of EU legislation leaves "a margin of discretion to the Member States, taking into account the diversity of their approaches as regards the place accorded to religion and beliefs within their respective systems".[150] Consequently, the Court concluded that "national provisions protecting the freedom of religion may be taken into account as more favourable provisions, within the meaning of Article 8(1) of that directive, in examining the appropriateness of a difference of treatment indirectly based on religion or belief".[151] On the surface, with this statement, the CJEU basically confirmed what the AG had previously held in his opinion. However, and perhaps more interestingly, this finding also speaks volumes about a "powerful cultural shift"[152] in FoRB litigation that the EU could probably conjure in the future.

In the wake of *WABE* and *Müller*, Andrea Pin has foreseen a pattern in which, while religious employees will increasingly turn to national laws to obtain protection of their rights, employers will, instead, begin to firmly rely on EU law in support of their freedom to conduct business.[153] This seems to suggest that Directive 2000/78/EC, typically known as a bastion for the protection of equality and non-discrimination laws in EU law, is now bound to become a key source for employers and their "neutral" business interests. As strange this might sound, the new strand of CJEU case law analysed above does not seem to exclude that this development is beyond the bounds of possibility. All that remains is to wait and see.

Conclusion

While Part I of this book articulated the intersection between business and religion in terms of the autonomy of churches to organise their own affairs (*business*) and invoke exemptions to protect their self-direction, this chapter has tried to

148 In this sense, see ibid 78; see also Candida Leone, 'Down the Rabbit Hole of Unequal Opportunities: Achbita and the Way Out' (*Transformative Private Law Blog*, 29 March 2021) <https://transformativeprivatelaw.com/down-the-rabbit-hole-of-unequal-opportunities-achbita-and-the-way-out/> accessed 5 August 2021.

149 Andrea Pin (n 141).

150 Joined Cases (n 140) 86.

151 ibid 90.

152 Andrea Pin (n 141).

153 ibid.

offer new insights on this relationship. Above and beyond churches per se, the goal has been to also demonstrate how secular for-profit corporations can claim and benefit from special conscience exemptions to advance their secular mission. It has been argued that, whenever a secular business enjoys as much immunity as churches do under the law, by logical extension, it itself becomes "religious" (legally speaking, at least).

To give a practical example, the implications of this "business turn" in law and religion have been evaluated using a supranational case study: the EU single market. In this context, it has been shown how recent CJEU case law implicitly offered a first extensive interpretation of Article 4(2) of Directive 2000/78/EC, leaving open important questions about whether secular for-profit corporations are also protected by this EU "ministerial exception".

To further strengthen this finding, considerations about how the competitive dynamics unleashed by the pursuit of profit might be justified on normative and, especially, moral grounds have been included in this analysis. In light of this, to the author's thinking, it would be ingenuous to exclude *a priori* the moral perceptions of business entities from the scope of Article 4(2) just because they lack the divine character that is generally attributed to conventional religions. Also, as noted elsewhere, treating for-profit entities as protected subjects under Article 4(2) would allow the CJEU to settle the conflicts between "neutrality-based companies" and their employees on more proportionate grounds.[154] For instance, it would be possible for the CJEU to assess the appropriateness of a corporate policy of neutrality in secular business through the same strict scrutiny test that it already developed and applied to the religious occupational requirements of church employers in *Egenberger* and *IR v JQ*.

Recently, in her "Shadow Opinion" on the *WABE* and *Müller* cases, the former AG Sharpston confirmed that the idea of importing the findings of the CJEU church-employment jurisprudence into an analysis of future disputes in secular employment is not beyond the bounds of possibility.[155]

At any rate, because Sharpston no longer serves as AG to the CJEU[156] (and, more trivially, that general opinions are not legally binding), doubts could be raised about whether the CJEU would follow this strategy. More recently, this was confirmed by the Court itself which, in its decisions in *WABE* and *Müller*, definitely proved to have turned a deaf ear to this proposition.

154 Matteo Corsalini (n 24) 49–55.

155 See Eleonor Sharpston QC, 'Shadow Opinion of Former Advocate-General Sharpston: Headscarves at Work (Cases C-804/18 and C-341/19)' (EU Law Analysis, 23 March 2021) para 260 <http://eulawanalysis.blogspot.com/2021/03/shadow-opinion-of-former-advocate.html> accessed 16 May 2021.

156 AG Sharpston was removed from office due to Brexit and through an internal procedure that she herself challenged on legal grounds. For a discussion see Dimitry Vladimirovich Kochenov and Graham Butler, 'The Illegal Appointment of a New Advocate General and What Can be Done to Uphold the Rule of Law in the EU' (*Verfassungsblog*, 3 September 2020). For criticism see the comments section.

Reference list

Allaux S. I., Christians L. L. and Lesch W. (eds), *Le Nouvel Esprit du Management Interrogations Interdisciplinaires sur la Spiritualite´ en Entreprise* (Presses Universitaires de Louvain, 2018).

Bainbridge S. M., *Corporate Law* (Foundation Press, 2002).

———, 'Director Primacy: The Means and Ends of Corporate Governance' (2002) 97(2) Northwestern University Law Review.

———, *Limited Liability: A Legal and Economic Analysis* (Edward Elgar Publishing, 2016).

Bishop J. D., 'Adam Smith's Invisible Hand Argument' (1995) 14(3) Journal of Business Ethics.

Bordieu P., 'Genesis and Structure of the Religious Field' in Craig Calhoun (ed) *Comparative Social Research. A Research Annual. Religious Institutions* (Jai Press, 1991).

Bribosia E., 'Ruling of the Belgian Court of Cassation (Cour de cassation) in the Achbita Case' (*European Network of Legal Experts in Gender Equality and Non-discrimination*, 23 October 2017).

——— and Rorive I., 'ECJ Headscarf Series (4): The Dark Side of Neutrality' (*Strasbourg Observers*, 14 September 2016).

Broberg M. and Fenger N., *Preliminary References to the European Court of Justice* (OxfordUniversityPress,2014)(DOI:10.1093/oso/9780198843580.001.0001).

Buccola V. S. J., 'Corporate Rights and Organizational Neutrality' (2016) 101(2) Iowa Law Review.

Calabresi G., *The Future of Law and Economics* (Yale University Press, 2016) (DOI: 10.12987/yale/9780300195897.001.0001).

Calhoun C. (ed), *Comparative Social Research. A Research Annual. Religious Institutions* (Jai Press, 1991).

Christians L. L., 'Ideologically Oriented Enterprises Faced with the Reconfiguration of Ethics and Spiritual Management' (2014) 1(3) Brigham Young University Law Review 565–584.

———, 'Le bien-être Spirituel en Management. Approches Juridiques' in Sophie Izoard- Allaux, Louis-Léon Christians and Walter Lesch (eds), *Le Nouvel Esprit du Management Interrogations Interdisciplinaires sur la Spiritualite´ en Entreprise* (Presses Universitaires de Louvain, 2018), 35–46.

Coase R., 'The Nature of The Firm' (1937) 4(16) Economica, 386–405 (DOI: 10.1111/j.1468-0335.1937.tb00002.x).

———, 'The Problem of Social Cost' (1960) 3(1) The Journal of Law and Economics, 1–44.

Corsalini M., 'Religious Freedom Inc: Business, Religion and the Law in the Secular Economy' (2020) 9(1) Oxford Journal of Law and Religion, 28–55 (DOI: 10.1093/ojlr/rwaa008).

Cranmer F., '*Achbita*: The (Interim) Domestic Outcome' (*Law & Religion UK*, 4 December 2017).

Daly E., 'Laïcite in the Private Sphere? French Religious Liberty After the Baby-Loup Affair' (2016) 5(2) Oxford Journal of Law and Religion, 211–229 (DOI: 10.1093/ojlr/rwv065).

Edmans A., *Grow the Pie. How Great Companies Deliver Both Purpose and Profit* (Cambridge University Press, 2020) (DOI: 10.1017/9781108860093).

Ekelund Jr., R. B. and others, *Sacred Trust: The Medieval Church as an Economic Firm* (Oxford University Press, 1996).
Epstein R. A., 'The Nature of the Religious Firm' (2018) 21(1) Journal of Markets & Morality, 141–166.
European Commission, 'Study on Director's Duties and Sustainable Corporate Governance' COMM (2020).
European Corporate Governance Institute, 'Call for Reflection on Sustainable Corporate Governance' <https://ecgi.global/content/call-reflection-sustainable-corporate-governance>.
Fama E. F., 'Agency Problems and the Theory of the Firm' (1980) 88(2) Journal of Political Economy, 288–307.
Fisch J. E. and Solomon S.D., 'The "Value" of a Public Benefit Corporation' (2020) Institute for Law and Economics Research Paper no 20-54, 1–24.
Freeman R. E., *Strategic Management. A Stakeholder Approach* (Boston Pitman, 1984).
Friedman M., 'The Social Responsibility of Business is to Increase its Profits' (*The New York Times*, 13 September 1970).
Garnett R. W., 'The Freedom of the Church: (Toward) An Exposition, Translation and Defense' in Micah Schwartzman, Chad Flanders and Zoë Robinson (eds), *The Rise of Corporate Religious Liberty* (Oxford University Press, 2016), 39–62.
Goodpaster K. E. and Matthews Jr J. B., 'Can a Corporation Have a Conscience?' (*Harvard Business Law Review*, January 1982) <https://hbr.org/1982/01/can-a-corporation-have-a-conscience#>.
Hinings C. R. and Raynard M., 'Organizational Form, Structure and Religious Organizations' in Paul Tracey, Nelson Phillips and Micheal Lounsbury (eds), *Religion and Organization Theory* (Emerald, 2014), 159–186.
Howard E., 'Islamic Headscarves and the CJEU: *Achbita* and *Bougnaoui*' (2017) 24(3) Maastricht Journal of European and Comparative Law, 2–19 (DOI: 10.1177/1023263X17722326).
Hunter-Henin M., 'Living Together in an Age of Religious Diversity: Lessons from Baby Loup and SAS' (2015) 4(1) Oxford Journal of Law and Religion, 94–118 (DOI: 10.1093/ojlr/rwu060).
Iannaccone L. R., 'Introduction to the Economics of Religions' (1998) 36(3) Journal of Economic Literature, 1465–1495.
Iyer S., *The Economics of Religion in India* (Harvard University Press, 2018).
Jensen M. C., 'Value Maximization, Stakeholder Theory, and the Corporate Objective Function' (2001) 14(3) Journal of Applied Corporate Finance, 8–21 (DOI: 10.1111/j.1745-6622.2001.tb00434.x).
——— and Meckling W. H., 'Theory of The Firm: Managerial Behaviour, Agency Costs and Ownership Structure' (1976) 3 Journal of Finance and Economics, 305–360 (DOI: 10.1016/0304-405X(76)90026-X).
Johnson R. H., 'Misguided Morality: Ethics and the Reagan Doctrine' (1988) 103(3) Political Science Quarterly, 509–529.
Jolly Q. C S., 'Islamic Headscarves and the Workplace Reach the CJEU: The Battle for Substantive Equality' (2016) 6(1) European Human Rights Law Review.
Karam A., 'Religion at the United Nations. Challenges or Opportunities?' in Sherrie M. Steiner and James T. Christie (eds), *Religious Soft Diplomacy and the United Nations. Religious Engagement as Loyal Opposition* (Lexington Books, 2021), 21–42.

Kéfer F., 'Religion at Work. The Belgian Experience' (2019) 41(1) Hungarian Labour Law E-Journal, 41–56.
Kochenov D. V. and Butler G., 'The Illegal Appointment of a New Advocate General and What Can be Done to Uphold the Rule of Law in the EU' (*Verfassungsblog*, 3 September 2020).
Kunde J., *Corporate Religion* (Pearson Education, 2000).
Leone C., 'Down the Rabbit Hole of Unequal Opportunities: Achbita and the Way Out' (*Transformative Private Law Blog*, 29 March 2021).
Lerner N., *Religion, Secular Beliefs and Human Rights: 25 Years After the 1981 Declaration* (Brill, 2006).
Luthens E., 'Racial Discrimination or Valid Business Judgments: Employment Discrimination and the Business Judgment Rule' (2017) 20(1) The Journal of Gender, Race & Justice, 381–401.
Mazzucato M., *Mission Economy. A Moonshot Guide to Changing Capitalism* (Allen Lane, 2021).
———, *The Value of Everything. Making and Taking in The Global Economy* (Penguin Books, 2018).
McCleary R. M. and Barro R. J., *The Wealth of Religions. The Political Economy of Believing and Belonging* (Princeton University Press, 2019).
McCrea R., *Religion and the Public Order of The European Union* (Oxford Scholarship Online, 2011) (DOI: 10.1093/acprof:oso/9780199595358.00 1.0001).
McMahon C., 'Morality and the Invisible Hand' (1981) 10(3) Philosophy & Public Affairs, 247–277.
Murray A., 'America's CEOs Seek a New Purpose for the Corporation' (*Fortune*, 19 August 2019).
Oman N. B., *The Dignity of Commerce. Markets and the Moral Foundations of Contract Law* (The University of Chicago Press, 2016).
Organization for Economic Cooperation and Development, *OECD Guidelines for Multinational Enterprises* (OECD Publishing, 2011).
Oslington P. (eds), *Adam Smith as Theologian* (Routledge, 2011).
Ouald C. S., 'Freedom of Religion in Conflict: Siebenhaar v. Germany' (*Strasbourg Observers*, 4 March 2011).
Pace E., *Religion as Communication. God's Talk* (Routledge, 2011).
Pin A., 'The EU Needs an RFRA: The Leftovers of Religious Freedom in the Case Law of the Court of Justice' (*Canopy Forum*, 3 August 2021).
Posner R. A., *Economic Analysis of Law* (Wolters Kluwer, 1986).
——— and McConnell M. W., 'An Economic Approach to Issues of Religious Freedom', 1–60 (1989) 56(1) University of Chicago Law Review.
Robertson D., *The Control of Industry* (James Nisbet and Co, 1923).
Robé J. P., 'The Legal Structure of The Firm' (2011) 1(1) Accounting, Economics and Law: A Convivium, 1–88 (DOI: 10.2202/2152-2820.1001).
Schwartzman M., Flanders C. and Robinson Z. (eds), *The Rise of Corporate Religious Liberty* (Oxford University Press, 2016) (DOI: 10.1093/acprof:oso/978019 0262525.001.0001).
Sharpston QC, 'Shadow Opinion of Former Advocate-General Sharpston: Headscarves at Work (Cases C-804/18 and C-341/19)' (*EU Law Analysis*, 23 March 2021).
Smith A., *An Inquiry into the Nature and Causes of the Wealth of Nations* (University of Chicago Press, 1976).

Smith C. N. and Lenssen G. (eds), *Mainstreaming Corporate Responsibility* (Wiley, 2009).
Steiner S. M. and Christie James T. (eds), *Religious Soft Diplomacy and the United Nations. Religious Engagement as Loyal Opposition* (Lexington Books, 2021).
Stout L. A., 'The Corporation as a Time Machine: Intergenerational Equity, Intergenerational Efficiency, and the Corporate Form' (2015) 38(2) Seattle University Law Review, 685–723.
Supiot A., *The Spirit of Philadelphia. Social Justice vs the Total Market* (Verso, 2012).
Sutcliffe-Braithwaite F., 'Neo-Liberalism and Morality in the Making of Thatcherite Social Policy' (2012) 55(2) The Historical Journal, 497–520.
Temperman J., *Corporate Religious Freedom and the Rights of Others* (Eleven, 2019).
Thatcher M., 'Speech to Conservative Women's Conference' (*Margaret Thatcher Foundation*, 22 May 1988).
Tracey P., Phillips N. and Lounsbury M. (eds), *Religion and Organization Theory* (Emerald, 2014).
Van Den Brink M., 'Preserving Prejudice in the Name of Profit. AG Rantos' Opinion in *IX* v *Wabe* and *MH Müller Handels GmbH*' (*Verfassungblog*, 1 March 2021).
Vermaelen T., 'Maximising Shareholder Value: An Ethical Responsibility?' in N. Craig Smith and Gilbert Lenssen (eds), *Mainstreaming Corporate Responsibility* (Wiley, 2009).
Ventura M., 'The Formula "Freedom of Religion or Belief" in the Laboratory of the European Union' (2020) 23(1) Studia z Prawa Wyznaniowego, 7–53.
———, *Nelle Mani di Dio. La Super-Religione del Mondo che Verrà* (Il Mulino, 2021).
Verhelst I. and Daniels L., 'Can Employers in Belgium Ban the Wearing of a Headscarf?' (*Mondaq*, 6 May 2021).
Vickers L., '*Achbita* and *Bougnaoui*: One Step Forward and Two Steps Back for Religious Diversity in the Workplace' (2017) 8(3) European Labour Law Journal 232–257 (DOI: 10.1177/2031952517724897).
———, 'Direct Discrimination and Indirect Discrimination: Headscarves and the CJEU' (*Oxford Human Rights Hub*, 15 March 2017).
———, *Religious Freedom, Religious Discrimination and the Workplace* (Hart Publishing, 2008) (DOI: 10.5040/9781474203395).
Vischer R. K., *Conscience and the Common Good. Reclaiming the Space Between Person and State* (Cambridge University Press, 2010).
Weiler J. H. H., 'Je Suis Achbita!' (2017) 15(4) International Journal of Constitutional Law, 279–906.
———, 'The Transformation of Europe' (1991) 100(8) The Yale Law Journal, 2403–2483 (DOI: 10.2307/796898).
Williamson O. E., *The Economic Institutions of Capitalism. Firms, Market, Relational Contracting* (The Free Press, 1985).

4 Faith-based companies

Matteo Corsalini

The previous chapter considered a new EU trend that is currently expanding the scope of religious exemptions for churches in employment to make room for business enterprises with a profit-motive and a secular corporate conscience. On the face of it, it might seem odd to speak of corporate entities having a "conscience", as if they were natural persons. Yet, as explained in Chapter I, one type of corporation (the religious institution) does, however, possess a "conscience" that derives from its members' ability to practice religion collectively and freely. Despite the inherent differences in the nature of not-for-profit religious institutions and for-profit corporations,[1] it is maintained, here, that it is not an irrationality to also apply the same "derivative" logic to the latter.

In this regard, it has to be noted that one standard economic view of the business enterprise has, in fact, described it as an aggregate of individuals representing, derivatively, their personal interests, liberties, goals, and, logically, beliefs.[2] A company, in this view, is merely a "fiction" that belies a set of individual and, as noted in Chapter III, contractual relationships among its business participants, with each participant motivated by self-interest. Without belabouring the point, all this is to say that, from the perspective of an "aggregate" theory of the firm, a company might be, in principle, assumed to embody the traits, views, and, therefore, the conscience of its human constituent parts. However, this purely

1 However, it remains that the for-profit/not-for-profit divide is more and more blurring, to say the least. No organisation can avoid making revenues entirely if it wants to survive in business. On this topic, see Henry B. Hansmann, 'The Role of Nonprofit Enterprise' (1980) 89(5) Yale Law Journal 835, 840–1. In any case, there is still a clear difference between the two sectors, and that is about how revenues are allocated. While a for-profit distributes income among its founders and owners, not-for-profit revenues are, instead, retained and recycled back into its social activities (i.e., the so-called "non-distribution constraint" doctrine).

2 See Eric W. Orts, *Business Persons. A Legal Theory of The Firm* (Oxford University Press, 2013) 10–13 (describing this theory as a "bottom-up" approach to the corporation, focusing exclusively on its individual participants rather than on its institutional characteristics). See also Christian List and Philippe Pettit, *Group Agency. The Possibility, Design and Status of Corporate Agents* (Oxford University Press, 2011) (describing a "theory of attitude aggregation", whereby the conscientious decisions of individuals in corporate groups are only attributable to the entity as such) 41–58.

DOI: 10.4324/9781003340829-7

atomistic and economic view of the corporation, in which only individuals are front and centre, is not yet a complete analysis.

A satisfactory explanation of corporate conscience requires an account of companies not just as simple combinations of assets, people, and contractual relationships but also as full-fledged juridical persons that are separate and distinct from their constituent members, stakeholders, and shareholders in particular. This view, in turn, is grounded on the assumption that, in order to encourage more investments in business ventures, the creation of an autonomous entity to insulate shareholders' capital contributions from the management's corporate risks, debts, and liabilities is economically indispensable.[3] Thus, this legal and "institutional" theory of the firm[4] (which is the preferred approach here) introduces a conceptual separation between the corporation (and its governance) from its investors (and their ownership of shares).[5] This is to say that, when it comes to considering what relationships are relevant for a discussion on corporate conscience, one should look to the governing body of the corporation (i.e., the board of directors (BoD)) rather than its investors.[6] It is the former, in fact, that "personifies the corporate entity",[7] as it plays a central role in charting a company's purpose and course of direction through its policies and actions. At any rate, it is also true that, under certain circumstances, even the views of shareholders might count as a source of corporate conscience. This situation will be revisited later in this chapter.

For now, the point to be gleaned is that, when seeking to determine the moral traits of a company, the principle of corporate separateness supplies reasons for focusing primarily on the beliefs and commitments under which its BOD operates. Having come this far, it is now easy to see how this preliminary analysis of corporate conscience resonates with the secularly minded board of G4S, the defendant company whose legal saga was extensively discussed in the previous

3 In corporate law, the limited liability doctrine holds that shareholders cannot be held responsible for the liabilities and torts incurred by the corporation. For a detailed discussion on this topic, see Stephen M. Bainbridge, *Limited Liability: A Legal and Economic Analysis* (Edward Elgar Publishing 2016).

4 This theory is advanced and explained in Eric W. Orts (n 2) 9–20. See also Abraham A. Singer, *The Form of the Firm. A Normative Political Theory of the Corporation* (Oxford University Press 2019) (describing the corporation as a "social phenomenon that exists by virtue of the rules, offices, and resources dedicated to an enterprise distinct from any individual".) 174.

5 For an introduction to corporate separateness and its main corollaries, see Colin Mayer, *Firm Commitment* (Oxford University Press 2013) 182–5. The founding text about the "separation of ownership and control" is Adolf A. Berle and Gardiner C. Means, *The Modern Corporation and Private Property* (Harcourt, Brace & World 1932).

6 In this sense, see Kent Greenfield, *Corporations Are People Too (and They Should Act Like It)* (Yale University Press, 2018) 96–100. See also James D. Nelson, 'The Trouble with Corporate Conscience' (2018) 71(5) Vanderbilt Law Review 1655, 1672–86 (discussing the role and influence of "managerial conscience" in corporate decision-making); Brett H. McDonnel, 'The Liberal Case for Hobby Lobby' (2015) 57(1) Arizona Law Review 777, 795.

7 Stephen M. Bainbridge, 'Director Primacy: The Means and Ends of Corporate Governance'(2002) 97(2) Northwestern University Law Review 547, 560.

chapter. Readers will recall how, motivated by the prospect of maximum profit, G4S's directors adopted a policy of neutrality with an eye to minimise inefficient (so it was felt) social expenditures. The end result was that, from then on, G4S de facto became "secular", harnessing its internal rules to impose its moral (and pecuniary) values onto its employees.

In any event, one need not be entirely negative about corporate conscience and rush to conclude that corporate moral judgement is all about the pursuit of efficiency gains. In fact, there is nothing in the nature of companies that legally obliges them to only maximise profits and shareholder wealth. This is not surprising, as corporate law's great flexibility also allows directors to consider a wide variety of stakeholder and community interests outside of shareholders.[8] What is more interesting for the scope of this discussion is that, in so doing, directors can imbue their corporate policies, statements, and bylaws with moral properties reflecting their socially responsible attitudes and convictions. Such convictions, in turn, might rest on an atheist, agnostic, humanist, or even a religious ethos.[9]

For instance, a corporate actor might draw on his religious belief to formulate policy decisions to then "translate" them into a business and secular language.[10] The Italian entrepreneur Adriano Olivetti (1901–60) is a case in point. Baptised Catholic in 1949, Olivetti's belief was that "human progress should have a religious aspect."[11] As a result, he implemented a corporate mission which implicitly relied on Catholic social teachings to promote employee satisfaction and other non-pecuniary objectives. The results, in terms of workforce productivity, were outstanding, while higher profits followed as a by-product of the company's social performance. Although Olivetti never made any explicit religious commitment within the charter and bylaws of his company, his business model, however, represents only one side of the spectrum of corporate religious

8 The literature describing how corporate law accords directors wide discretion to consider non-shareholder values in decision-making is extensive. For a recent summary about the "shareholders vs stakeholders" debate in Europe and the US, see Martin Petrin, 'Beyond Shareholder Value: Exploring Justifications for a Broader Corporate Purpose' in Elizabeth Pollman and Robert B. Thompson (eds), *Research Handbook of Corporate Purpose and Personhood* (Edward Elgar Publishing, 2021).

9 Lyman PQ Johnson, 'Faith and Faithfulness in Corporate Theory' (2006) 56(1) Catholic University Law Review (discussing the role of religion in corporate law) 1–46. Ronald J. Colombo, 'Religious Conception of Corporate Purpose' (2017) 72(2) Washington and Lee Law Review. 813, 831. More specifically, some US legal scholars have also explored the intersection between Catholic social doctrine and corporate conduct. See Stephen Bainbridge, 'Catholic Social Thought and the Corporation' (2003) UCLA School of Law Research Paper no 03-20 <https://papers.ssrn.com/sol3/papers.cfm?abstract_id=461100> accessed 29 May 2021; Susan J. Stabile, 'A Catholic Vision of the Corporation' (2005) St. John's Legal Studies Research Paper <https://papers.ssrn.com/sol3/papers.cfm?abstract_id=761605> accessed 29 May 2021.

10 This hypothesis is discussed in Lyman PQ Johnson (n 9) 4.

11 Claudia Nasini, 'Adriano Olivetti: A "Socialist" Industrialist in Postwar Italy' in Stefania Lucamante (eds), *Italy and the Bourgeoisie. The Re-Thinking of a Class* (Fairleigh Dickinson University Press 2009) 101, fn 4.

conscience. In fact, other corporate actors might want to chart a corporate mission that, unlike Olivetti's, uses overtly religious language to frame their vision and goals. Companies of this kind typically operate for a profit, but, at the same time, serve faith-based (and social) needs for the benefit of their communities. For this purpose, they might establish a wide array of non-monetary objectives in their corporate mission, such as religious observance, and sacrifice short-term profits to attain these goals. Examples include kosher-/halal-certified restaurants, whose choice not to serve pork and alcohol reflects religious dietary laws, or Islamic banks that forbid charging interest rates to facilitate access to credit and attract socially responsible investors.[12]

But however religiously committed a company might be, it would be ingenuous not to acknowledge that, after all, the relationship between religious conscience and profits is ambivalent and cuts both ways. This should be taken to mean that, while, in principle, religious conscience in business might be a noble exemplar of corporate social responsibility, it can also defy *public* commitments and become a smokescreen for maximising *private* commercial interest. It bears note, in this regard, that, in challenging state social welfare objectives embodied in laws of general applicability, some "faith-based companies"[13] have recently begun to invoke corporate religious freedom in the form of religious exemptions.[14] Once granted, such exemptions could facilitate claimant companies in taking efforts to increase their revenues and competitive advantages by reducing the costs of directing economic resources to social goals.[15] If cases on point

12 In drawing a close analogy between Islamic baking and sustainable finance, S&P Global has recently suggested that Islamic financial products can make a decisive contribution to help address the impact of COVID-19 on companies, banks, and households by compensating them for lost income. See S&P Global Ratings, 'Islamic Finance 2020-2021: COVID-19 Offers an Opportunity for Transformative Developments' available at <https://www.spglobal.com/ratings/en/research/articles/200615-islamic-finance-2020-2021-covid-19-offers-an-opportunity-for-transformative-developments-11533355> accessed 30 May 2021.

13 This term can be traced back to Rex Ahdar, 'Companies as Religious Liberty Claimants' (2016) 5(1) Oxford Journal of Law and Religion 1, 4.

14 This topic is subject of a rapidly expanding body of literature. To cite but a few examples, see Ronald J. Colombo, *The First Amendment and the Business Corporation* (Oxford University Press, 2014); Elizabeth A. Clark and W. Cole Durham, Jr., 'The Emergence of Corporate Religious Freedom' in Malcolm D. Evans, Peter Petkoff, and Julian Rivers (eds), *The Changing Nature of Religious Rights under International Law* (Oxford University Press, 2015) 256–85. See also the collection of essays in Micah Schwartzman, Chad Flanders, and Zoë Robinson (eds), *The Rise of Corporate Religious Liberty* (Oxford University Press 2016). Rex Ahdar (n 13) 1–27; Jeroen Temperman, *Corporate Religious Freedom and the Rights of Others* (Eleven, 2019); Winnifred Fallers Sullivan, *Church State Corporation: Construing Religion in US Law* (The University of Chicago Press 2020).

15 Elizabeth Sepper and James D. Nelson, 'Why Corporate Religious Exemptions Are Not Corporate Social Responsibility' (*Canopy Forum*, 18 May 2021) <https://canopyforum.org/2021/05/18/why-corporate-religious-exemptions-are-not-corporate-social-responsibility/> accessed 31 May 2021 (discussing corporate religious exemptions as a means to promote profit-maximisation and shareholder wealth in US litigation).

are not numerous in Europe, one should then look to the US, where the link between free-market liberalism and, in particular, Christian conservatism is more explicit and straightforward.[16]

Against this background, the goal of this chapter is to explore the US version of that "business turn" in law and religion which, as discussed in Chapter III, is stretching the scope of religious exemptions beyond conventional houses of worship to include for-profit corporations. The first part begins by discussing the USSC decision in *Burwell v Hobby Lobby Stores, Inc.* In this 2014 judgement, the USSC exempted two Christian businesses, with a religious objection to contraceptives, from including birth control coverage within their employee health insurance plan. Despite claims to the contrary,[17] part of the criticism, here, is that, for the first time ever, the USSC allowed corporate religious objectors to externalise the costs of their business (in this case, those arising from supplying contraceptives for free) onto the state or, worse, the employees themselves.[18] Understood this way, US faith-based companies that pursue their own self-interest in the form of corporate freedom *of* religion look no different from European neutrality-based enterprises couching their profit-oriented objectives in terms of corporate freedom *from* religion. In other words, it is the argument of this

16 One reason for this might be the increasing salience of religion in American culture, politics, and capitalism as opposed to the less religious societies that dominate Western Europe in particular. See Pippa Norris and Ronald Inglehart, 'Uneven Secularization in the United States and Western Europe' in Thomas Banchoff (eds), *Democracy and the New Religious Pluralism* (Oxford University Press, 2007) 31–57. On this topic, see also Peter Berger, Gracie Davie, and Effie Fokas, *Religious America, Secular Europe? A Theme and Variation* (Ashgate, 2008). Empirical research about the influence of religion in the business life of American CEOs seems to further confirm this point. See Bradley C. Smith, *Baptizing Business. Evangelical Executives & the Sacred Pursuit of Profits* (Oxford University Press 2020) (collecting interviews with evangelical Christian CEOs describing money-making as a religious duty that is anchored in biblical scriptures). See also the investigative essay Katherine Stewart, *The Powers of Worshippers. Inside The Dangerous Rise of Religious Nationalism* (Bloomsbury Publishing, 2020) (discussing how American Christian nationalists found theological justifications for attacking governmental redistributive programmes and supporting free-markets in the biblical commandment: "Thou shalt not steal") 115–16. For a historical reconstruction of the enmeshment between religion and capitalism in America, see Kevin M. Kruse, *One Nation under God. How Corporate America Invented Christian America* (Basic Books, 2015).

17 Some scholars described the *Hobby Lobby* case as an endorsement of corporate social responsibility by the USSC. See, for example, Holly Fernandez Lynch & Gregory Curfman, 'Bosses in the Bedroom: Religious Employers and the Future of Employer-Sponsored Health Care' in Holly Fernandez Lynch, I. Glenn Cohen, and Elizabeth Sepper (eds), *Law, Religion and Health in the United States* (Cambridge University Press, 2017) 154–69; Lyman Johnson and David Millon, 'Corporate Law after Hobby Lobby' (2014) 70(1) The Business Lawyer 1–31.

18 *Burwell v Hobby Lobby Stores, Inc* 134 S Ct 2751 (2014) 148 (Justices Ginsburg and Kagan, dissenting). See also Frederick Mark Gedicks and Andrew Koppelman, 'Invisible Women: Why an Exemption for Hobby Lobby Would Violate the Establishment Clause' (2014) 67(1) Vanderbilt Law Review En Banc 51–66.

chapter that the USSC decision in *Hobby Lobby* represents the religious counterpart to the CJEU *Achbita* case. All that said, some USSC developments that post-dated *Hobby Lobby* are also considered to then contrast them with relevant case law of the ECtHR in the second part of the chapter.

The United States Supreme Court

Readers will recall how the USSC, in its 2011 decision in *Hosanna-Tabor*, carved out a "ministerial exception" from the Free Exercise and Establishment Clauses of the First Amendment to the US Constitution. This special concession, in turn, gave churches and their affiliated organisations a wide latitude in hiring and firing their religious staff free from anti-discrimination laws.[19] Taken together, it is now widely accepted that *Hosanna-Tabor* provided fuel for a new regime of constitutional religious autonomy rights in US corporate law and religion.[20]

What is more, some scholars went so as far as to entertain the possibility that *Hosanna-Tabor* could have also offered a strong push for accommodating the corporate religious claims of another type of entity: the faith-based company.[21] For others, instead, this reading of *Hosanna-Tabor* was excessively broad and implausible. By its own terms, the argument goes, the ministerial exception applies only to "ministers".[22] Thus, any exemption for entities that, unlike churches, lack a primary religious purpose (such as the for-profit companies in *Hobby Lobby*) would go beyond the boundaries of the USSC's decision in *Hosanna-Tabor*.[23]

19 See Chapter II, 93–95.

20 Some scholars refer to this movement as a "new religious institutionalism". See Gregory P. Magarian, 'The New Religious Institutionalism Meets the Old Establishment Clause' in Micah Schwartzman, Chad Flanders, and Zoë Robinson (n 14) 441–63; Paul Horwitz, 'Defending (Religious) Institutionalism (2013) 99(5) Virginia Law Review 1049–63; Richard Schragger and Micah Schwartzman, 'Against Religious Institutionalism' (2013) 99(5) Virginia Law Review 917–85.

21 Michael W. McConnell, 'Reflections on *Hosanna-Tabor*' (2012) 35(3) Harvard Journal of Law and Public Policy (suggesting that *Hosanna-Tabor* could be a jurisprudential basis for expanding religious exemptions to faith-based employers objecting against health insurance coverage for their workforce, such as Hobby Lobby) 821, 835. For arguments in support of narrow exemptions, see also Zoë Robinson, '*Hosanna-Tabor* after *Hobby Lobby*' in Micah Schwartzman, Chad Flanders, and Zoë Robinson (n 14) 173–91. For critics, see Ira C. Lupu and Robert W. Tuttle, 'Religious Exemptions and the Limited Relevance of Corporate Religious Identity' in ibid 373, 375.

22 In this sense, see B. Jessie Hill, 'Kingdom without End? The Inevitable Expansion of Religious Sovereignty Claims' (2017) 20(4) Lewis & Clark Law Review 1177, 1186; *Hosanna-Tabor Evangelical Lutheran Church & School v. Equal Employment Opportunity Commission*, 132 S. Ct. 694 (2012) ("We express no view on whether the exception bars other types of suits, including actions by employees alleging breach of contract or tortious conduct by their religious employers. There will be time enough to address the applicability of the exception to other circumstances if and when they arise") 21.

23 See Gregory P. Magarian (n 20) (suggesting that a narrow reading of the "ministerial exemption" as limited to the activities of churches and other religious institutions is more plausible and normatively appealing) 458.

Finally, several other circumstances supported a narrow reading of the ministerial exception to exclude the FoRB claims of commercial businesses from its range of protection.

For some, the primary reason was that for-profit entities (including faith-based ones) have no valid claim for exemption under First Amendment law. In their dissent opinion in *Hobby Lobby*, Justices Ginsburg and Kagan explained that any Free Exercise claim that the applicant companies would assert would be completely foreclosed.[24] To see why, one should go back as far as 1990, when the USSC decided one of the most important Free Exercise cases of the twentieth century: *Employment Division v Smith*.[25] In brief summary, *Smith* presented a free-exercise claim by two members of the Native American Church who were fired from the private workplace for consuming peyote (a banned substance in Oregon) for sacramental purposes. Without belabouring the point, the USSC did not favour the applicants. In fact, it rejected the possibility that free-exercise claims entitle faith-based actors to a categorical exemption from provisions that do not explicitly target religion and are, therefore, neutral in scope (like Oregon's drug laws). In a word, with this decision, the USSC restricted the scope of the Free Exercise clause, concluding that neutral laws that are not motivated by an explicit anti-religious animus do not violate the Constitution, despite the possibility that de facto they might have an indirect adverse effect on religion.[26] Seen in this way, *Smith* ushered in a trend that Marc O. De Girolami dubs a "contraction of the constitutional law of religious freedom".[27] Scholarly speculations aside, all this goes to show that, drawing on *Smith*, business entities objecting against healthcare laws of general applicability on conscience grounds (such as those in *Hobby Lobby*) would also be barred from obtaining protection under the Free Exercise Clause.[28]

Others went on further to explain that the religious accommodation of faith-based companies also violates the Establishment Clause. Here, the reason is that exemptions for objecting religious businesses are likely to impose substantial economic costs on third parties: whether employees (such as Hobby Lobby's workforce saddled with out-of-pocket expenses for contraceptives) or society as a whole (read: taxpayers). Understood this way, the argument is that, when a civil authority recognises excessively burdensome religious exemptions, this, in

24 *Hobby Lobby* (Justices Ginsburg and Kagan, dissenting) (n 18) 2790.

25 494 US 872 (1990).

26 In this sense, see Kent Greenfield (n 6) 95.

27 Marc O. De Girolami, 'Constitutional Contraction: Religion and the Roberts Court' (2015) 26(2) Stanford Law & Policy Review 385, 388.

28 *Burwell v Hobby Lobby Stores, Inc* (n 18) 2790. See also Kent Greenfield (n 6) (arguing that under *Smith*, Hobby Lobby had no free exercise claim at all') 96. For a critique of this argument, see Marc O. De Girolami, '"The Bishops" Statement on Religious Freedom and Widespread Misunderstanding of the State of Free Exercise' (Mirror of Justice, 14 April 2012) <https://mirrorofjustice.blogs.com/mirrorofjustice/2012/04/the-bishops-statement-on-religious-freedom-and-widespread-misunderstanding-of-the-state-of-free-exer.html> accessed 3 June 2021 (explaining why the *Smith* rule does not apply to *Hobby Lobby*).

turn, should trigger the constitutional scrutiny under the Establishment Clause because exceptional treatments amount to favouring one religion over another.[29]

For all the reasons above, and perhaps to obviate issues of constitutional nature, the USSC did not decide *Hobby Lobby* under the First Amendment, instead resolving it under the Religious Freedom Restoration Act (RFRA) (this will be discussed more later in this chapter).[30] On its face, this latter provision was passed by Congress as a way to restore pre-*Smith* standards of review that offered more generous protection to free-exercise claims.[31] With that being said, the point here is that *Hobby Lobby* was not framed as a constitutional case but, rather, as a statutory one. In fact, the applicant companies could not, in principle, benefit from a constitutional ministerial exception such as if they were out-and-out ecclesiastical entities. Yet, in *Hobby Lobby*, the unprecedented and expansive interpretation of RFRA rights that the USSC gave to protect the business (and religious) autonomy of faith-based companies virtually resembled a constitutional ministerial exception case. From there, it is but a short step to the claim that *Hobby Lobby* de facto looks like "an expansion of *Hosanna-Tabor* to the context of for-profit corporations".[32] This is discussed below.

Burwell v Hobby Lobby Stores, Inc.: a constitutional law analysis

Having clarified that *Hobby Lobby*'s RFRA claim was statutory and not constitutional in nature, it is true that this sub-section's title ("a constitutional law analysis") might be somewhat misleading. In the author's opinion, however, the heading might help emphasise how RFRA shares many characteristics of what some scholars have called "super-statutes" functioning in a quasi-constitutional manner.[33]

29 Some scholars dub this theory as "third-party harm" doctrine. For arguments in favour, see Frederick Mark Gedicks and Andrew Koppelman (n 18); Micah Schwartzman, Nelson Tebbe, and Richard Schragger, 'The Costs of Conscience' (2018) 106(4) Kentucky Law Journal 782–812. For argument against, see Marc O. De Girolami, 'Free Exercise by Moonlight' (2016) 53(105) San Diego Law Review (arguing that '[t]he third-party-harms theory is implausible as a doctrinal matter')105, 132.

30 42 USC ss 2000bb (1993). In this sense, see Marc O. De Girolami (n 27) (arguing that 'possibly for reasons of constitutional avoidance, the majority in *Hobby Lobby* expressly declined to address the free exercise claims that were raised') 407. See also *Hobby Lobby* (n 18) (arguing that '[l]acking a tenable claim under the Free Exercise Clause, Hobby Lobby and Conestoga rely on RFRA') 2791.

31 For a discussion on the RFRA, see Micah Schwartzman, 'What Did RFRA Restore?' (*Cornerstone Forum*, 30 June 2016) <https://static1.squarespace.com/static/57052f155559869b68a4f0e6/t/5f244d5597df9830c22e3b08/1596214613994/Cornerstone+Forum+_+No.+77+_+Schwartzman+_+What+Did+RFRA+Restore_.docx+%281%29.pdf> accessed 3 June 2021.

32 In this sense, see B. Jessie Hill (n 22) 1185.

33 In this sense, see ibid 1186. For a discussion on 'super-statues', see William N. Eskridge, Jr, and John Ferejohn, 'Super-Statutes' (2001) 50(5) Duke Law Journal 1215, 1216–17.

By design, super-statutes indicate a set of laws capable of (1) trumping ordinary legislation via a balancing act and (2) establishing normative frameworks for advancing new readings of the Constitution.[34] In the wake of *Hobby Lobby*, these readings now also recognise the existence of a "church-like" exemption that commercial businesses enjoy, derivatively, from the constitutional free-exercise rights of the human members holding their offices.[35] However, to see how this exemption was crafted in practice, one must first consider *Hobby Lobby*'s merits, which are discussed below.[36]

Facts

The controversy surrounding *Burwell v Hobby Lobby Stores, Inc.*[37] revolved around objections raised by three[38] family-owned Christian companies regarding compliance with the Patient Protection and Affordable Care Act 2010 (ACA or the so-called "Obamacare").[39] This piece of legislation requires employers with 50 or more employees to provide "minimum essential coverage requirements",[40] amongst which the Health Resources and Services Administration specifically prescribed 20 methods of FDA-approved contraception (including two types of "morning after" pills and intrauterine devices).[41] Failure to comply with this compulsory scheme would make firms liable to a fine of $100 per day for each employee affected.[42] The Department of Health and Human Services (HHS) included an exemption for ecclesiastical employers who were likely to raise religious objections, such as churches and their non-profit offshoots (e.g., religious universities or hospitals) provided that they certified their eligibility for such dispensation.[43] The HHS also clarified that for-profit corporations were not included within this exemption. The primarily economic purpose of businesses is, in fact, considered a secular activity and, consequently, excludes profit-making entities from any "exercise of religion".[44] To state the obvious, this analysis

34 William N. Eskridge, Jr. and John Ferejohn (n 33) 1216–17.
35 In this sense, see Amy J. Sepinwall, 'Corporate Piety and Impropriety. Hobby Lobby's Extension of RFRA Rights to the For-Profit Corporation' (2015) 5(2) Harvard Business Law Review 173, 174.
36 The following sub-sections contain excepts from the author's prior published work in Matteo Corsalini, 'Religious Freedom Inc: Business, Religion and the Law in the Secular Economy' (2020) 9(1) Oxford Journal of Law and Religion 28, 18–21.
37 134 S Ct 2751 (2014).
38 Note here that only two of the cases (*Conestoga* and *Hobby Lobby*) were heard (i.e., granted certiorari) and consolidated into a single action before the USSC.
39 Patient Protection and Affordable Care Act 2010 Public Law III-148, 124 Stat 119.
40 ibid s 1501.
41 *Hobby Lobby* (n 37) 2763.
42 ibid 2762.
43 *Hobby Lobby* (n 37) 2763.
44 For example, see *Newland v Sebelius* 881 F Supp 2d 1287 (D Colo 2012) (No 1:12-cv-01 123-JLK) 1296.

ignores that, alongside companies that follow pure shareholder-value thinking, there are numerous businesses which adhere to non-profit and profit objectives at the same time. Examples include faith-based businesses, such as the family-owned *Conestoga Wood Specialties Corporation*, *Hobby Lobby Stores Inc.*, and *Mardel*, which sued invoking a religious exemption to protect their FoRB rights through RFRA.

Analysis

As noted, the goal of RFRA was to restore higher standards of FoRB protection that existed before the USSC decision in *Smith*.[45] For this purpose, RFRA introduced a two-part scrutiny standard whereby the government might substantially burden a person's exercise of religion only if FoRB restrictions constitute (1) the less restrictive means of (2) serving a compelling government interest. On first glance, what clearly emerges from this statutory language and terminology is the importance of demonstrating that businesses are "persons" under RFRA to rule on cases such as *Hobby Lobby*. Toward that aim, Justice Alito examined the attribution of legal personhood to firms under corporate law and, partly, under the Dictionary Act, which states that, for acts of Congress, "the wor[d] 'person' include[s] corporations, companies, associations, firms, partnerships, societies, and joint stock companies, as well as individuals (...) unless there is something about RFRA context that "indicates otherwise".[46] Having taken the word "person" to also include, by logical extension, the applicant companies, the USSC turned to consider whether the ACA requirement to pay for insurance coverage of contraception substantially burdened their FoRB rights. On this point, Justice Alito, writing for the majority, found evidence of the existence of a burden, stressing how the applicants' objection to contraceptives was based on their conviction that certain drugs and devices covered by the mandate are abortifacients and, consequently, against their Christian principles. Also, and relatedly, Justice Alito heavily relied on the companies' willingness to suffer severe economic consequences for breaching the ACA requirement to highlight how sincere they religious beliefs really were.[47]

At this point, guided by the convictions of the plaintiffs, the USSC had to balance their corporate religious rights under the RFRA compelling interest test.[48] In this regard, the Court admitted that the HHS met *prima facie* the "compelling state interest" standard, as the government had a crucial concern in ensuring that all female employees could access FDA-approved contraceptives for free.[49]

45 In this sense, see Micah Schwartzman (n 31).
46 *Hobby Lobby* (n 37) 2768.
47 ibid 2770; 2775–6.
48 For insights and critics about the USSC's balancing exercise, see Kent Greenawalt, 'Hobby Lobby. Its Flawed Interpretative Technique and Standards of Application' in Micah Schwartzman, Chad Flanders, and Zoë Robinson (n 14) 125–47.
49 *Hobby Lobby* (n 37) 2779.

This notwithstanding, in its eyes, the HHS failed the "less-restrictive means" standard.[50] The Court noted that the Obama Administration had already devised and implemented an exemption for religious non-profit organisations from providing contraceptives.[51] Based on this, the Court then concluded that there was no reason why the same accommodation mechanism could not be extended to for-profit businesses. Regarded in this light, the Court ultimately ruled that the HHS failed to prove why this less restrictive alternative to the mandate of providing contraception was not extended to Hobby Lobby and Conestoga, thus, finding in the latter's favour.[52]

The main thing here is that the USSC virtually elided the distinction between non-profit and for-profit enterprises. With little explanation, the Court held that the profit-making objective itself did not constitute a bar to the corporate exercise of religion. If it is true that, in principle, corporations can follow a religious end in addition to making money, nevertheless, one line of critique is that the USSC would have done better to examine the mixture between profit and religion more carefully. In this way, some criticised how, in assessing whether the burden suffered by the applicant companies counted as "substantial", Justice Alito limited his analysis to a purely economic reasoning (i.e., the applicants' acceptance of fines for non-compliance to the ACA requirement).[53] Commentators voicing this argument seem to suggest that, by quantifying religious burdens primarily in economic terms, the risk is to open the door wider for companies to strategically use religion for avoiding compliance with rules that they consider detrimental to financial performance, regardless of how sincere their religious claims actually are.[54] Be that as it may, the USSC ignored this possibility. Rather, the Court went so far as to recognise, for the first time, the RFRA rights of two family-owned businesses; the logic being that the latter derivatively hold and enjoy the FoRB rights of the shareholder families that own them.

50 ibid 2759.
51 ibid.
52 ibid 2780–83.
53 See Elizabeth Sepper, 'The Risky Business of RFRAs after Hobby Lobby' in Robin Fretwell Wilson (eds), *The Contested Place of Religion in Family Law* (Cambridge University Press, 2018) 27–31 (analysing and criticising the USSC's "penalty approach" to religious burdens). In this sense, see also Frederick Mark Gedicks, '"Substantial" Burdens: How Courts May (and Why They Must) Judge Burdens on Religion under RFRA' (2017) 85(1) The George Washington Law Review (arguing that "the presence of substantial secular costs proves literally nothing about the presence of substantial religious costs") 94, 98.
54 In this sense, some authors discuss how an economically oriented approach to religious burdens de facto converts conscience objections into tax objections, ibid 31; see also ibid 98–104. See also 'Brief of Corporate and Criminal Law Professors as Amici Curiae in Support of Petitioners, *Burwell v Hobby Lobby Stores, Inc.* (No 13-354 and 13-356)' <https://law.wm.edu/news/stories/2014/documents-2014/hobbylobbybrief.pdf> accessed 10 June 2021 (arguing that "If this Court were to accept Hobby Lobby's and Conestoga's arguments, what would prevent a corporation from invoking religion essentially at will in order to obtain exemptions from generally applicable laws and regulations that the corporation finds too costly?") 26–7.

Burwell v Hobby Lobby Stores, Inc.: a corporate law analysis

In matching the applicant companies with their shareholders' religious beliefs, the USSC seemed to have circumvented a basic principle of corporate personality which, as discussed in the introduction to this chapter, introduces a legal separation between a company and its investors. There might, however, be situations in which religious shareholders, such as those in *Hobby Lobby*, are allowed to imbue the corporation with their moral values without violating the principle of corporate separateness. This is discussed below.

Closely held companies as FoRB claimants

As noted, Justice Alito's main argument was that, because RFRA protects "persons" and, in turn, for-profit companies are "persons" under corporate law, the applicant businesses deserved FoRB protection. But, as Kent Greenfield explained, "the fact that corporations are 'persons' should have led to the opposite conclusion".[55]

This would be no surprise because both corporate personality and separateness emphasise a clear-cut distinction between those who *own* shares in a company (i.e., shareholders) and those who *control* its management (i.e., the BOD).[56] This means that, when it comes to matters of corporate conscience, it is the latter that has most authority to determine and adopt corporate policies and mission statements (including religious ones) not the shareholders.[57] Hence, for business claims of corporate religious freedom to have standing under RFRA, as Kent Greenfield explained, they must be connected solely and exclusively to the religious views and commitments that a company's directors have enshrined within the corporate statutes and by-laws.[58] With this in mind, and turning back to *Hobby Lobby*, it has to be noted how both the Hahn family (Conestoga) and the Green family (Hobby Lobby and Mardel) own all shares of the corporation's stock.[59] Applying Greenfield's argument, it would seem that these corporations cannot take on the religious identity of their controlling shareholders precisely because of the "separation of ownership and control" doctrine.[60] As a consequence, neither Hobby Lobby nor Conestoga should be exempted from the ACA's contraceptive mandate. Furthermore, to do otherwise would risk giving unfair competitive advantages to their shareholders vis-à-vis other secular companies in the market.

55 Kent Greenfield (n 6) 97.

56 On this point, see the introduction to this chapter.

57 In this sense, see Brett H. McDonnel (n 6) 795.

58 Kent Greenfield (n 6) 96–100. In support of this contention, an illustrative example might be the case of a company with a clear religious mission statement whose majority shares are then bought, at some point, by atheist shareholders. In such an example, the company will remain formally religious until its new shareholders appoint a more secularly minded board which, in turn, might decide to revoke the religious statements of the former directors. This hypothetical scenario is discussed in ibid 800.

59 *Hobby Lobby* (n 37) 2764–5.

60 In this sense, see also 'Brief of Corporate and Criminal Law Professors' (n 54).

The accommodation of their religious claims would, in fact, enable them to shirk healthcare costs on conscience grounds while, at the same time, benefitting from legal separateness (in the form of limited liability for corporate debts).[61]

In any case, these arguments lost. Importantly, the USSC found in favour of Hobby Lobby and Conestoga because they are "closely held corporations",[62] namely family-owned businesses whose shareholders serve as directors and officers as well. All that said, it bears note that, in closely held companies, the fact that shareholders also sit on the board of directors de facto "vitiates the rationale for separating ownership and control".[63] Understood this way, the USSC reasoned that awarding a religious exemption to closely held companies was in no way equivalent to an idiosyncratic deviation from the principle of corporate separateness.[64] Rather, because both companies have clear religious mission statements[65] and trade products that are closely linked to their family owners' Christian principles,[66] in the Court's view, it was completely reasonable to attribute to the plaintiff companies the beliefs of their shareholders/controllers.

Veil piercing

Based on the above analysis, the end result of *Hobby Lobby* was that, for the Court, the shareholders of the claimant companies had such a strong control over them that they were virtually indistinguishable from their respective corporate entities. In criticising this decision, a group of corporate and criminal law professors submitted an *amicus curiae* brief explaining that *Hobby Lobby* was, instead, an unfair attempt to "reverse veil pierce".[67] That is to say, the USSC de facto lifted the "veil" of corporate separateness that characterises limited liability entities to then allow their shareholders to avail themselves of human rights protection at the expenses of other public interests at stake.

In brief, "reverse veil piercing" is a variation of the corporate law's "alter-ego" doctrine, which, in legal jargon, is better known as "piercing the corporate veil". Under this, a creditor of a shareholder (corporate *outsiders*, such as banks) is allowed to disregard the principles of corporate separateness and limited liability to personally sue the debtor/shareholder for his business debts.[68] Understood in this way, the corporate entity and the debtor/shareholder are virtually indistinguishable.

61 ibid. On the issues arising from the combination of limited liability with corporate religion, see Mark Tushnet, 'Do For-Profit Corporations Have Rights of Religious Conscience' (2013) 99(1) Cornell Law Review Online 70, 80.
62 *Hobby Lobby* (n 37) 2773. The principal hallmarks of closely held corporations are (i) the small number of shareholders and (ii) the absence of a secondary market in which corporate stocks are traded. See Stephen M. Bainbridge, *Corporate Law* (Foundation Press 2002) 485.
63 Stephen M. Bainbridge (n 62) 485.
64 *Hobby Lobby* (n 37) 2768.
65 ibid 2764, 2766.
66 ibid 2768.
67 'Brief of Corporate and Criminal Law Professors' (n 54) 2.
68 This doctrine is explained in Stephen Bainbridge (n 62) 53–75.

At this point, it is easy to see how "reverse piercing" overturns this logic. This time, in fact, it will be a corporate *insider* (e.g., a shareholder) to pierce the corporate veil (in reverse) to satisfy his personal interests (such as claiming FoRB rights) through the medium of the corporation.[69] Despite criticisms, the application of the "reverse veil piercing" doctrine to faith-based companies appears not only to be gaining favour but also to provide a meaningful backstop to corporate religious freedom protection.[70] Of course, certain caveats should apply.

To state the obvious, and if taken seriously by courts, this doctrine must be handled carefully to also give justice to the competing rights of the others (such as those of employees who do not always share the religious perspective of their faith-based employers). More exactly, Stephen Bainbridge pointed out three criteria for a correct and lawful application of "reverse veil piercing" with faith-based companies. The first requirement is to verify the existence of a substantial correspondence between the shareholders' religious beliefs and the manner in which their corporation is operated. The second is to appraise the strength and reasonability of the government's "compelling interest" in not accommodating faith-based companies on religious grounds. Third, and relatedly, it would be necessary to consider whether allowing shareholders to pierce the corporate veil would impose too heavy a burden on third parties.[71]This third prong seems not to have been met in *Hobby Lobby*. Rather, by granting a blanket religious immunity to closely held companies without properly discussing third-party harms, the USSC set a precedent for significantly reducing human rights and equality standards in future faith-based employment disputes. This is discussed below.

Sequel: in the aftermath of *Burwell v Hobby Lobby Stores, Inc.*

The previous section detailed the high-profile *Hobby Lobby* case from both a constitutional and corporate law perspective. All things considered, in the author's opinion, the USSC was correct, as a matter of corporate law, to ascribe to closely held companies the religious attributes of their shareholders/controllers.[72] As noted, in closely held companies, shareholder families have a significant percentage of shares, along with substantial, if not complete, managerial control over the manner in which their companies are operated. In light of this, it would be plausible, in principle, to confer free-exercise rights on closely held businesses as a way to respect the FoRB rights of the physical members who have the most authority

69 For a discussion on this topic, see Gregory S. Crespi, 'The Reverse Pierce Doctrine: Applying Appropriate Standards (1991) 16(1) The Journal of Corporation Law 34–69.

70 For instance, one scholar discussed "reverse veil piercing" in relation to *Hobby Lobby*. See Stephen Bainbridge, 'Using Reverse Veil Piercing to Vindicate the Free Exercise of Incorporated Employers' (2013) 16(3) The Green Bag 235–49.

71 ibid 246.

72 In support of this contention, see Amy J. Sepinwall (n 35) 191–198; Stephen Bainbridge (n 70).

over their governance and identity.[73] In any case, it was from a constitutional law perspective that the USSC's reasoning could seem unconvincing, if not mistaken.

A genuine commitment to proportionality should have led the Court to evaluate not only the costs of the applicants' religious adherence (in the form of penalties for refusing to provide contraceptive coverage) but also the costs that a religious exemption threatens to impose upon the others. That is to say, the USSC could have struck a more careful balance of competing rights to then dismiss corporate exemptions that risk resulting in excessively broad immunities from social welfare's governmental duties and employment anti-discrimination laws.[74] For all these reasons, the dissent and others argue that the extension of religious exemptions to for-profit corporations in *Hobby Lobby* is bound to have "untoward effects"[75] in the near future. This ruling risks not only having negative implications for employment insurance and family law issues (affecting the decision whether and when to bear children),[76] so the dissenting justices predict, but will also risk further extending religious immunities "to corporations of any size, public or private."[77] As a result, corporate religion could become a powerful economic tool to challenge state laws in pursuit of maximum profit and shareholder value.[78] And because some events that post-date *Hobby Lobby* seem to suggest that the universe of institutions eligible for religious exemptions is actually expanding, what follows turns to discuss how the above predictions have come true.

Legal exemptions

In the wake of *Hobby Lobby*, the USSC took up a number of claims involving religious non-profits refusing to distribute birth control, consolidating them under the 2016 case of *Zubik v Burwell*.[79] The protagonists in this case included Bishop David Zubik of the Diocese of Pittsburgh, the Roman Catholic Archbishop of Washington, three Christian schools (East Texas Baptist School, Southern Nazarene University, and Geneva College), one Catholic institute (Little Sisters of the Poor Home for the Aged), and one Catholic network promoting pro-life

73 In support of this contention, see Amy J. Sepinwall (n 35) 191–198; 200; Stephen Bainbridge (n 70); Frank Cranmer, 'Can Secular Non-Natural Persons be Said to Have a 'Conscience'? in John Adenitire (eds), *Religious Beliefs and Conscientious Exemptions in a Liberal State* (Hart, 2019) 231, 242, Rex Ahdar (n 13) 27.

74 In this sense, see Kent Greenawalt (n 48) 146–147; Elizabeth Sepper (n 53) (arguing that "[t]he negative effects of religious exemptions for businesses and institutions will fall particularly hard on religious minorities, who do not frequently share the religious perspective of powerful institutions.") 19.

75 *Hobby Lobby* (Justices Ginsburg and Kagan, dissenting) (n 18) 2797.

76 In this sense, see Elizabeth Sepper (n 53) 19.

77 *Hobby Lobby* (Justices Ginsburg and Kagan, dissenting) (n 18) 2797.

78 Kent Greenfield (n 6) (arguing that the risk of decisions such as *Hobby Lobby* is that they "would elevate constitutional wisdom about shareholder primacy to constitutional doctrine") 94.

79 136 S. Ct. 1557 (2016).

activism (Priests for Life). Against this background, one might now wonder what these subjects have to do with religious exemptions for business corporations. In fact, although *Zubik* considered RFRA claims by non-profits, it did have a crucial role in further expanding the ACA's religious exemption within the for-profit sector. This religious overreaching in business is discussed below.

As already noted, the ACA requires employers and their insurance companies to cover all costs of providing contraceptives in the private workplace. Although the underlying rationale of this provision is to make it easier for employees to access private healthcare services (which are particularly expansive in the US), the ACA, nevertheless, contains an all-out exemption for churches and houses of worship to provide birth control devices. Instead, in order for other religiously affiliated non-profits (schools, hospitals, and the like) to benefit from the same "church exemption", they should notify their health insurance companies of their objections. This is done by filing in and sending a special form, known as "EBSA Form 700", that, after *Hobby Lobby*, can also be submitted by faith-based closely held businesses. In any case, the point here is that this form virtually transfers the responsibility of providing contraceptive coverage to the insurance companies of the objecting institutions without imposing any cost-sharing fee on the latter or involving them in any way.[80] On top of that, after the USSC's decision in *Wheaton College v Burwell*,[81] religious non-profits can assert their objections also by means of a letter addressed to the federal government as an alternative to the special form mentioned above.

At issue in *Zubik* was precisely the fact that, in the eyes of the applicants, even just filling in a form (or putting their objections in writing) would have made them complicit in sinful behaviour.[82] In other words, by notifying their insurance companies of their objections, the applicants believed that they would, thereby, assist them in the provision of contraception— practice that they oppose on conscience grounds.[83] In light of this, they sued, alleging that the self-certification that they were required to deliver under the ACA forced them to offer contraceptive coverage against their will, thus substantially burdening their religious free-exercise under RFRA. On the whole, the federate appeals courts rejected the

80 The text of this form can be found in Robert Pear and Alicia Parlapiano, 'Opting Out of Contraceptive Coverage' (*New York Times*, 12 July 2014) <https://www.nytimes.com/interactive/2014/07/09/us/opting-out-of-contraceptive-coverage.html?_r=0> accessed 10 June 2021.

81 134 SCt 2806.

82 This is what some US scholars call "complicity-based claims". For a discussion on this topic, see Douglas Nejaime and Reva Siegel, 'Conscience Wars: Complicity-Based Conscience Claims in Religion and Politics' (2015) 124(7) Yale Law Journal 2516, 2519.

83 ibid 3. See also 'Brief Amicus Curiae of United States Conference of Catholic Bishops; Institutional Religious Freedom Alliance; World Vision, Inc; Catholic Relief Services; Family Research Council; Association of Catholic Colleges and Universities; Thomas More Society; and the Cardinal Newman Society in support of Petitioners and Supporting Reversal' Nos. 14-1418, 14-1453, 14-1505, 15-35, 15-105, 15-119, & 15-191 <https://www.scotusblog.com/wp-content/uploads/2016/01/Zubik-USCCB-brief.pdf> accessed 10 June 2021, 27.

applicants' arguments, finding that the ACA self-certification requirement did not constitute a substantial burden. Only one court, the Eighth Circuit, ruled in favour of the applicants. And this, in turn, set up a "circuit split"[84] that, ultimately, required the USSC to step in.

In brief summary, instead of addressing the merits of *Zubik*, the USSC vacated all the appeal judgements at the preliminary hearing stage and remanded them to their respective courts. Taking such an approach, the Court instructed the appeal tribunals to give the parties an opportunity to find a middle ground between accommodating the petitioners' religious exercise while, at the same time, ensuring that women covered by petitioners' health plans "receive full and equal health coverage, including contraceptive coverage".[85] In practice, the Court simply directed the parties to seek a compromise solution to advance both religious liberty and reproductive autonomy simultaneously. In so doing, it said nothing about "whether petitioners' religious exercise has been substantially burdened, whether the Government has a compelling interest, or whether the current regulations are the least restrictive means of serving that interest".[86] Ultimately, and months after remand, the government announced that no compromise was found on the possibility of amending the ACA accommodation procedure to resolve the applicants' objections while ensuring contraceptive coverage to their employees.[87] This led to a stalemate, with the risk of taking the substantial burden issue back to the USSC as originally presented in *Zubik*, which was finally resolved in 2017, as will be detailed below.

Exemptions from contraceptive coverage

In picking up on this theme, the Trump administration released two ***interim*** final rules that, in light of *Hobby Lobby* and *Zubik*, now recognise a total exemption for any religious employer, be it a church, a non-profit, or a closely held business, without the need to self-certify any objection.[88] In this way, the new rules (final-

84 In this sense, see Sarah Smith and Nina Martin, '10 Things to Know about the Supreme Court Showdown over Contraception and Religious Freedom' (*Mother Jones*, 22 March 2016) <https://www.motherjones.com/politics/2016/03/10-things-you-need-know-about-supreme-court-contraception-showdown/> accessed 11 June 2021.

85 *Zubik* (n 79) 4.

86 ibid 4–5.

87 See US Department of Labor, Employee Benefit Security Administration, 'FAQs about Affordable Care Act Implementation Part 36' (9 January 2017) <https://www.dol.gov/sites/dolgov/files/EBSA/about-ebsa/our-activities/resource-center/faqs/aca-part-36.pdfZ > accessed 11 June 2021, 4–5.

88 See US Department of the Treasury, Department of Labor; Department of Health and Human Services, 'Religious Exemptions and Accommodations for Coverage of Certain Preventive Services under the Affordable Care Act' (13 October 2017) <https://www.govinfo.gov/content/pkg/FR-2017-10-13/pdf/2017-21851.pdf> accessed 11 June 2021. For a comment on these rules, see Dylan Scott and Sarah Kliff, 'Leaked Regulation: Trump Plans to Roll back Obamacare Birth Control Mandate' (*Vox*, 11 June 2021) <https://www.vox.com/policy-and-politics/2017/5/31/15716778/trump-birth-control-regulation> accessed 11 June 2021.

ised in 2018)[89] put to rest the question of substantial religious burdens stemming from affirmative actions such as filing paperwork in *Zubik*.[90] Clearly, the most immediate consequence of this was that the rules widened religious exemptions also for closely held businesses that, after *Hobby Lobby*, enjoy the same mechanisms of religious accommodation of religious non-profits. What is more, and to complete this picture, the Trump administration extended religious exemptions to also include another type of commercial business: publicly traded companies.

The latter are large-scale corporations that, in principle, are entirely profit-making and have their original shareholder ownership dispersed among many (and sometimes even non-religious) investors trading their shares in financial stock markets.[91] Within publicly traded companies, this class of financial investors is often criticised for its limited dedication to corporate management and its lack of interest in the long-term success of the enterprise (i.e., short-term shareholders). Consequently, if the corporation is deemed incapable of producing immediate profits during their investing lifetime, investors will quickly sell their shares and seize the opportunity of an immediate return on their investment elsewhere.[92] For this reason, it is unlikely that the shareholders of publicly traded companies will look to the corporation as a way of expressing their religious beliefs, being more interested in achieving a profitable return on their investments. Further, dispersed ownership in publicly traded companies determines such a complete separation of ownership and control that, unlike close companies, would make their shareholders implausible candidates for corporate claims of religious freedom.[93] On the flip side, however, it is not unconceivable (although unlikely) that religious shareholders with enough stock to exercise voting rights in a public company could use these powers to elect themselves to the board to then give a religious character to the corporation's governance.[94]

89 See US Department of the Treasury, Department of Labor; Department of Health and Human Services, 'Religious Exemptions and Accommodations for Coverage of Certain Preventive Services under the Affordable Care Act' <https://www.govinfo.gov/content/pkg/FR-2018-11-15/pdf/2018-24512.pdf> accessed 11 June 2021.

90 In this sense, see Elizabeth Sepper (n 53) 24.

91 This is explained in Stephen M. Bainbridge (n 62) 485.

92 This phenomenon is described in a derogatory sense as the modern "financialisation of the real economy". See Mariana Mazzucato, *The Value of Everything. Making and Taking in the Global Economy* (Penguin Books 2018) 161–83.

93 See Nicholas B. Allen, 'Reverse Piercing of the Corporate Veil: A Straightforward Path to Justice' (2011) 83(3) St. John's Law Review (arguing that courts rarely pierce the veil of publicly traded companies, as in the latter, "it is difficult to satisfy the domination element of the alter ego doctrine") 1147, 1151, fn 29. See also Jeroen Temperman (n 14) 59; Rex Adhar (n 13) 27 (arguing that corporate religious freedom claims can be supported only with respect to sole proprietors and closely held companies from which it is possible to distil the conscience of their shareholders).

94 Edward B. Rock and Michael L. Wachter, 'Islands of Conscious Power: Law, Norms, and the Self-Governing Corporation' (2001) 149(6) University of Pennsylvania Law Review (discussing controlling shareholders' voting powers)1619, 1657.

This was precisely one of the arguments behind the logic of the Trump administration's rules.[95] Because America is a country comprised by "a supermajority of religious persons", as the rules read, it is entirely reasonable that some publicly traded companies might have an objection to providing contraception coverage in their health insurance plans.[96] Understood this way, the first rule significantly broadened the definition of an exempt religious employer to include all kinds of business entities, be they closely or publicly held ones. While the second rule did not specifically address religion, it did, however, introduce a broader "moral exemption" for any private organisation with sincerely held objections to providing some or all forms of birth control devices.[97]

One week after the promulgation of the 2017 rules, the state of Pennsylvania sued. In seeking an injunction, it asserted that such rules were procedurally and substantively invalid under the Administrative Procedures Act (APA).[98] Further, and after the Trump administration finalised the rules in November 2018, New Jersey joined the suit. Together, the applicants filed an amended complaint, arguing that the rules were unlawful because the departments responsible for promulgating them lacked statutory authority under either the ACA or RFRA. Further, because the rules were preceded by a document entitled *Interim Final Rules with Request for Comments* instead of *General Notice of Proposed Rulemaking*, they observed, the departments did not comply with the notice and rulemaking process that is required under the ACA.[99] For this reason, they maintained that the rules were not only unlawful but also procedurally defective. Overall, the District Court found in favour of the applicants, thereby issuing an injunction that kept the rules from going into effect and which was, subsequently, upheld by the Third Circuit.

At that point, the federal government appealed, and so did the Little Sisters of the Poor, an international congregation of Roman Catholic women, and other religious non-profits to defend the religious exemption.

On 8 July 2020, the USSC agreed to hear their claims, consolidating them in the case of *Little Sisters of the Poor Saint Peters and Paul Home v Pennsylvania et al.*[100] In brief summary, the USSC reversed and remanded the judgement of the Third Circuit. Writing the majority opinion for the Court, Justice Thomas held that the departments had authority under the ACA to promulgate the religious and moral exemptions. In this way, he explained that the ACA includes language that gives the departments "broad discretion to define preventive care

95 US Department of the Treasury, Department of Labor; Department of Health and Human Services (n 88) section 147.132(a)(1)(i)(D), 47810.

96 ibid; US Department of the Treasury (n 89) section 147.132(a)(1)(i)(D), 57562.

97 US Department of the Treasury (n 88) 4784; 47850; 47861 and 47862. US Department of the Treasury (n 89) section 147.132(a)(1)(i)(E) 57563.

98 5 USC §551 et seq. (1946).

99 *Trump, President of the United States, et al. v. Pennsylvania et al.* F. Supp. 3d 553, 563.

100 140 S. Ct. 2367 (2020) consolidated with: ibid.

and screenings and to create the religious and moral exemptions".[101] At that stage, and having clarified that the ACA provided a legal basis for the exemptions, Justice Thomas found unnecessary to assess whether the rules were authorised by the RFRA.[102] However, he took this occasion to clarify how, in promulgating the rules, the government was right to take into account RFRA in order to guarantee "very broad protection for religious liberty".[103] Finally, the USSC acknowledged that the rules creating the exemptions were also procedurally valid. Although the rules were preceded by a document entitled *Interim Final Rules with Request for Comments* rather that *General Notice of Proposed Rulemaking*, Justice Thomas considered that their formal title did not matter at all.

According to Justice Thomas, this was because "[f]ormal labels aside, the rules contained all of the elements of a notice of proposed rulemaking as required by the APA".[104] Based on this analysis, one could now see how the USSC recognised the lawfulness of a newly defined regulatory environment that, together with RFRA, inflated the powers of exemptions for faith-based entities objecting to the distribution of contraceptives in healthcare, regardless of whether they operate for a profit, are small "mom-and-pop" businesses, or large-scale public companies. Thus, it can be said, as Justice Ginsburg wrote in her dissent, that for the very first time, the USSC totally cast aside countervailing rights and interests "in its zeal to secure religious rights to the *nth* degree."[105] But apart from completely disregarding the for-profit/non-profit divide, what is more is that, with this decision, the USSC also supported a broader "moral exemption" that now extends protection to virtually any potential corporate objector, be it religious or not.

Exemptions from employment discrimination

Much as *Hobby Lobby* and litigation in its wake expanded religious exemptions from providing coverage for contraception, a parallel strand of USSC case law strengthened the statutory defences that faith-based companies can raise against lesbian, gay, bisexual, and transgender (LGBT) discrimination claims. In so doing, the USSC gave them a wide margin to manoeuvre in their employment choices that, to state the obvious, are likely to have longstanding and negative implications for the LGBT community. The case of *Bostock v. Clayton County*,[106] which the USSC consolidated with *Altitude Express Inc. v Zarda*,[107] and *Harris*

101 ibid 2373.
102 ibid 2382.
103 ibid 2383.
104 ibid 2384.
105 *Little Sisters of the Poor Saint Peters and Paul Home v Pennsylvania et al.* (Justice Ginsburg, dissenting) 2400.
106 140 S. Ct. 1731 (2020).
107 883 F.3d 100 (2d Cir. 2018).

Funeral Homes Inc. v. Equal Employment Opportunity Commission,[108] is an illustrative example in this regard.

All three cases were decided by the Court on 15 June 2020 (almost one month before *Little Sisters of the Poor*) and shared a similar factual background: the employers terminated long-time workers after they revealed that they are gay or transgender. More precisely, in *Bostock*, the plaintiff was a child welfare advocate who was fired after his employer, Clayton County (a board of commissioners charged with administering the county government of Georgia) found out about his participation in a gay recreational softball league. The applicant in *Zarda*, a skydiving instructor at Altitude Express in New York, was dismissed upon disclosing his homosexuality to a female customer who later told Zarda's employer. The plaintiff in *Funeral Homes* was dismissed shortly after informing her superiors of her plan to transition from male to female. It was against this background that each applicant filed a lawsuit asserting unlawful sex discrimination under Title VII of the 1964 Civil Rights Act.

On the face of it, in deciding these three cases, the USSC seems to have reached a very progressive outcome. The majority opinion gave a broad interpretation of the word "sex" under the text of Title VII, to then find that the prohibition of sex discrimination under this piece of legislation should be taken to also include homosexual and transgender status. In other words, "sex" should not be read simply in terms of a biological distinction between male and female because, the Court reasoned, "it is impossible to discriminate against a person for being homosexual or transgender without discriminating against that individual based on sex".[109] In light of this, the USSC concluded that sex did play a critical role in the employers' choice to dismiss, which is exactly what Title VII forbids.

All things considered, as Marci A. Hamilton explains, this decision should not be seen as a "shocker", as a broad reading of Title VII had already been embraced by two of the three circuit courts at the lower level.[110] Also, evolutionary interpretations of Title VII aside, *Bostock* is perfectly coherent with a positive narrative about same-sex marriage in US case law ushered in by *Obergefell v. Hodges*,[111] the historic USSC decision affirming the freedom to marry for same-sex couples nationwide.[112] *Bostock* does, however, have a religious exemption-related side on which Hamilton invites reflection. In this sense, she considered how Justice Gorsuch, writing the majority for the Court, took this case as an opportunity to

108 884 F.3d 560 (6th Cir. 2018).
109 ibid 1741.
110 Marci A. Hamilton, 'The Scope of *Bostock v. Clayton County*'s Contribution to LGBTQ Rights Is Not as Broad as You Might Think: Beware the "Super Statute" RFRA' (*Verdict*, 18 June 2020) <https://verdict.justia.com/2020/06/18/the-scope-of-bostock-v-clayton-countys-contribution-to-lgbtq-rights-is-not-as-broad-as-you-might-think> accessed 14 June 2021.
111 135 S. Ct. 2584 (2015).
112 In this sense, see Evan Wolfson, 'Five Years Later, How *Obergefell* Paved the Way for *Bostock* and the DACA Decision' (*Slate*, 24 June 2020) <https://slate.com/news-and-politics/2020/06/obergefell-fifth-anniversary-supreme-court-marriage-equality-daca.html> accessed 14 June 2021.

strengthen claims for religious exemptions by faith-based employers.[113] To understand this, one should look at the end of Gorsuch's opinion, in which he went out of his way to suggest some available defences for employers wishing to fire someone simply for being homosexual or transgender. In this way, he first pointed out the First Amendment's "ministerial exception" for churches and their affiliated non-profits that, as discussed in Chapter II, the USSC further strengthened with its decision in *Our Lady of Guadalupe School v Morrisey-Berru*.[114]

In addition, Justice Gorsuch also mentioned another "escape hatch":[115] RFRA. What bears note here is that Justice Gorsuch recalled how the latter "operates as a kind of super statute",[116] meaning that, however broadly the notion of "sex" has been defined to protect homosexual and transgender people, RFRA can de facto displace "the normal operation of other federal laws", and thereby "supersede Title VII's commands in appropriate cases".[117] Seen from this angle, it becomes clear that *Bostock*, read in light of RFRA, seems to encourage, rather than prevent, discriminatory practices in employment by indicating to religious entities some strategies to sidestep Title VII of the federal Civil Rights Act.[118] But to top it all off, and in the aftermath of *Hobby Lobby*, the door also remains open for commercial businesses to avail themselves of RFRA and, thereby, opt out from Title VII under the guise of their religious scruples. Essentially, this is how (in the words of Marci A. Hamilton) *Hobby Lobby* and its successors "have built a functional and operational establishment"[119] for religious bosses to discriminate at will, be they a church, a non-profit, or a for-profit corporation.

Constitutional exemptions

In the previous sub-sections, it was considered how, with a conservative majority secured,[120] the USSC has progressively expanded statuary exemptions for reli-

113 See Marci A. Hamilton, 'Religious Entities Flex Their Muscles through the Roberts Court, Playing Both Sides of the Discrimination Coin' (*Verdict*, 4 August 2020) <https://verdict.justia.com/2020/08/04/religious-entities-flex-their-muscles-through-the-roberts-court-playing-both-sides-of-the-discrimination-coin> accessed 14 June 2021.

114 See Chapter II, 96–98.

115 In this sense, see ibid.

116 *Bostock v. Clayton County* (n 106) 1754.

117 ibid.

118 In this sense, see Marci A. Hamilton (n 113).

119 ibid.

120 After the death of Justice Scalia in 2016, Donald Trump has been steadfast in appointing conservative justices who would uphold not only religious freedom, but (in the words of Hobby Lobby CEO David Green) "all that have emanated from it". David Green, 'One Judge away from Losing Religious Liberty: Hobby Lobby CEO' (USA Today, 1 September 2016) <https://eu.usatoday.com/story/opinion/2016/09/01/hobby-lobby-religious-freedom-liberty-obamacare-christian-david-green/89597214/> accessed 15 July 2021. For an intriguing discussion about how Donald Trump has strategically cultivated the support of conservative voters through securing conservative appointments to the USSC, see Katherine Stewart (n 16) 169–84.

gious entities whose consciences tell them to not accommodate abortion and LGBTQ+ rights. However, to complete this brief picture of US corporate religious rights, one should note that, after *Hobby Lobby*, the Court began to uphold not only statutory but also constitutional religious exemptions for faith-based companies under the First Amendment's Free Exercise Clause. The USSC decision in *Masterpiece Cakeshop, Ltd. v. Colo. Civil Rights Comm'n* (2018)[121] is a case in point and will be analysed in what follows.

One thing to note before proceeding further is that, before *Hobby Lobby*, the USSC by and large resisted businesses' claims to religious exemptions, whether statutory or constitutional ones.[122] For instance, as early as 1968, the Court declared "patently frivolous" the request for a religious exemption from the 1964 Civil Rights Act by Piggie Park BBQ, a chain of barbecue restaurants in South Carolina refusing to serve African American customers on conscience grounds.[123] More recently, in 2013, the USSC refused to review the appeal of Elane Photography, a wedding photography studio claiming that forcing it to photograph a gay wedding infringed its First Amendment right not to speak and to religious free-exercise. Despite the lower court assumption that even a business entity, in principle, has First Amendment rights, it, nevertheless, denied that the law had interfered with the applicant's constitutional liberties, thereby leading the latter to seek relief before the USSC.[124] While Elane Photography's effort was in vain, things are, however, starting to change. The USSC is, in fact, progressively accommodating corporate religious claims that threaten to become the undoing of this previous case law. It only remains to be seen how this is happening in practice.

Free Exercise exemptions

Similar to Elane Photography, Masterpiece Cakeshop, a bakery in Colorado, asked the USSC for a religious exemption under the First Amendment to refuse service to a gay couple on religious grounds. More exactly, Mr. Jack Phillips, the company's owner, refused to bake a wedding cake for a gay couple's wedding reception. It was his belief that "to create a wedding cake for an event that celebrates something that directly goes against the teachings of the Bible", would have been tantamount to "a personal endorsement and participation in the ceremony and relationship that they were entering into".[125] The couple filed a charge with the Colorado Civil Rights Commission pursuant to the Colorado Anti-Discrimination Act (CADA),[126] which prohibits sexual discrimination, among

121 138 S. Ct. 1719 (2018).
122 In this sense, see Elizabeth Sepper, 'Reports of Accommodation's Death Have Been Greatly Exaggerated' (2014) 128(1) Harvard Law Review 24, 25.
123 *Newman v. Piggie Park Enters., Inc.*, 390 U.S. 400 (1968) 402, fn 5.
124 *Elane Photography v Willock, 309 P.3d 53* (2013), 73.
125 *Masterpiece* (n 121) 1724.
126 CO Rev Stat § 24-34-601 (2016).

other things, in "any place of business engaged in any sales to the public and any place offering services (...) to the public".[127] For this reason, the Commission found it proper to refer the couple's complaint before a state Administrative Law Judge (ALG) that, in turn, determined that Mr. Phillips had violated the CADA. The ALG, thereby, dismissed the baker's First Amendment claim that requiring him to create a wedding cake for a gay couple violated his rights of religious free-exercise and not to speak. As to this latter claim, Mr. Phillips, in fact, believes that using his artistic skills to make an expressive endorsement of gay marriage, "has a significant First Amendment speech component".[128] Be that as it may, the Colorado lower courts also found against the religious baker. The USSC accepted the case and heard the first ever First Amendment claim from a faith-based company,[129] which it, ultimately, reversed.

All things considered, one might argue that finding in favour of Mr. Phillips, a religious objector opposing anti-discrimination laws of general applicability, is all the more surprising given the particularly narrow scope of the constitutional Free Exercise Clause. As already discussed, the USSC's precedent in *Smith* made it clear that a law does not violate the Free Exercise Clause unless it had shown an explicit and discriminatory anti-religious bias. So, for Mr. Phillips to win an exemption under the Free Exercise Clause, he should have proven that the CADA was not neutral but showed elements of a clear and impermissible hostility toward religion. Toward that aim, the USSC's precedent in *Church of the Lukumi Babalu Aye, Inc. v. City of Hialeah*[130] did the trick for him.[131] Briefly put, in *Lukumi*, the USSC found that a city council's ordinances banning religious animal sacrifice were unconstitutional because they specifically targeted the Afro-Caribbean-based religion of Santeria and its religious practices. In practice, as Leslie Kendrick and Micah Schwartzman explained, with this ruling, the Court reiterated a basic constitutional principle prohibiting the government to act on the basis of animosity toward religion.[132]

Returning now to *Masterpiece*, the Court availed itself precisely of this principle in examining the trial bundle of the case to then point out how the records of the Commission's proceeding were muddled by statements that where neither tolerant nor respectful of Mr. Phillips's beliefs.[133] Based on this straightforward application of the *Lukumi* precedent, the USSC held that "the Commission's

127 ibid part 6.
128 *Masterpiece* (n 121) 1721.
129 In this sense, see Leslie Kendrick and Micah Schwartzman, 'The Etiquette of Animus' (2018) 132(1) Harvard Law Review (arguing that: "*Masterpiece* was the first wedding-vendor case taken up by the Supreme Court") 133, 133.
130 508 U.S. 520 (1993).
131 *Masterpiece* (n 121) 1731.
132 Leslie Kendrick and Micah Schwartzman (n 129) 137.
133 *Masterpiece* (n 121) (arguing that "[t]he Commission gave 'every appearance' (...) of adjudicating Phillips' religious objection based on a negative normative 'evaluation of the particular justification' for his objection and the religious grounds for it") 1731.

treatment of Phillips' case violated the State's duty under the First Amendment not to base laws or regulations on hostility to a religion or religious viewpoint".[134] It was on these procedural grounds that the Court ultimately ruled in Mr. Phillips's favour. However, in doing so, the Court focused solely and exclusively on the Commission's statements and personal attacks on Mr. Phillips and, thereby, "largely skirted"[135] the legal question that was at the heart of the matter—to wit, whether closely held companies also have a First Amendment right under the Constitution to not comply with anti-discrimination laws. For this reason, some would say that this decision will provide "almost no guidance for lower courts facing similar cases", being based on a rationale that is too case-specific (i.e., the "hostility" of the Colorado Civil Rights Commission).[136] However, not everyone is buying this argument.

In fact, for others, the "unprecedented carve-outs proposed by Masterpiece" have the potential to cast a wider net for "other businesses that are also arguably engaged in expressive activities, such as culinary arts, interior design and architecture firms, fashion boutiques, beauty salons",[137] and the list goes on. Based on this analysis, it is clear that the USSC has generated some confusion among legal scholars and professionals by not explicitly addressing constitutional questions over the proper relationship between First Amendment rights and corporate religious exemptions. Regardless, it will soon be called upon to clarify this matter, as at the time of writing, other religiously devout bosses are trying to make their way to the Court, with some hoping to establish *Masterpiece* as a precedent in their fight for religious liberty.

Further developments

At the same time the USSC decided *Masterpiece* in 2018, the case of another religious wedding-service provider was pending before the Court: *State v. Arlene's Flowers, Inc.*[138] Ms. Baronelle Stutzman, the owner of Arlene's Flowers, refused to sell flowers to a gay couple for their wedding, telling them that doing so would

134 ibid.

135 in this sense see Raphael A. Friedman, 'Stop Accusing Religious Conservatives of 'Using' Religion' (*Canopy Forum*, 9 June 2021) <https://canopyforum.org/2021/06/09/stop-accusing-religious-conservatives-of-using-religion/> accessed 16 June 2021.

136 Garrett Epps, 'Justice Kennedy's *Masterpiece* Ruling' (*The Atlantic*, 4 June 2018) <https://www.theatlantic.com/ideas/archive/2018/06/the-court-slices-a-narrow-ruling-out-of-masterpiece-cakeshop/561986/> accessed 16 June 2021.

137 'Brief for Lawyers' Committee for Civil Rights Under Law, Asian American Legal Defense and Education Fund, Center for Constitutional Rights, Color of Change, the Leadership Conference on Civil and Human Rights, National Action Network, National Association for the Advancement of Colored People, National Urban League, and Southern Poverty Law Center As Amici Curiae Supporting Respondents'(No. 16-111) <https://lawyerscommittee.org/wp-content/uploads/2017/10/16-111-bsac-Lawyers-Committee-for-Civil-Rights-Under-Law-2.pdf> 29, accessed 16 June 2021.

138 138 S. Ct. 2448 (2018).

violate her religious beliefs. After that, Ms. Stutzman also issued the corporate policy of not arranging flowers for same-sex marriages, even if she would have continued to sell them to same-sex couples.

In brief summary, the Washington Supreme Court rejected Ms. Stutzman's religious freedom constitutional defences, principally grounded on the Free Speech and Free Exercises Clauses of the First Amendment.[139] As a response, Ms. Stutzman asked the USSC to take up her case, filing a petition for a writ of certiorari. Meanwhile, the Court found in favour of Jack Phillips, the Christian baker in *Masterpiece.* As noted, this ruling was made on procedural grounds because the Colorado Civil Rights Commission showed hostility to Mr Phillips's religious belief instead of impartially analysing his claim. On this news, Ms. Stutzman filed a supplemental briefing with the USSC, arguing that, in a similar way to Phillips, her religious views had been treated with hostility by the State of Washington. At that stage, the USSC apparently found significant similarities between *Masterpiece* and *Arlene's Flowers*, as it vacated and remanded the latter to the Washington Supreme Court, with instructions to reconsider it "in light of" Masterpiece Cakeshop.[140]

In the end, the Washington Supreme Court ruled against Ms. Stutzman a second time in June 2019,[141] while the USSC ultimately dismissed the applicant's petition for rehearing on 22 November 2021, thus refusing to entertain further review of this case.[142]

Another dispute that recently relied on *Masterpiece* to reinforce its request for a First Amendment religious exemption from accommodating same-sex couples is *Fulton v. City of Philadelphia*.[143] This was a case in which Catholic Social Services (CSS), a public, faith-based agency affiliated with the Archdiocese of Philadelphia, declined to interview same-sex couples interested in becoming foster parents. The foster care system in the City of Philadelphia ("the City") relies on cooperation with private agencies, including the applicant, to place children in need. However, because CSS holds the belief that marriage is a sacred bond between a man and a woman, it refuses to certify individuals who are cohabitating and unmarried as foster-care parents. By logical extension, this also includes same-sex couples, as CSS does not recognise same-sex marriage and, therefore, views such couples as unmarried. Having become aware of CSS's religious objections, the City informed the applicant that it would no longer refer foster children to it in the future unless CSS agreed to certify same-sex couples. It also clarified that CSS's objection violated a non-discrimination requirement contained in the contractual arrangement between the parties, as well as the City's Fair Practices Ordinance. In response, CSS sued the City, saying that the decision to stop

139 See *State v. Arlene's Flowers, Inc.*, 389 P.3d 543, 550 (Wash. 2017).
140 *State v. Arlene's Flowers* (n 138) 2671–2.
141 *State v. Arlene's Flowers* 441 P.3d 1203 (Wash. 2019).
142 See <https://www.supremecourt.gov/search.aspx?filename=/docket/docketfiles/html/public/19-333.html>.
143 593 U. S. (2021).

placing children with it violated its First Amendment rights to religious freedom and free speech. Further, and as a backup for its claim that the City's anti-discrimination rules were religiously biased, CSS invoked *Lukumi* and *Masterpiece* which, as discussed, inhibit the application of governmental rules that are not neutral but motivated by "ill will towards a specific religious group".[144] This notwithstanding, CSS's complaint was dismissed by the District Court and lost on appeal. The lower courts reasoned that the City's anti-discrimination laws were both of general applicability and did not specifically target the applicant on religious grounds. Thus, the courts held that the City satisfied the neutrality requirement that the USSC set in *Smith*.

However, in an interesting turn of events, on 17 June 2021, the USSC ultimately reversed the decision, siding with the applicant Christian agency. The Court, thus, unanimously ruled that the City's refusal to continue to contract with CSS unless it agreed to certify same-sex couples violated the Free Exercise Clause of the First Amendment. In reaching this conclusion, the Court first considered that the contracts between the City and its agencies typically contain a non-discrimination requirement from which a contractor can only be exempted "at the sole discretion"[145] of the City. From there, it logically deduced that CSS's non-discrimination requirement was far from being neutral and generally applicable. Understood this way, the USSC then found it necessary to subject the City's contractual exemption mechanism to a "rigorous" scrutiny test to verify whether the governmental refusal to offer exceptional treatment to CSS served a compelling state interest.[146] The Court found that the City's asserted reasons did not pass muster because CSS only sought an exemption to work in a manner coherent with its religious convictions; convictions which CSS did not seek to impose on anyone else.[147] Thus, absent a sufficiently "weighty"[148] compelling interest, the USSC then ruled that Philadelphia's decision not to extended exemptions to CSS unfairly burdened its religious free-exercise, therefore, violating the First Amendment.

Needless to say, for critics, this decision was an evident setback for gay rights "and further evidence that religious groups almost always prevail in the current court".[149] More to the point, *Fulton* seems to replace the neutrality test under *Smith* (i.e., a Free Exercise claim cannot trump a valid, neutral, and generally applicable law) with a heightened strict scrutiny test. Under this latter regime, the practical advantage for faith-based entities is that, in a similar manner to

144 See *Fulton v. City of Philadelphia*, 2 F.3d 140 (3d Cir. 2019) 153–4.
145 *Fulton v. City of Philadelphia* (n 143) 7.
146 ibid 13.
147 ibid 15.
148 ibid 14.
149 Adam Liptak, 'Supreme Court Backs Catholic Agency in Case on Gay Rights and Foster Care' (*New York Times*, 17 June 2021) <https://www.nytimes.com/2021/06/17/us/supreme-court-gay-rights-foster-care.html?action=click&module=Top%20Stories&pgtype=Homepage> accessed 17 June 2021.

RFRA, a law that burdens religion would be unconstitutional solely and exclusively if it is "narrowly tailored to meet a compelling interest".[150] However, this should not be taken to mean that *Fulton* overruled *Smith* (there is no passage in the judgement to this effect) or that it opened the door wider to constitutional religious exemptions from LGBTQ+ anti-discrimination laws.[151] In fact, *Fulton* is similar to *Masterpiece* in that it did not explicitly clarify whether faith-based entities are entitled to religious exemptions under the First Amendment, ruling once again, on procedural and case-specific grounds (i.e., the "hostility" toward the applicant).[152] In light of this, a pattern seems to emerge in which the USSC is going out of its way to accommodate faith-based entities and business on very narrow grounds, instead of tackling broader issues of constitutional nature.[153] With that being said, all that remains is to wait for the Court to give a clearer answer as to whether faith-based entities have a First Amendment right to not comply on religious grounds. New *Fulton*-like cases will soon return to the Supreme Court, as Justice Alito predicted in his 77-page concurring opinion, so, apparently there is more happening here.[154]

The European Commission and Court of Human Rights

The previous section considered how the USSC progressively expanded the reach of corporate religious freedom, allowing commercial businesses to demand religious exemptions not only under statutory laws (RFRA) but under the Constitution as well. As to the latter, it was clarified, however, that the Court has not yet established clear standards for constitutional exemption, as the *Masterpiece* and *Fulton* decisions were fairly narrow in scope. But technicalities aside, the upshot of this analysis is that, in the wake of *Hobby Lobby*, the USSC has signalled the start of something new—to wit, a "business turn" in US law and religion in which the Court moved initially to protect the *religious autonomy* of churches and their non-profit offshoots to then recognise the *business autonomy* of commercial enterprises with a corporate vision that mixes profits

150 ibid 13.

151 Mark Joseph Stern, 'John Roberts Just Pulled Off His Greatest Judicial Magic Trick' (*Slate*, 17 June 2021) <https://slate.com/news-and-politics/2021/06/john-roberts-philadelphia-adoption-supreme-court.html> accessed 17 June 2021 (explaining that *Fulton* "does not imperil most LGBTQ non-discrimination laws, which usually lack an exception that would trigger strict scrutiny").

152 In this sense, see Jo Yurcaba, 'Court's Foster Care Ruling Has Experts, Advocates Split on Potential LGBTQ Impact' (*NBC News*, 17 June 2021) <https://www.nbcnews.com/nbc-out/courts-foster-care-ruling-experts-advocates-split-potential-lgbtq-impa-rcna1210> accessed 18 June 2021.

153 ibid.

154 See *Fulton v City of Philadelphia* (Justice Alito, concurring). In this sense, see also Elizabeth Sepper and James D. Nelson, '*Fulton v. Philadelphia*: A Masterpiece of an Opinion?' (*American Constitutional Society*, 18 June 2021) <https://www.acslaw.org/expertforum/fulton-v-philadelphia-a-masterpiece-of-an-opinion/' > accessed 18 June 2021.

and religion. Understood this way, this book has suggested that *Hobby Lobby* and litigation in its wake should be seen as the American and religious counterpart to the European "neutrality-based companies" discussed in Chapter III. In fact, by incorporating free-market principles under FoRB doctrine, American "faith-based" and European "neutrality-based" companies, respectively, invoked their freedom *of* and *from* religion as a means to advance shareholder self-interest above other social concerns within US and EU markets. It is in this sense that these two types of ideological enterprises are diametrically opposed but, nevertheless, complementary expressions of the same legal phenomenon of corporate religious freedom. With this in mind, it is now easy to see how the parallel between the US and the EU single market helps to provide a fuller account of the different variations in which corporate religious freedom is manifested under the law. However, to get a fuller picture, one should also include in this analysis on business religious freedom the position of another European legal order: the Council of Europe (CoE)

On the whole, the question of whether enterprises that are based on a religious or philosophical belief (and, at the same time, are *entirely* profit-making) can claim FoRB rights under Article 9 of the ECHR "is not yet completely clear"[155] at this level of jurisdiction. This notwithstanding, first the ECommHR and now the ECtHR have developed an approach that, unlike the USSC, seems to view the relationship between profit and religion with suspicion. This is because, in the eyes of the Strasbourg judges, the basic assumption is that "an individual establishes a profit-making corporation for the purpose of making profit and not with the goal to further a religious objective".[156] Furthermore, this attitude of "Strasbourg" is at odds with the EU "competitive approach" to FoRB that, as discussed in Chapters I and II, accommodates religion precisely when it satisfies the economic and commercial goals of the EU single market.[157] All told, "Strasbourg" case law on this subject is still in its infancy and, therefore, quite scarce. In light of this, what follows concludes this chapter by giving an overview of the state-of-the-art of this jurisprudence, looking forward for future developments.

The European Commission of Human Rights

As discussed in Chapter I, the refusal to grant FoRB rights to churches and their non-profit offshoots was the prevailing trend in the ECommHR's jurisprudence until the late 1970s. Religious freedom is by its own nature a human right that only applies to *physical* persons, the Commission reasoned, meaning that this

155 See Council of Europe/European Court of Human Rights, 'Guide on Article 9 of the European Convention on Human Rights' 1, 9 (31 August 2020) <https://www.echr.coe.int/Documents/Guide_Art_9_ENG.pdf> accessed 24 June 2021.

156 In this sense, see Ioana Cismas and Stacy Cammarano, 'Whose Right and Who's Right? The US Supreme Court v. the European Court of Human Rights on Corporate Exercise of Religion' (2016) 34(1) Boston University International Law Journal 1, 10.

157 See Chapter I, 37–39; Chapter II, 31–33.

right is not susceptible to being exercised by *legal* persons such as churches and other institutional entities. Consistent with this train of thought, it is, therefore, hardly surprising that the ECommHR initially denied the applicability of corporate religious freedom even to for-profit corporations. Because the Commission had the opportunity to discuss the relationship between FoRB and profit on two occasions in the late 1970s, it is with this case law that this section begins.

Case law (late 1970s)

In the first case, *Company X v Switzerland*[158] (1979), the applicant was a limited liability enterprise running a printing office in the Canton of Zürich. Company X complained that the Swiss federal authorities violated its freedom *from* religion under Article 9 of the ECHR, in that the former forced it to pay ecclesiastical taxes intended for the Catholic and Protestant cantonal state churches. In a brief opinion, the ECommHR summarily rejected the applicant's claim. It held that:

> Even supposing that the applicant's claim may fall within the ambit of Article 9 of the Convention, the Commission is nevertheless of the opinion that a limited liability company given the fact that it concerns a profit-making corporate body, can neither enjoy nor rely on the rights referred to in Article 9, paragraphe [sic] 1, of the Convention.[159]

Given the succinctness of this finding, the ECommHR appeared to leave open some basic questions. Was the profit-seeking character of the applicant the sole and only justification for denying it protection under Article 9 of the ECHR? Or was it also because of its juridical and "artificial" nature that the appeal was rejected? A few months later, the ECommHR confirmed the first of the two hypotheses in its decision in *X and Church of Scientology v. Sweden*.[160]

Readers will recall from Chapter I that, in this case, the ECommHR was challenged with the question of whether Article 9 of the ECHR also covers statements of religious belief appearing in marketing and promotional strategies.[161] More exactly, the Swedish Church of Scientology objected to an administrative injunction requiring it to amend some commercial advertisements for being misleading. In fact, in the eyes of the government, such advertisements contained religious references precisely to leverage the faith of potential consumers in a bid to persuade them to buy so-called "E-Meters", religious tools used in Scientology "liturgical" practices. Overall, in taking up this case, the ECommHR reversed its denial of FoRB rights for corporate entities that characterised its earlier case law. As a preliminary matter, it considered that "a church body is capable of pos-

158 App no 7865/77 (ECommHR, 27 February 1979).
159 ibid 87.
160 App no 7805/77 (ECommHR, 17 December 1979) 16 DR 68.
161 See Chapter I, 28–30.

sessing and exercising the rights contained in Article 9(1) in its own capacity as a representative of its members".[162] This means that, other things being equal, "the Church of Scientology, as a non-governmental organisation, can properly be considered to be an applicant within the meaning of Article 25 (1) of the Convention".[163] This notwithstanding, the ECommHR also clarified that religious freedom under the ECHR "does not confer protection on statements of purported religious belief which appear as selling 'arguments' in advertisements of a purely commercial nature by a religious group".[164] It was on these grounds that it confirmed. once again. that for-profit entities are barred from the scope of FoRB protection under the Convention.

Case law (late 1990s)

The ECommHR again considered the link between profit and FoRB in 1997, while deciding the case of *Kustannus Oy Vapaa Ajattelija AB et al. v. Finland.*[165]

This case is similar to *Company X v Switzerland* in that it involved a limited liability company, Publishing Company Freethinker Ltd., once again challenging an ecclesiastical tax regime. Overall, this company claimed to be secular in nature and to have among its objectives the propagation of the doctrine for church–state separation in Finland. Toward that aim, Freethinkers Ltd. publishes and sells books to raise awareness on this topic. However, despite the earning that it made, the company contended that it did not "aim at producing profit"[166] (outside the need to generate an operating surplus to support costly activities), as its mission was solely and exclusively focused on the propagation of secular ideas. All told, it was against this background that Freethinkers Ltd. filed an application before the ECommHR, claiming that its compelled performance of an obligation to pay a church tax violated its freedom *from* religion under Article 9 of the ECHR. Two other applicants, Freethinkers Association and one Finnish citizen joined the suit. In brief summary, the ECommHR rejected the applicant company's claim. It ruled that Freethinkers Ltd. could "not enjoy nor rely" on Article 9 of the ECHR because of its inherently commercial nature, regardless of how modest its economic activities actually were.[167] This all came, however, with a caveat: the ECommHR conceded that:

> The general right to freedom of religion includes, *inter alia*, freedom to manifest a religion or "belief" either alone or "in community with others" whether in public or in private. *The Commission would therefore not exclude*

162 *X and Church of Scientology v. Sweden* (n 160) 70.
163 ibid.
164 ibid 72.
165 App no 20471/92 (ECommHR, 15 April 1996).
166 ibid 39.
167 ibid 44.

> *that the applicant association is in principle capable of possessing and exercising rights under Article 9 para. 1.*[168]

This notwithstanding, the Commission went on to consider that the applicant incorporated as a private limited liability entity, and because of the financial benefits that Freethinkers Ltd. derived from this legal form, it was, in principle, "required by domestic law to pay tax as any other corporate body, regardless of the underlying purpose of its activities".[169] This taxation regime, in turn, might also include church tithes when governments so decide.[170] Following from this, the Commission then refused to consider the FoRB rights of the natural persons behind the corporate entity (or, as one would say in legal jargon, it did not "pierce the corporate veil" in favour of the company's owners). Thus, while in the end, the ECommHR recognised that there is not an innate incompatibility between profits and FoRB, nevertheless, it established that commercial business cannot invoke their religious (or non-religious) rights to challenge the levying of corporate taxes.

The European Court of Human Rights

The previous section considered how the ECommHR has progressively conceded that, in some circumstances, even for-profit entities can plead Article 9 of the ECHR (although it rejected all the cases brought to its attention on taxation issues). Shortly after the ECommHR's ruling in *Kustannus*, the ECtHR also had the opportunity to further clarify the conditions under which business entities might rely on religious freedom protection under Article 9 of the ECHR. This is discussed below.

Case law (early 2000s)

On 27 June 2000, the ECtHR decided *Cha'are Shalom Ve Tsedek v France*.[171] In this case, the Court was challenged with the question of whether a corporate entity that has some (but not exclusive) commercial purposes is eligible for protection under Article 9 of the ECHR.

The dispute arose from the claim by *Cha'are Shalom Ve Tsedek* (an ultra-orthodox Jewish association) that French authorities violated its Article 9 ECHR right. More exactly, the applicant objected to the governmental refusal to grant it access to slaughterhouses with a view to performing religious animal slaughter in the strictest Jewish orthodoxy and for business purposes as well. This ritual, in fact,

168 ibid 43 (emphasis added).
169 ibid.
170 In this sense, see Ioana Cismas, *Religious Actors and International Law* (Oxford University Press 2014) 103.
171 App no 27417/95 (ECtHR, 27 June 2000).

has inherent commercial implications since *Cha'are Shalom* performs it to make *kosher* meat available for sale in the butcher shops of its members. For this reason, the applicant association also employs *kashrut* inspectors to verify the compliance of its meat with Jewish religious dietary requirements. More than this, and as a consequence of the legal restrictions on *halal* slaughtering rites in France, *Cha'are Shalom* engages in commercial imports of meat stocks from Belgium.[172]

All that said, in deciding this case, the ECtHR emphasised as a preliminary remark that *Cha'are Shalom* set itself up as a liturgical association. Following from this, it then went on to consider that "ritual slaughter, as indeed its name indicates, constitutes a rite (…) whose purpose is to provide Jews with meat from animals slaughtered in accordance with religious prescriptions".[173] In light of this, the Court did not find unreasonable the applicant's claim that ritual slaughter was an essential aspect of practice of the Jewish religion, regardless of its commercial implications. And because of this, it ultimately found in favour of *Cha'are Shalom*, recognising, for the first time ever, that a corporate entity that is not entirely profit-making but also pursues purely religious objectives, such as the applicant, deserves FoRB protection under the ECHR. In conclusion, and in the words of Jeroen Temperman, "[t]his is the nearest the Court has come to embracing corporate religious freedom"[174] for commercial businesses so far.

Case law (early 2022—Lee v the United Kingdom)

If the ECtHR has not yet decided whether corporate entities that are *entirely* profit-making (e.g., US-style closely held corporations) are eligible under Article 9 of the ECHR, this is confirmed by the fact that in January 2022, the Court missed another opportunity to do so. To understand why, it is necessary to travel back to March 2020 when the First Section of the ECtHR notified the British Government that an application against it had been lodged with the Court (i.e., "communication procedure")[175] under the heading of *Lee v the United Kingdom.*[176]

The case was brought by Mr. Gareth Lee, a gay rights activist who volunteers for QueerSpace (a LGBTQ+ organisation in Belfast) that, in 2014, placed an order for a cake from Ashers Baking Company Limited with the words "Support Gay Marriage" on it. Ashers's bakery provides a "Build-a-Cake" service, whereby a cake could be iced with a personalised graphic of the customer's choice. Although there are no limitations on the cake graphics available (or, at least, so according to an Ashers promotional flyer), Mr. Lee later received a telephone call

172 ibid 33.
173 ibid 73.
174 Jeroen Temperman (n 14) 26.
175 For an introduction to this procedure see Council of Europe/European Court of Human Rights, 'Rules of Court' (2021) 29–30 <https://www.echr.coe.int/documents/rules_court_eng.pdf> accessed 26 June 2021.
176 App no 18860/19 (First Section, 23 March 2020).

from the bakery indicating that his order could not be fulfilled. The reason given was that Ashers is a Christian business and, on that basis, should not have taken Mr. Lee's order.

At this point, it is not difficult to see that *Lee v the United Kingdom* represents the European counterpart to the US decision in *Masterpiece*. The most striking difference being that, while *Masterpiece* was about a company's refusal to create a cake to celebrate same-sex marriages (whatever its design), the bakers in *Lee* instead had no objections to crafting sweets for LGBTQ+ couples, provided, however, that they were not forced to decorate them with slogans conflicting with their Christian beliefs.[177]

Lady Hale, who gave the judgement in the UK Supreme Court (UKSC), zeroed in on this critical comparison to clarify that the McArthurs' objection "was to the message, not to the messenger".[178] Understood this way, she then rejected the preposition that the McArthurs' refusal to bake a cake amounted to direct discrimination because, in her view, the caption "Support Gay Marriage" was "indissociable" from Mr. Lee's sexual orientation. Because people of any sexual orientation, be they gay, straight, or bisexual, can stand for same-sex unions as much as oppose them, the UKSC reasoned, the formula "Support Gay Marriage" is not "an exact proxy for any particular sexual orientation".[179] For this reason, the UKSC held that Mr. Lee was not discriminated against because of his sex.[180] More than this, Lady Hale went further to consider whether the bakery discriminated on the grounds of Mr. Lee's political opinion. For the Court, there was, in fact, no doubt that the wording "Support Gay Marriage" also had an inherent political connotation. Be that as it may, the UKSC answered this question in the same way as it answered the previous one, namely that the McArthurs' objection was directed neither at Mr. Lee nor at his political views but at the cake's message alone: a message with which the McArthurs deeply disagree because of their faith. For this reason, the Court concluded that no discrimination on the grounds of political opinion occurred either.[181]

On the face of it, the dispute in *Lee* involved "entirely trivial matters",[182] quantifiable in terms of a cake worth approximately 30£. However, on closer inspection, this case is, nonetheless, interesting in its own way and deserves further attention. For one thing, *Lee*, in fact, conceals deeper ideological clashes between conservative and liberal society actors who more frequently fight their "culture

177 In this sense see René Reyes, 'Masterpiece Cakeshop and Ashers Baking Company: A Comparative Analysis of Constitutional Confections' (2020) 16(1) Stanford Journal of Civil Rights & Civil Liberties 113, 135.

178 *Lee v Ashers Baking Company Ltd [*2018] UKSC 49, 22.

179 ibid 25.

180 ibid 35.

181 iid 47.

182 Rex Ahdar and Jessica Jiles, 'The Supreme Courts' Icing on the Trans-Atlantic Cakes' (2020) 9(1) Oxford Journal of Law and Religion 1, 11.

wars" (*kulturkampf*) in courtrooms to seek publicity for their political causes.[183] For another, and more relevant to the scope of this discussion, for the first time ever, *Lee* transposed questions about the corporate religious rights of for-profit companies to the ECtHR level. These are questions which, as already discussed, have been obsessing American scholars since *Hobby Lobby* and, more recently, *Masterpiece*.

This notwithstanding, Lady Hale chose not to explore further the issue of whether Ashers Baking Company Limited *qua* a corporate legal entity should enjoy FoRB rights in its own terms under the Convention. In fact, she found the matter completely irrelevant because, in her view, holding Ashers Baking Company Ltd not liable was tantamount to upholding the rights of its physical owners, the McArthurs.[184]

The ball was then passed to the Strasbourg Court which, on 6 January 2022, was expected *inter alia* to elaborate more on the relationship between the corporate personality of the defendant company and Article 9 of the ECHR. Expectations have, however, been disappointed, as the Court hastily declared the case inadmissible for failure to exhaust domestic remedies under Article 35 of the ECHR. As a rule of thumb, this latter provision sets out that, for an application to be declared admissible by the Court, applicants must have first raised (explicitly or in substance) all their ECHR-based arguments before national tribunals. In the case at hand, however, the Court noted that Mr. Lee "did not invoke his Convention rights expressly at any point in the domestic proceedings"[185] because his submissions at the national level relied in substance only on British anti-discrimination law. In conclusion, and borrowing from Mark Hill QC, the key practical point to take from this case is that "if there are human rights arguments, they should be taken openly and expressly before the domestic courts".[186] Hence the Court's silence on questions concerning the cloaking of commercial businesses with Convention rights generally, and FoRB in particular in *Lee*.

Conclusion

While in Chapter III, this book explored the emergence of what has been dubbed a new "business turn" in EU law and religion, this chapter has considered the American counterpart to this trend. Starting from an analysis of the high-profile decision in *Hobby Lobby*, it considered how the USSC began to extend religious exemptions beyond conventional houses-of-worship contexts to include secular for-profit corporations run by conservative Christian CEOs. Although European

183 In this sense see ibid 11.
184 *Lee* (n 178) 57.
185 *Lee v the United Kingdom*, App no 18860/19 (ECtHR, 6 January 2022).
186 Mark Hill QC, 'The Great Strasbourg Bake Off' (*Law & Religion UK*, 6 January 2022) <https://lawandreligionuk.com/2022/01/06/the-great-strasbourg-bake-off/> accessed 8 January 2022.

readers (who are generally not accustomed to such an explicit relationship between free-market liberalism and Christian conservatism) may consider *Hobby Lobby* a far-fetched and isolated case, litigation in its wake has demonstrated that quite the opposite is true. In fact, under the Trump administration, the USSC further strengthened statutory exemption mechanisms for both closely held and publicly traded businesses, whose negative effects will hit female employees looking for contraceptive coverage particularly hard. More than this, and outside the specific context of healthcare, it has been shown how the Court is also crafting new exemptions under the Constitution, empowering faith-based employers to refuse services to same-sex couples and make discriminatory employment decisions on religious grounds.

All that said, this chapter has turned to contrast this American extensive regime of religious exemptions for businesses with relevant case law of the ECommHR and ECtHR on the matter. The results of this comparison have shown that the USSC and "Strasbourg" approaches are oppositional to one another, their major disagreement being about matters of corporate form. Overall, the USSC adopted an extensive view of religious exercise that sidestepped the distinction between religious non-profits and for-profits, churches and commercial businesses, thus disregarding how the latter have self-interested (and sometimes even religiously insincere) objectives. On the contrary, the "Strasbourg" courts took a more cautious approach that established stricter parameters for what kind of corporations can exercise religion. In this way, the ECommHR rejected virtually every business religious freedom brought to its attention by limited liability companies (treating with particular suspicion their objections to the levying of taxes on conscience grounds). Instead, the ECtHR has, so far, only recognised the FoRB claims of religious institutions that carry out commercial activities but do not have exclusively profit-making objectives.

Reference list

Adenitire J. (ed), *Religious Beliefs and Conscientious Exemptions in a Liberal State* (Hart, 2019).

Ahdar R., 'Companies as Religious Liberty Claimants' (2016) 5(1) Oxford Journal of Law and Religion, 1–27 (DOI: 10.1093/ojlr/rww001).

——— and Jiles J., 'The Supreme Courts' Icing on the Trans-Atlantic Cakes' (2020) 9(1) Oxford Journal of Law and Religion, 212–228 (DOI: 10.1093/ojlr/rwaa005).

Allen N. B., 'Reverse Piercing of the Corporate Veil: A Straightforward Path to Justice' (2011) 83(3) St. John's Law Review, 1148–1188.

Bainbridge S. M., 'Catholic Social Thought and the Corporation' (2003) UCLA School of Law Research Paper no 03-20.

———, *Corporate Law* (Foundation Press, 2002).

———, 'Director Primacy: The Means and Ends of Corporate Governance' (2002) 97(2) Northwestern University Law Review, 547–606.

———, *Limited Liability: A Legal and Economic Analysis* (Edward Elgar Publishing, 2016) (DOI: 10.4337/9781783473038).

———, 'Using Reverse Veil Piercing to Vindicate the Free Exercise of Incorporated Employers' (2013) 16(3) The Green Bag, 235–249.

Banchoff T. (eds), *Democracy and the New Religious Pluralism* (Oxford University Press, 2007) (DOI: 10.1093/acprof:oso/9780195307221.001.0001).

Berger P., Davie G. and Fokas E., *Religious America, Secular Europe? A Theme and Variation* (Ashgate, 2008).

Berle A. A. and Means G. C., *The Modern Corporation and Private Property* (Harcourt, Brace & World, 1932).

Cismas I., *Religious Actors and International Law* (Oxford University Press, 2014).

——— and Cammarano S., 'Whose Right and Who's Right? The US Supreme Court v. The European Court of Human Rights on Corporate Exercise of Religion' (2016) 34(1) Boston University International Law Journal, 2–44.

Clark E. A. and Durham Jr. W. C., 'The Emergence of Corporate Religious Freedom' in Malcolm D. Evans, Peter Petkoff and Julian Rivers (eds), *The Changing Nature of Religious Rights Under International Law* (Oxford University Press, 2015), 256–285.

Colombo R. J., *The First Amendment and the Business Corporation* (Oxford University Press, 2014) (DOI: 10.1093/acprof:oso/9780199335671.001.0001).

———, 'Religious Conception of Corporate Purpose' (2017) 72(2) Washington and Lee Law Review, 813–845.

Corsalini M., 'Religious Freedom Inc: Business, Religion and the Law in the Secular Economy' (2020) 9(1) Oxford Journal of Law and Religion, 28–55 (DOI: 10.1093/ojlr/rwaa008).

Cranmer F., 'Can Secular Non-Natural Persons be Said to Have a "Conscience"?' in John Adenitire (eds), *Religious Beliefs and Conscientious Exemptions in a Liberal State* (Hart, 2019).

Crespi G. S., 'The Reverse Pierce Doctrine: Applying Appropriate Standards' (1991) 16(1) The Journal of Corporation Law, 34–69.

De Girolami M. O., 'Constitutional Contraction: Religion and the Roberts Court' (2015) 26(2) Stanford Law & Policy Review, 385–410.

———, 'Free Exercise by Moonlight' (2016) 53(105) San Diego Law Review, 105–146.

———, 'The Bishops' Statement on Religious Freedom and Widespread Misunderstanding of the State of Free Exercise' (*Mirror of Justice*, 14 April 2012).

Epps G., 'Justice Kennedy's *Masterpiece* Ruling' (*The Atlantic*, 4 June 2018).

Eskridge Jr. W. N. and Ferejohn John 'Super-Statutes' (2001) 50(5) Duke Law Journal, 1215–1276.

Evans D. M., Petkoff P. and Rivers J. (eds), *The Changing Nature of Religious Rights Under International Law* (Oxford University Press, 2015) (DOI: 10.1093/acprof:oso/9780199684229.001.0001).

Friedman R. A., 'Stop Accusing Religious Conservatives of "Using" Religion' (*Canopy Forum*, 9 June 2021).

Gedicks F. M., '"Substantial" Burdens: How Courts May (and Why They Must) Judge Burdens on Religion Under RFRA' (2017) 85(1) The George Washington Law Review, 94–151.

———, and Koppelman A., 'Invisible Women: Why an Exemption for Hobby Lobby Would Violate the Establishment Clause' (2014) 67(1) Vanderbilt Law Review En Banc, 51–66.

Greenawalt K., '*Hobby Lobby*. Its Flawed Interpretative Technique and Standards of Application' in Micah Schwartzman, Chad Flanders and Zoë Robinson (eds), *The Rise of Corporate Religious Liberty* (Oxford University Press, 2016), 125–147.

Greenfield K., *Corporations Are People Too (And They Should Act Like It)* (Yale University Press, 2018) (DOI: 10.2307/j.ctv6hp3qr).

Green D., 'One Judge Away from Losing Religious Liberty: Hobby Lobby CEO' (*USA Today*, 1 September 2016).

Hamilton M. A., 'Religious Entities Flex Their Muscles Through the Roberts Court, Playing Both Sides of the Discrimination Coin' (*Justia*, 4 August 2020).

———, 'The Scope of *Bostock v. Clayton County*'s Contribution to LGBTQ Rights Is Not as Broad as You Might Think: Beware the "Super Statute" RFRA' (*Verdict*, 18 June 2020).

Hansmann H. B., 'The Role of Nonprofit Enterprise' (1980) 89(5) Yale Law Journal, 835–901.

Hill J. B., 'Kingdom Without End? The Inevitable Expansion of Religious Sovereignty Claims' (2017) 20(4) Lewis & Clark Law Review, 1177–1204.

Hill M. Q. C., 'The Great Strasbourg Bake Off' (*Law & Religion UK*, 6 January 2022).

Horwitz P., 'Defending (Religious) Institutionalism' (2013) 99(5) Virginia Law Review, 1049–1063.

Kendrick L. and Schwartzman M., 'The Etiquette of Animus' (2018) 132(1) Harvard Law Review, 33–70.

Kruse K. M., *One Nation Under God. How Corporate America Invented Christian America* (Basic Books, 2015).

Liptak A., 'Supreme Court Backs Catholic Agency in Case on Gay Rights and Foster Care' (*New York Times*, 17 June 2021).

List C. and Pettit P. *Group Agency. The Possibility, Design and Status of Corporate Agents* (Oxford University Press, 2011).

Lucamante S. (eds), *Italy and the Bourgeoisie. The Re-Thinking of a Class* (Fairleigh Dickinson University Press, 2009).

Lupu Ira C. and Tuttle Robert W., 'Religious Exemptions and the Limited Relevance of Corporate Religious Identity' in Micah Schwartzman, Chad Flanders and Zoë Robinson (eds), *The Rise of Corporate Religious Liberty* (Oxford University Press, 2016), 373–397.

Lyman J, 'Faith and Faithfulness in Corporate Theory' (2006) 56(1) Catholic University Law Review, 1–46.

Lynch H. F., Cohen I. and Sepper E. (eds), *Law, Religion and Health in the United States* (Cambridge University Press, 2017).

——— and Curfman G., 'Bosses in the Bedroom: Religious Employers and the Future of Employer-Sponsored Health Care' in Holly Fernandez Lynch, I. Glenn Cohen andElizabeth Sepper (eds), *Law, Religion and Health in the United States* (Cambridge University Press, 2017), 154–167.

Magarian G. P., 'The New Religious Institutionalism Meets the Old Establishment Clause' in Micah Schwartzman, Chad Flanders and Zoë Robinson (eds), *The Rise of Corporate Religious Liberty* (Oxford University Press, 2016), 441–463.

Mayer C., *Firm Commitment* (Oxford University Press, 2013).

Mazzucato M., *The Value of Everything. Making and Taking in The Global Economy* (Penguin Books, 2018).

McConnell M. W, 'Reflections on *Hosanna-Tabor*' (2012) 35(3) Harvard Journal of Law and Public Policy, 821–837.
McDonnel Brett H., 'The Liberal Case for Hobby Lobby' (2015) 57(1) Arizona Law Review, 788–822.
Nasini C., 'Adriano Olivetti: A "Socialist" Industrialist in Postwar Italy' in Stefania Lucamante (eds), *Italy and the Bourgeoisie. The Re-Thinking of a Class* (Fairleigh Dickinson University Press, 2009).
Nelson J. D., 'The Trouble with Corporate Conscience' (2018) 71(5) Vanderbilt Law Review, 1656–1702.
Nejaime D. and Siegel R., 'Conscience Wars: Complicity-Based Conscience Claims in Religion and Politics' (2015) 124(7) Yale Law Journal, 2518–2589.
Norris P. and Inglehart R., 'Uneven Secularization in the United States and Western Europe' in Thomas Banchoff (eds), *Democracy and the New Religious Pluralism* (Oxford University Press, 2007), 31–57.
Orts E. W., *Business Persons. A Legal Theory of the Firm* (Oxford University Press, 2013) (DOI: 10.1093/acprof:oso/9780199670918.001.0001).
Pear R. and Parlapiano A., 'Opting Out of Contraceptive Coverage' (*New York Times*, 12 July 2014).
Petrin M., 'Beyond Shareholder Value: Exploring Justifications for a Broader Corporate Purpose' in Elizabeth Pollman and Robert B. Thompson (eds), *Research Handbook of Corporate Purpose and Personhood* (Edward Elgar Publishing, 2021), 345–362.
Pollman E. and Thompson R. B. (eds), *Research Handbook of Corporate Purpose and Personhood* (Edward Elgar Publishing, 2021).
Reyes R., 'Masterpiece Cakeshop and Ashers Baking Company: A Comparative Analysis of Constitutional Confections', (2020) 16(1) Stanford Journal of Civil Rights & Civil Liberties, 113–146.
Robinson Z., '*Hosanna-Tabor* after *Hobby Lobby*' in Micah Schwartzman, Chad Flanders and Zoë Robinson (eds), *The Rise of Corporate Religious Liberty* (Oxford University Press, 2016), 173–191.
Rock E. B. and Wachter M. L., 'Islands of Conscious Power: Law, Norms, and the Self-Governing Corporation' (2001) 149(6) University of Pennsylvania Law Review, 1619–1700.
Schragger R. and Schwartzman M., 'Against Religious Institutionalism' (2013) 99(5) Virginia Law Review, 917–985.
Schwartzman M., 'What Did RFRA Restore?' (*Cornerstone Forum*, 30 June 2016).
———, Flanders C. and Robinson Z. (eds), *The Rise of Corporate Religious Liberty* (Oxford University Press, 2016) (DOI: 10.1093/acprof:oso/9780190262525.001.0001).
Scott D. and Kliff S., 'Leaked Regulation: Trump Plans to Roll Back Obamacare Birth Control Mandate' (*Vox*, 11 June 2021).
Sepinwall A. J., 'Corporate Piety and Impropriety. Hobby Lobby's Extension of RFRA Rights to the For-Profit Corporation' (2015) 5(2) Harvard Business Law Review, 174–204.
Sepper E., 'Reports of Accommodation's Death Have Been Greatly Exaggerated' (2014) 128(1) Harvard Law Review, 24–30
———, The Risky Business of RFRAs After *Hobby Lobby*' in Robin Fretwell Wilson (ed), *The Contested Place of Religion in Family Law* (Cambridge University Press, 2018), 17–39.

———, and Nelson James D., '*Fulton v. Philadelphia*: A Masterpiece of an Opinion?' (*American Constitutional Society*, 18 June 2021).
Singer A. A., *The Form of the Firm. A Normative Political Theory of the Corporation* (Oxford University Press, 2019) (DOI: 10.1093/oso/9780190698348.001.0001).
Smith B. C., *Baptizing Business. Evangelical Executives & the Sacred Pursuit of Profits* (Oxford University Press, 2020) (DOI: 10.1093/oso/9780190055776.001.0001).
Stabile S. J., 'A Catholic Vision of the Corporation' (2005) St. John's Legal Studies Research Paper, 181–224.
Smith S. and Martin N., '10 Things to Know About the Supreme Court Showdown Over Contraception and Religious Freedom' (*Mother Jones*, 22 March 2016).
Stern M. J., 'John Roberts Just Pulled Off His Greatest Judicial Magic Trick' (*Slate*, 17 June 2021).
Stewards K., *The Power Worshippers. Inside the Dangerous Rise of American Nationalism* (Bloomsbury Publishing, 2020).
Sullivan W. F., *Church State Corporation: Construing Religion in US Law* (The University of Chicago Press, 2020).
Tebbe N. and Schragger R., 'The Costs of Conscience' (2018) 106(4) Kentucky Law Journal, 781–812.
Temperman J., *Corporate Religious Freedom and the Rights of Others* (Eleven, 2019).
Tushnet M., 'Do For-Profit Corporations Have Rights of Religious Conscience?' (2013) 99(1) Cornell Law Review Online, 70–86.
Wilson R. F. (ed), *The Contested Place of Religion in Family Law* (Cambridge University Press, 2018) (DOI: 10.1017/9781108277976).
Wolfson E., 'Five Years Later, How *Obergefell* Paved the Way for *Bostock* and the DACA Decision' (*Slate*, 24 June 2020).
Yurcaba J., 'Court's Foster Care Ruling Has Experts, Advocates Split on Potential LGBTQ Impact' (*NBC News*, 17 June 2021).

Concluding remarks

Matteo Corsalini

This book has examined the intersection between business and religion from a legal perspective. Toward that aim, the idea has been to draw a roadmap tracking how legal and judicially created exemptions for faith-based entities have evolved over time and across international legal orders. The decision to establish doctrinal legal scholarship and case law on corporate religious freedom (and, more specifically, on religious exemptions) as the theoretical framework for a study on business and religion has not been a random choice.

Quite the contrary, and as mentioned in the introductory bits of this volume, justifications for this approach have been found precisely within classic literature on corporate law and religion. In fact, scholarly debates in this field have gone in a long way to explain that there are certain zones of ecclesiastical governance that are the *business* of churches not of governments. Other things being equal: religious institutions, be they churches or their non-profit offshoots, should, in principle, enjoy autonomy rights in organising and managing their spiritual affairs (i.e., their *business*) without intrusion by state regulation.[1] In this perspective, this body of literature has offered input for a definition of "business" in the broadest sense of the word to describe the internal spiritual domain of ecclesiastical entities and, relatedly, their autonomy claims vis-à-vis state regulation. It is on this broad definition of "business" that Part I of this thesis has been built.

In light of this, to think of the relation between religion and "business" in a legal sense, this book has argued, first of all, to think of the role of religious freedom in preserving "the option of a religious way of life by enabling a group to self-define and self-direct according to religion".[2] This is what scholars on both sides of the Atlantic call "corporate religious freedom".[3]

Within this space of legal protection, of greatest interest has been problematising the regime of religious exemptions that might result from the recognition of corporate autonomy rights. In fact, more and more occasions exist for conflicts between

1 See the bibliography quoted in the introduction to this book, 2 (fn 2).

2 Jane Calderwood Norton, *Freedom of Religious Organisations* (Oxford University Press 2016) 194.

3 For one of the most recent studies on the issue see: Jeroen Temperman, *Corporate Religious Freedom and the Rights of Others* (Eleven 2019).

DOI: 10.4324/9781003340829-8

governments and corporate religious actors that, by virtue of their self-determination rights, ask civil courts for exemptions from state laws that they deem to be at odds with their religious mission and objectives (read: business). And because the appointment of spiritually qualified ministers and lay personnel is not only one among these objectives, but is also at the heart of religious self-determination, very often tensions between the state and religious entities revolve around discriminatory practices in employment. To state the obvious, a typical example in this context is the dismissal of ministers and lay staff for carrying out practices disapproved of by the official church, be they the teaching of doctrines at odds with the orthodox one or engagement in extra-marital relationships. Also relevant are corporate religious objections to providing goods and services to third parties, most notably because of the sexual orientation of the latter. While writing this book, parallel developments in the US and Italy are a good reminder of how these conflicts are topical and timeless. While the US Supreme Court (USSC) allowed a Catholic agency to refuse to work with same-sex couples in one of its most recent rulings[4] on 17 June 2021, on the same day, the Vatican argued that an Italian "anti-homophobia" bill, as currently written, limits the Catholic Church's ability to operate free from state regulation.[5] Both examples offer an important "reality check" on the topic at hand.

Bringing these issues one stage further, new lines of research are now also considering the question of whether religious autonomy rights, and, by logical extension, claims for religious exemptions, could be "taken out of the physical house-of-worship context".[6] In more practical terms, the basic question here is can other secular organisational structures, and more specifically commercial *businesses*, exercise FoRB rights? And if so, should they be deemed to be new "religious" actors in international law and religion?[7] It is in the context of these lines of research that Part II of this investigation has been situated.

By exploring how some jurisdictions answered the above questions in the affirmative, a central aim for this book has been to present an overall evolutionary picture of corporate religious freedom on both sides of the Atlantic. A pattern emerged, it has been explained, in which some US and EU commercial enterprises are now re-conceptualising religious freedom as an economic tool to maximise profits in business above other social concerns. Hence, at first glance and on a level of purely methodological observation, the theme of corporate religious exemptions here has been imagined as the red thread connecting the two parts of this book. The theoretical framework on *church autonomy* in Part I has been used

4 *Fulton v. City of Philadelphia*, 593 U. S. (2021).

5 See Hannah Brockhaus, 'Vatican Intervenes in Proposed 'Anti-Homophobia' Law in Italy' (Catholic News Agency, 22 June 2021) <https://www.catholicnewsagency.com/news/248088/vatican-intervenes-in-proposed-anti-homophobia-law-in-italy?fbclid=IwAR286T4Nc63X12e1vbMho_cY0EuF43tZWg_zKnqvHrZVX5fZQp7_qfZ9xMA> accessed 28 June 2021.

6 Jeroen Temperman (n 3) 21. This topic is the subject of a rapidly expanding body of literature (see the bibliography cited in Chapter IV, 4 (fn 14).

7 Always in this sense, see Jeroen Temperman (n 3) 2.

to unpack insights for answering questions on the *business autonomy* of ideologically oriented commercial enterprises introduced and explored in Part II.

Findings

The conclusions reached regarding the above, after a critical appraisal of the evolution of the legal category of "corporate religious freedom" are summarised in what follows. Part I has been divided into two chapters.

Chapter I has offered a comparative legal analysis of how four international legal orders (the UN, the OSCE, the CoE, and the EU) address calls for corporate religious autonomy by ecclesiastical entities. This preliminary analysis has been foundational, allowing the groundwork to be set for a discussion on religious exemptions in Chapter II. Analysing these four models, it has been found that only two of them (the CoE and the EU) exhibited sufficient legal and judicial strength to accommodate requests for corporate religious exemptions from otherwise applicable state laws.[8] Having established that, Chapter II then restricted the field of inquiry to these two models and their respective courts: the European Court of Human Rights (ECtHR) and the Court of Justice of the European Union (CJEU). The goal has been to critically assess how both tribunals handled calls for corporate religious exemptions from ecclesiastical bodies in employment matters. All things considered, the results obtained have indicated that their approaches are oppositional to one another.

On the one hand, the current trend of ECtHR case law is toward an increased entitlement of religious exemptions to church employers strengthening their autonomy in their hiring and firing practices. As explained, one reason for this is that the ECtHR felt for some time the influence of American jurisprudence and, in particular, the USSC's "ministerial exception" doctrine, defined as a broad immunity that puts church autonomy beyond the reach of a proportionality balancing. Although the ECtHR has now returned to its conventional "balancing approach" (grounded on the requirements of legality, legitimacy, and necessity/proportionality of an interference), however, the Court still seems to be applying proportionality in a way that gives special favour to church employers.

On the other hand, an analysis of EU case law on this subject has revealed a restrictive approach by the CJEU that, in marked contrast to the ECtHR, narrowed down exemptions for religious employers on proportionality grounds in two major decisions on church employment. It has been assumed that the main reason for this is that the CJEU has developed, over time, a "competitive" approach[9] to FoRB that values and protects religion only insomuch as it meets

8 For the sake of succinctness, only the most relevant results are reported. For a summary of the positions of each four models on corporate religious freedom see Chapter I, 61–62.

9 This term can be traced back to Marco Ventura, *La Laicità dell'Unione Europea. Diritti, Mercato e Religione* (Giappichelli Editore 2001) 149–55. Ronan McCrea, *Religion and the Public Order of the European Union* (Oxford Scholarship Online 2011) (discussing how the CJEU protects FoRB in light of an assessment of its suitability to meet and facilitate the economic goals of the Union) 143–96.

the economic and commercial goals of the EU single market and not otherwise. Among these objectives, of crucial importance is also the protection of free access to the labour market which, as explained, is considered a strategic factor toward the achievement of an "highly competitive economy".[10] From here, it has been inferred that the CJEU limited the managerial discretion of church employers precisely to prevent their religious occupational requirements from hindering the ability of potential (and lay) employees to enter employment relationships with them. In any case, and despite a narrow approach to religious autonomy rights, the most striking finding to emerge from CJEU case law on this subject is what this book has called a "business turn" in EU law and religion—to wit, a progressive recognition of the religious freedom rights of another corporate entity: the for-profit corporation. It is this new trend of corporate religious freedom that has constituted the central theme of Part II of this book. Also, the latter has been structured in two chapters.

In Chapter III, a pattern has been observed: on the one hand, the CJEU restricted ***church autonomy*** through a narrow interpretation of the exemption mechanisms for churches contained under its anti-discrimination legislation (i.e., Directive 2000/78/EC). While on the other, it extended this same regime of religious exemptions to protect the ***business autonomy*** of so-called "neutrality-based companies". As explained, the latter are a type of corporation with a pure focus on profit-maximisation that incorporate so-called "policies of neutrality" within their statutes and by-laws in pursuit of higher revenues. By preventing employees from showing any sign of political, ideological, and religious affiliation in the workplace, "neutrality-based companies"[11] aim to present a secular corporate image to customers and investors as part of their purely efficiency-oriented business model. In this way, it has been suggested that corporate policies of neutrality should be seen as the "secular" version of the religious occupational requirements used by churches to limit employee "deviance" form the orthodoxy of their mission. In practice, while the working contexts in which churches and enterprises operate are different, nonetheless, they give rise to the same normative and legal phenomenon. Namely, a growing recognition of the right of commercial enterprises to assert before the law the religious (or non-religious)[12] beliefs and identities that inspire their business models. Phrased differently, just as churches and "faith-based companies" are capable of exercising corporate free-

10 See Consolidated Version of the Treaty on European Union [2012] OJ C 326/13, art 3(3).

11 In a similar vein, one author describes "neutral" businesses as "ideologically-oriented companies"; see Louis-Leon Christians, 'Ideologically Oriented Enterprises Faced with the Reconfiguration of Ethics and Spiritual Management' (2014) 1(3) Brigham Young University Law Review 565–84.

12 As one author explains "secular organisations are erroneously considered 'neutral', when they are themselves guided by values and ideologies which, incidentally, may not always be transparent". Azza Karam, 'Religion at the United Nations. Challenges or Opportunities?' in Sherrie M. Steiner and James T. Christie (eds), *Religious Soft Diplomacy and the United Nations. Religious Engagement as Loyal Opposition* (Lexington Books, 2021) 24.

dom *of* religion, in a perfectly symmetrical fashion, "neutrality-based companies" can similarly invoke corporate freedom *from* religion to preserve a secular workplace environment.

Against this background, this chapter has done five things.[13] First, it has reviewed the interpretation of the first CJEU decision on a "neutrality-based company" (*Achbita v G4S Secure Solutions*) as discussed by the most relevant doctrine on the subject. This analysis has been complemented by an overview of its "sister" case *Bougnaoui v Micropole* to highlight the differences between the two.

Second, it has offered an "alternative" reading of *Achbita* as a case about corporate religious freedom in its negative modality (corporate freedom *from* religion). This analysis has then made it possible to argue that, for the first time ever, the CJEU extended religious exemptions that categorically shield churches from anti-discrimination laws to a "neutral" company refusing to accommodate religious employees at work for efficiency-related reasons. And to the extent that a for-profit enterprise enjoyed immunities that are typically available to churches, a presumption should exist that commercial businesses are now becoming "religious" (in a legal sense, at least) under EU law.

Third, and combining these findings in *Achbita* with economic theory, an interrelated sub-issue has been identified: the existence of an important debate in economic doctrine on the "moral" character of profit-making. Based on these considerations, it has been seen as germane to a revised study on corporate religious freedom to entertain the possibility that even the so-called "moral obligation of profit-maximisation" should fall within the category of "freedom of religion or belief".

However, there is a caveat, as this argument should not be interpreted as a blind endorsement of dogmatic assertions of "market fundamentalism".[14]

Rather, and fourth, the goal has been to adopt this perspective to suggest an alternative approach to resolve employer/employee disputes on more proportionate grounds. In practice, by treating "neutral" companies as FoRB claimants under EU law, the argument goes, it would be possible for the CJEU to transpose the "proportionality-oriented" approach as laid down in its church-autonomy jurisprudence into an analysis of future disputes on business autonomy. And because former AG Sharpston herself also proposed this same solution

13 This chapter has been built on material previously analysed in Matteo Corsalini, 'Religious Freedom Inc: Business, Religion and the Law in the Secular Economy' (2020) 9(1) Oxford Journal of Law and Religion 28–55.

14 This term has been generally used in pejorative terms to describe an exaggerated "faith" in the idea that the highest level of prosperity occurs when there is a free-market economy and a minimum of government regulation. In this sense, see George Soros, 'Capitalism versus Open Society' (*Financial Times*, 30 October 2009) <https://www.ft.com/content/d55926e8-bfea-11de-aed2-00144feab49a> accessed 1 July 2021.

more recently,[15] it only remains to be seen whether this suggestion will remain unheeded.

Fifth, this chapter has examined two new CJEU cases to conclude that, contrary to the above expectations, broad "church-like" exemptions for "neutral" businesses under EU law seem to be an upward trend for now.[16]

To complete this study on corporate religious freedom, Chapter IV has turned to consider the American version of the "business turn" in law and religion explored in Chapter III. Here, at stake have been the FoRB rights of so-called "faith-based companies":[17] the religious counterpart to the European "neutrality-based companies". On the whole, US "faith-based companies" are characterised by governance structures and business models that explicitly merge principles of free-market liberalism and, in particular, Christian conservatism in a unique "American way". This mix of profit and religion, in turn, gave rise to heated debates among legal scholars, especially after the USSC's decision in *Hobby Lobby* to include commercial businesses among the recipients of corporate religious exemptions in a way that placed them on a par with churches. It is these debates on the role of corporate religion in American constitutional and business law that have constituted the focus of this chapter. For the purpose of this discussion, the high-profile *Hobby Lobby* case and litigation in its wake have been explored in detail. The results obtained from this analysis have shown that the USSC progressively expanded the universe of religious exemptions typically available to churches to all types of "faith-based companies", whether closely held or publicly traded. It was explained in the literature that the escalation of this exceptional treatment for religious businesses went hand in hand with the progressive unfolding of the Trump administration's ultra-conservative agenda. This also provided authority to the proposition that, during Trump's four years as a president, the USSC (now with a conservative majority) and the government engaged in a mutually supportive relationship.[18] Based on this analysis, the goal has been to highlight how the USSC's case law on business religious freedom is following an expansive pattern that is similar, although diametrically opposed, to that of the CJEU.

15 Eleonor Sharpston QC, 'Shadow Opinion of Former Advocate-General Sharpston: Headscarves at Work (Cases C-804/18 and C-341/19)' (EU Law Analysis, 23 March 2021) para 260 <http://eulawanalysis.blogspot.com/2021/03/shadow-opinion-of-former-advocate.html> accessed 3 July 2021.

16 See Opinion of Advocate General Rantos in Joined Cases C-804/18, *IX v WABE e.V* and *C-341/19 MH Müller Handels GmbH v MJ*, [2021] EU:C:2021:144.

17 This term can be traced back to Rex Ahdar, 'Companies as Religious Liberty Claimants' (2016) 5(1) Oxford Journal of Law and Religion 11–27; 4.

18 Katherine Stewart, *The Powers of Worshippers. Inside The Dangerous Rise of Religious Nationalism* (Bloomsbury Publishing, 2020) 177. For an empirical analysis of Trump's relationship with the USSC see: Adam Fieldman, 'Empirical SCOTUS: 365 days of Trump and the Supreme Court' (SCOTUS blog, 27 December 2018) <https://www.scotusblog.com/2018/12/empirical-scotus-365-days-of-trump-and-the-supreme-court/> accessed 2 July 2021.

Ultimately, this chapter concluded by considering the position on business religious exemptions of the last model covered by this study: the Council of Europe (CoE). Compared to the breadth of US and EU business exemptions, it has been shown that the CoE took a more cautious stance on the relationship between profit and religion. First, the ECommHR, and then the ECtHR, reiterated on several occasions that FoRB rights can be exercised by religious entities that are not *entirely* profit-making (e.g., the commercial subsidiary of a church established to generate income to support other faith-based and non-profit activities). While for now, the question whether corporate bodies that are *entirely* profit-making can also claim FoRB rights "is not yet completely clear"[19] at this level of jurisdiction.

Looking forward (to being in good "company")

The for-profit corporation is a time-machine: a legal institution that transfers wealth between time, periods and generations.[20] It is with this metaphor that Lynn A. Stout praised the ability of companies to pass resources, assets, and goods "forward through time to benefit those who will live in the future".[21] With a trivial example, Steve Jobs might have passed away ten years ago, but his MacBooks still make hundreds of PhD students in the dreary throes of finals and deadlines faster typists. Needless to say, the goods that companies put on the market for the benefit of future generations go well beyond simple consumer electronics. Consider, for instance, the pharmaceutical industry's contribution to global health over time (net of "Big Pharma" conspiracy theories) and how, more recently, some private drugmakers have even pledged to provide coronavirus vaccines on a non-profit basis.[22]

But just as companies can embark on long-term projects to generate wealth for those who will live in the future, they can similarly squander such potential wealth to serve the short-term and opportunistic interests of those who live in the present. Thus, in a process that works in reverse to the one described above, the corporation/time-machine can also "shift wealth backward in time to benefit earlier generations".[23] It is at this point that the same pharmaceutical companies pre-

19 See Council of Europe/European Court of Human Rights, 'Guide on Article 9 of the European Convention on Human Rights' 1, 9 (31 August 2020) <https://www.echr.coe.int/Documents/Guide_Art_9_ENG.pdf> accessed 28 July 2021.

20 Lynn A. Stout, 'The Corporation as a Time Machine: Intergenerational Equity, Intergenerational Efficiency, and the Corporate Form (2015) 38(2) Seattle University Law Review 685, 686.

21 ibid 686.

22 See Stephanie Baker and Suzi Ring, 'The World Needs the Not-For-Profit AstraZeneca Vaccine, Minus the AstraZeneca Drama' (Bloomberg, 8 April 2021) <https://www.bloomberg.com/news/features/2021-04-08/why-astrazeneca-azn-covid-vaccine-was-plagued-with-errors> accessed 4 July 2021.

23 Lynn A. Stout (n 20) 686.

sented earlier as innovators can also be criticised for, say, increasing drugs prices (a boon for profits) instead of making it easier for underdeveloped countries to access medical supplies, be they coronavirus vaccines or other drugs.[24] Increasing access to medicines for developing countries (to support their *future* economic development)[25] is, in fact, a long-term project from which *present* shareholders are likely to reap benefits only after a long time—perhaps too long a time for the financial interests of some of them.

All things considered, this is not to say that companies (and their shareholders) should not focus on profits. In fact, it would be truly ingenuous to think that businesses could really break new ground without the capital necessary to survive in the market or the incentive of higher revenues. Also, without profit, companies would not be able to pay back their shareholders who, apart from the conventional capitalist, also include parents saving for their children or any other ordinary citizen investing his or her retirement savings into pensions and mutual funds that bear the risks of the market. The crucial role that profits play in social improvement, therefore, cannot be ignored. What is problematic, however, is how the "mantra" of profit-maximisation in the modern business world, taken at its extreme, encourages more and more investors to prioritise ventures promising immediate returns *today* over long-term projects to the benefit of those who will be born *tomorrow*.[26] Moreover, and by virtue of substantial ownership of a company's shares, investors have de facto gained the ability to exert strategic influence to bring about desired changes in corporate management that, at worst, will reflect precisely their short-term and self-interested desires.[27]

It is against this background that Part II of this book has tried to make sense of how even religion can play a role within this "shareholder-centric" paradigm

24 See Michael Erman and Carl O'Donnel, 'Exclusive: Drugmakers to Hike Prices for 2021 as Pandemic, Political Pressure Put Revenues at Risk' (Reuters, 30 December 2020) <https://www.reuters.com/article/us-usa-healthcare-drugpricing-exclusive-idUSKBN2951Q2> accessed 04 July 2021.

25 For an empirical analysis of the correlation between strengthened healthcare systems in underdeveloped countries and their overall economic performance, see C. James Attridge and Alexander S. Preker, 'Improving Access to Medicines in Developing Countries. Application of New Institutional Economics to the Analysis of Manufacturing and Distribution Issues' (2005) The International Bank for Reconstruction and Development/The World Bank, Health, Nutrition and Population (HNP) Discussion Paper <https://openknowledge.worldbank.org/bitstream/handle/10986/13668/320380AttridgeImprovingAccessFinal.pdf?sequence=1&isAllowed=y> accessed 4 July 2021.

26 Lynn A. Stout (n 20) (arguing that the modern embrace of "shareholder value" as the only corporate objective and "shareholder democracy" as the ideal of corporate governance is damaging the corporate form's ability to serve this economically and ethically important function.) 685.

27 This is what some law and economics scholars have called "shareholder primacy". That is, a theory of corporate governance according to which investors both *own* and *control* the corporation, thus, reducing directors to mere agents with fiduciary duties toward the former. Among the first proponents of this theory, see Frank H. Easterbrook and Daniel R. Fischel, *The Economic Structure of Corporate Law* (Harvard University Press, 1991).

of the for-profit corporation/time-machine. Although, in principle, one should be open to the possibility that a commercial entity mixing business and religion in good faith, Chapter III has shown, nonetheless, how the risk of corporate religion becoming a disingenuous guise for short-term profits is real. The American retail company Hobby Lobby is perhaps the epitome of the "backwards time-shifting function" of certain commercial businesses. For Hobby Lobby shareholders' objection *today* to providing contraceptives on religious (and financial) grounds will restrict the ability of hundreds of female employees to freely choose whether and when to bear children *tomorrow*.

Instead, in a slightly different way, Chapter III has tried to take the discussion on the relationship between profits and religion one stage further. The position has been advanced that purely secular European companies and their shareholders have themselves become "religious" (legally speaking, at least) to the extent that they now enjoy "church-like" legal immunities to freely carry out their efficiency-oriented and short-term goals. Irrespective of whether this argument has been satisfactorily justified, one thing is certain: namely, that both the American "faith-based" and the European "neutrality-based" companies discussed in this book carry out "shareholder-centric" business models that not only harm people and communities but also damage their corporate private interests in the long run.

In a time when human rights violations, environmental disasters, emergencies, and epidemics are at a peak, business professionals and scholars[28] predict that greater opportunities to boost profitability will come precisely for those who, surprisingly, will put "purpose" over "profits".

Overall, at the heart of these prepositions lies a radical shift in thinking. "Corporate purpose", as Alex Edmans explains, is precisely the commitment to create a business revolving around individuals (from workers, suppliers, and investors) projected toward shared, long-term goals rather than short-term profits.[29] By employing human values as the measuring stick of corporate performance, not revenues, this approach radically flips traditional doctrines supporting a pure profit focus of the corporation on their head. This, however, does not mean that "corporate purpose" must be at the expense of profits. In fact, "corporate purpose" serves both profits and society and does so by creating *social* value for communities (i.e., stakeholders) and *financial* value for shareholders at the same time.

To understand this, a growing body of literature (including Edmans's works) is presenting empirical evidence explaining that higher profits will come precisely

28 Recent academic works on this subject include Colin Mayer, *Prosperity. Better Business Makes the Greater Good* (Oxford University Press, 2018); Alex Edmans, *Grow the Pie. How Great Companies Deliver Both Purpose and Profit* (Cambridge University Press, 2020); Mariana Mazzucato, *Mission Economy. A Moonshot Guide to Changing Capitalism* (Allen Lane, 2021). See also the collection of essays in Elizabeth Pollman and Robert B. Thompson, *Research Handbook on Corporate Purpose and Personhood* (Edward Elgar Publishing, 2021).

29 Alex Edmans (n 28) 3.

as a "by-product"[30] of serving society. Because of the ability of companies acting for the long-term to create value not just for their shareholders, but for the economy as a whole, the argument goes that a "corporate purpose" will enable businesses to attract more investments and market opportunities. Whether religion will be able to meet the challenge of fostering long-term thinking in business is still an open question that, for now, is better left to another writing.

Reference list

Adam F., 'Empirical SCOTUS: 365 Days of Trump and the Supreme Court' (*SCOTUS blog*, 27 December 2018).

Ahdar R., 'Companies as Religious Liberty Claimants' (2016) 5(1) Oxford Journal of Law and Religion, 1–27 (DOI: 10.1093/ojlr/rww001).

Baker S. and Ring S., 'The World Needs the Not-For-Profit AstraZeneca Vaccine, Minus the AstraZeneca Drama' (*Bloomberg*, 8 April 2021).

Brockhaus Hannah, 'Vatican Intervenes in Proposed "Anti-Homophobia" Law in Italy' (*Catholic News Agency*, 22 June 2021).

Christians L. L., 'Ideologically Oriented Enterprises Faced with the Reconfiguration of Ethics and Spiritual Management' (2014) 1(3) Brigham Young University Law Review, 565–584.

Corsalini M., 'Religious Freedom Inc: Business, Religion and the Law in the Secular Economy' (2020) 9(1) Oxford Journal of Law and Religion, 28–55 (DOI: 10.1093/ojlr/rwaa008).

Easterbrook F. H. and Fischel D. R., *The Economic Structure of Corporate Law* (Harvard University Press, 1991).

Edmans A., *Grow the Pie. How Great Companies Deliver Both Purpose and Profit* (Cambridge University Press, 2020) (DOI: 10.1017/9781108860093).

Erman M. and O'Donnel C., 'Exclusive: Drugmakers to Hike Prices for 2021 as Pandemic, Political Pressure Put Revenues at Risk' (*Reuters*, 30 December 2020).

Karam A., 'Religion at the United Nations. Challenges or Opportunities?' in Sherrie M. Steiner and James T. Christie (eds), *Religious Soft Diplomacy and the United Nations. Religious Engagement as Loyal Opposition* (Lexington Books, 2021), 21–43.

James Attridge C. and Preker Alexander S., 'Improving Access to Medicines in Developing Countries. Application of New Institutional Economics to the Analysis of Manufacturing and Distribution Issues' (2005) The International Bank for Reconstruction and Development/The World Bank, Health, Nutrition and Population (HNP) Discussion Paper.

Mayer C., *Prosperity. Better Business Makes the Greater Good* (Oxford University Press, 2018).

Mazzucato M., *Mission Economy. A Moonshot Guide to Changing Capitalism* (Allen Lane, 2021).

McCrea R, *Religion and the Public Order of the European Union* (Oxford Scholarship Online, 2011) (DOI: 10.1093/acprof:oso/9780199595358.001.0001).

Norton J. C., *Freedom of Religious Organisations* (Oxford University Press, 2016).

30 ibid 4.

Pollman E. and Thompson R. B. (eds), *Research Handbook of Corporate Purpose and Personhood* (Edward Elgar Publishing, 2021).
Sharpston QC, 'Shadow Opinion of Former Advocate-General Sharpston: Headscarves at Work (Cases C-804/18 and C-341/19)' (*EU Law Analysis*, 23 March 2021).
Soros G., 'Capitalism versus Open Society' (*Financial Times*, 30 October 2009).
Steiner S. M. and Christie James T. (eds), *Religious Soft Diplomacy and the United Nations. Religious Engagement as Loyal Opposition* (Lexington Books, 2021).
Stewards K., *The Power Worshippers. Inside the Dangerous Rise of American Nationalism* (Bloomsbury Publishing, 2020).
Stout Lynn A., 'The Corporation as a Time Machine: Intergenerational Equity, Intergenerational Efficiency, and the Corporate Form' (2015) 38(2) Seattle University Law Review, 385–723.
Temperman J., *Corporate Religious Freedom and the Rights of Others* (Eleven, 2019).
Ventura M., *La Laicità dell'Unione Europea. Diritti, Mercato e Religione* (Giappichelli Editore, 2001).

Index

For Product Safety Concerns and Information please contact our EU representative GPSR@taylorandfrancis.com
Taylor & Francis Verlag GmbH, Kaufingerstraße 24, 80331 München, Germany

www.ingramcontent.com/pod-product-compliance
Ingram Content Group UK Ltd.
Pitfield, Milton Keynes, MK11 3LW, UK
UKHW020141200926
475702UK00005B/846

* 9 7 8 1 0 3 2 3 7 5 6 2 5 *